The Arams of Idaho

THE
ARAMS OF IDAHO

PIONEERS OF CAMAS PRAIRIE

AND

JOSEPH PLAINS

KRISTI M. YOUNGDAHL

University of Idaho Press/Moscow, Idaho
1995

Library of Congress Cataloging-in-Publication Data

Youngdahl, Kristi M., 1948–
    The Arams of Idaho : pioneers of Camas Prairie and Joseph
Plains / by Kristi M. Youngdahl.
        p.   cm.
    Includes bibliographical references and index.
    ISBN 0-89301-186-X (alk. paper)
    1. Pioneers—Idaho—Joseph Plains—Biography.   2. Aram
family.   3. Joseph Plains (Idaho)—Biography.   4. Camas
Prairie (Idaho)—History.   5. Frontier and pioneer life—Idaho
—Joseph Plains.   I. Title.
F752.I2Y68   1995
979.6'82—dc20   95-18894
                                                                          CIP

99 98 97 96 95   5 4 3 2 1

In Memory of
James H. and Phebe Aram

Contents

FOREWORD

*There is a divinity that shapes our ends—but we can
help by listening to its voice.* —Kathleen Norris

In the early part of this century when our parents, Phebe Smith
and James Aram, settled on Joseph Plains they were each pursuing the
ambitious, entrepreneurial spirit of their pioneer families. As a single
woman, Mother was creating a nest egg for herself by claiming a federal timber grant and teaching school. Our father, on the other hand,
aspired from his meager beginning to build a cattle empire. Both were
captivated by nature's bountiful landscape.

This area of central Idaho, named in honor of the great Nez Perce
Indian chief, is isolated from the Camas Prairie region, where the natural flow of transportation and communication brought people together. Joseph Plains and its sister ridge, Doumecq Plains, are locked
away from "the outside," as we called the prairie region, by Camp
Howard on the south and the deep and perilous canyons of the Snake
River to the west and the Salmon to the north and east. Joseph is further isolated by Rice Creek Canyon, which separates it from Doumecq
Plains.

In the minds of most "outsiders" Joseph was a strange and faraway
place, although as the crow flies the county seat of Grangeville is less
than 30 miles away. White Bird, located in the canyon of White Bird
Creek, supplied area ranchers and homesteaders with their basic needs.
This little frontier community was not considered outside even though
it marked the halfway point to Grangeville.

We had few visitors from outside, except an occasional surveyor or
bank representative. I do not remember any county officials ever coming to the ranch; we had to go to Grangeville to conduct business with
the government. Even the Native Americans stayed away, only making
an occasional visit during the fall grouse and deer hunting seasons.

One time a community of Gypsies excited us by camping near Sunset School while traveling across the plateau, but they didn't stay long.

Reflecting upon my boyhood experiences on Joseph Plains and the Getta Creek ranch, I sense a vision of wonder and beauty—a vision as in a dream rather than reality. In retrospect the Aram family and each of the other resident families were struggling for survival. At that time we did not realize the survival issue, since most of us came from pioneer families and did not know that many people living elsewhere enjoyed greater comforts.

During Christmas vacation of 1933, I lived in a cloud of depression and anxiety. Father insisted that I leave the university and return to the ranch to help him. Because I was midway through my junior year, he agreed to allow me to graduate. However, he didn't approve of my doing so. I considered his requests to return thoughtfully. The love of our family, nostalgic memories, and a hope that the ranching business could succeed and provide a more comfortable life tempted me to oblige him. With intense effort, hour by hour, I tried to imagine a scenario that would be profitable and successful, much as I had in 1930 when I chose college over ranch life. I couldn't find one. I had enjoyed the comforts of the outside, so I had to say no to Father.

When my brother, James Smith Aram, finally left Joseph Plains, he explored several entrepreneurial ventures and triumphed in a successful real estate business. As his investments matured and returns from the hard work came more easily, Jim's recollection of his youth stirred him to record anecdotes of life on Joseph. His first narrative was written in 1971. He urged me and our surviving sister, Narcie, to contribute.

Jim wasn't able to decide between writing and publishing a factual history of family experience or attempting to write the story in fiction. His sense of humor may have been in the way. With his friend, Hilton Thrapp, Jim started the book, but Hilton's failing health eventually stopped progress. Narcie, who was at first reluctant to consider presenting written accounts of her childhood, took an interest in Jim's work and she challenged me to assist Jim. I started recording boyhood tales in 1983.

We ask ourselves why we have spent the time to tell our family story. Only by "going home" to the old abandoned ranch house and barn where we were born and grew to adulthood can we answer even to ourselves. The country's beauty beckons. Standing by the old home, looking across the Kerlee place and Rice Creek southerly to Camp Howard and the Seven Devils Mountains, or across Rice Creek over Doumecq Plains to Camas Prairie and Grangeville, remembering the Grangeville lights at night, or standing at the top of Fir Gulch Trail viewing Getta Creek and Oregon's Copper Mountain—all this inspires us. When author Kristi Youngdahl saw this vast country with us and heard our stories, she, too, became enthused.

In presenting *The Arams of Idaho*, Narcie, Jim, and I do so, acknowledging the guidance of our parents for contributions of motivation, energy, integrity, the ability to work and serve others, and especially our abiding faith in God. Our prayers are being answered, as were Mother's who ceaselessly prayed for our safety and well-being.

Narcie and I dedicate our interest in this book to Jim and his lovely wife, Ruth. Jim is still respected and admired by those living on Joseph, then and now. With Ruth by his side, he has taken all the good from Joseph and turned it into a wonderful life with a great family and abundant resources. Jim's life, interests, and writings started this book, but it was Ruth's leadership that led to its production. She encouraged Jim to write, typed his copy, suggested numerous approaches, and provided inspiration. Ruth also did most of the family research until Kristi Youngdahl took the helm, conducted detailed research, and compiled our various memoirs into this story.

Jim and Ruth, we salute you for being you. We admire, respect, and love you.

John L. Aram

P.S. My brother Jim did not live to see this book in its final form for he passed away suddenly at his home in Lewiston on 9/6/95.

PREFACE

❧

The Aram family enjoyed the distinction of being among the first to blaze a trail into the unsettled regions, a trail later used by thousands.—Grangeville Globe Thursday, January 20, 1921, Obituary of Sarah A. Aram

ON A HOT day in August 1991 I stood at the crest of a rolling hill on Joseph Plains. Spread below me in a sloping meadow of bunchgrass, timothy, and wildflowers was what remains of the James H. Aram ranch.

Near a small grove of pine trees on the higher side of the meadow stood a two-story ranch house, its siding weathered to hues of gray and brown. Tattered curtains hung in broken windows. Rotten steps led to an open front door.

Beyond the house a meadow dotted with relic farm equipment sloped toward the barn. Once magnificent, the building was now missing much of its exterior siding, providing a partial view of the meadow on the other side through its dark interior.

Although only a whisper of what they had once been, the ranch buildings stood their ground. Each supported a gleaming metal roof, added in the 1940s as protection from wildfires. Those created a stark but picturesque contrast to the broken, decaying structures holding them aloft.

Sharing the view of the ranch with me that August day were James Aram's three surviving children, John, Jim, and Narcie Aram See, then in their 70s. They pointed out where they had planted fields of hay or ridden their horses across steep slopes, down draws, through canyons and into high forested areas while they pursued their daily chores.

The fields were gone, reclaimed by a mixture of timothy and bluegrass. Where once a rough dirt road led to the ranch, a deeply rutted two-wheel track, barely visible under three-foot-high prairie grasses, twisted through pastures now grazed by horses and cattle.

The land surrounding the ranch was made up of gentle hills and sloping meadows, crisscrossed with deep canyons and gullies. Higher ranges, capped with forests of pine and fir, dominated the skyline. The ranches and homesteads found on Joseph Plains in the years between the two world wars had long since disappeared into vast ranching operations. Old-growth timber, where the Aram cattle once took refuge from the elements, was gone—logged long ago by the lumber companies who had built the roads now leading to Joseph. No trace was left of the Sunset School attended by the Arams or the wagon and horse trails they had traversed daily.

From the ranch, we continued across the plateau. We met only cattle. We saw no sign of humans until, rounding a bend in the road, we came upon an inhabited house. In a pasture nearby, four cowboys were inoculating cattle. On closer inspection, I realized the cowboys were actually three young women and one man.

We stopped at an old schoolhouse where Narcie remembered attending dances as a teenager. There, in the shady yard, we enjoyed a picnic lunch brought with us from Lewiston. Later, we drove across part of the original Aram ranchlands to a pasture where we parked the car and climbed to the top of a steep hill. The land ended abruptly in a deep canyon. Some three miles below lay the site of their father's Getta Creek ranch. The narrow, treacherous Fir Gulch Trail leading down to the ranch site started a few feet from where we stood. Even as small children, the Arams had ridden horseback down that trail, often leading packhorses.

The Snake River is approximately a mile from the former ranch site, but we could not see the river from where we stood. It was obscured by high bluffs on both sides where Oregon's Copper Mountain forms a dramatic section of Hells Canyon. Standing on that lofty plateau overlooking the western edge of Idaho, I tried to imagine what it must have been like for the Arams to grow up in such a ruggedly beautiful land— wild, remote, and now even more sparsely populated than in their day. The rigors of ranch life had ruled their childhood, for they lived much as their grandparents, without electricity or running water. Horses, mules, and their own strong bodies supplied all their power and transportation.

Well into the 20th century the Arams were pioneers, cowboys, and entrepreneurs. For three generations they took an active part in the development of Idaho County. They had a great love for good horses and cattle and spent much of their lives tending both. Each generation forged ahead in a variety of business adventures, never hesitating to assume the risk of a new idea.

Although this is the story of only one family who helped build the American West, it is really the story of many—all those whose lives paralleled the Arams'. It is a story that deserves to be told.

Kristi M. Youngdahl
Paradise, California
October 1991

ACKNOWLEDGMENTS

OTHER THAN HISTORICAL facts gleaned from Idaho County's colorful history, this work is based largely on family records and the memories of the surviving Aram children. Jim, the most prolific, supplied memoir after memoir and spent hours answering questions. His wife, Ruth, furnished her original family research and continued seeking information, even as the work progressed. Narcie pursued family records in Oregon, collected information on the Smith family, and provided the feminine viewpoint. John, after spending many hours taping his memoirs, coordinated all efforts.

Special thanks go to Verna Geary McGrane of Grangeville—daughter of Edna Johnson Geary and granddaughter of Henry Clay and Mary Frances Aram Johnson—who willingly shared family history, as well as her own vast knowledge of Camas Prairie; Verna's daughter, Linda McGrane Junes, who enthusiastically helped with research in Grangeville; Carmelita Spencer, current owner of the original Aram homestead on Camas Prairie, who provided a tour of the site and information on its early history; and Patricia Kuhn, who edited the manuscript for the Aram family.

A heartfelt thanks goes to the "Inklings of Paradise"—writers Pat Brice, Ann Doro, Lynn Hartsell, Maida Parr, and Betty Platko, whose encouragement, suggestions, and editing helped me every step of the way, and to my family—my parents, Ken and Margaret Hvistendahl, who instilled in me a love of history, my daughters, Sonja and Shana, for their patience, and my husband, Doug, who provided wise counsel and who, because he first saw Joseph with me, always understood.

FROM THE GALLOWS OF YORK
TO THE CANYONS OF IDAHO

On August 1, 1758, a human skeleton was unearthed at Thistle Hill near Knaresbrough in Yorkshire, England. The gruesome discovery reopened an investigation into of the disappearance of Daniel Clarke, a wealthy shoemaker, some 13 years before. Authorities arrested Richard Houseman, a petty thief, who was seen with Clarke on the night he disappeared.

Houseman denied any knowledge of Clarke, and when the bones proved not to be those of the shoemaker, he was released. But the discovery at Thistle Hill rekindled an interest in Clarke's disappearance. When some of his valuables surfaced and were traced back to Houseman, the thief was arrested again.

This time Houseman confessed his participation in the murder of Clarke, but he vowed the actual deed had been carried out by one Eugene Aram. The thief then led authorities to St. Robert's Cave, where he told them he saw Aram beat Clarke about the head and chest until he died. Clarke's remains were found in the cave and authorities turned their attention to finding Eugene Aram.

Quite by accident, a Knaresbrough constable—who was visiting in King's Lynn—discovered Aram living there under an assumed name. He arrested the 55-year-old schoolteacher and returned him in chains to Knaresbrough. Aram's trial for the murder of Daniel Clarke became one of the century's most sensational and stamped the name of Eugene Aram onto the pages of British criminal history.

Before Eugene Aram turned to crime, his family had dwelt quietly in England for many generations. In Eugene's own words his ancestors were of "great antiquity and consideration."[1] Eugene's father, Peter Aram, was a highly regarded gardener and draftsman who had, in his lifetime, been in the employ of Sir Edward Blackett for 30 years.

Eugene became a scholar and was well respected in that community.

A man of noteworthy ability and intellect, he was a self-taught authority in French, Arabic, Hebrew, Chaldee, and the Celtic dialects. He was among the first scholars to point out the relationship of Celtic to the Indo-European languages and to dispute that Latin was derived from Greek.

Before Daniel Clarke disappeared, Eugene was an assistant schoolteacher—then known as an usher—in Knaresbrough. Despairing of ever supporting his wife Anna and seven children on his small income, he turned to robbery and enlisted the aid of other local thieves. He was a friend of Daniel Clarke's, sharing with him an interest in books, botany, and gardening. On the night Clarke disappeared, Eugene was seen with the shoemaker. Later, Aram and his group of thieves were arrested on suspicion of possessing some of Clarke's valuables, but they were released due to lack of evidence.

Eugene then fled Knaresbrough, abandoning his family. He changed his name and moved from London to Middlesex to King's Lynn, taking teaching positions in each town. At King's Lynn, according to one of his students, he often lectured them on the subject of murder.[2]

Once apprehended, Eugene prepared his own clever and eloquent defense, saying at one point, "I concerted not schemes of fraud, projected not violence, injured no man's person or property. My days were honestly laborious and my nights intensely studious." He went on to say that no man living such a purposeful life could "plunge into the very depth of profligacy, precipitately. . . . Mankind is never corrupted at once. Villainy is always progressive."[3]

Houseman stuck to his story, swearing Daniel Clarke had met a violent death at the hands of Eugene Aram. This story was corroborated by another thief, Henry Terry. On the strength of their testimony, as well as the questions raised by Aram's conflicting statements concerning his involvement with Clarke, Houseman, and Terry, Eugene was convicted. He was hanged at York on August 6, 1759, going to the gallows calmly. Later, his body hung in chains at Knaresbrough where it was left to rot. There it remained for many years, a reminder to the public of the crimes of Eugene Aram.

The schoolteacher's sensational story caught the imagination of the people and he became a folk hero. Seventy years after Aram's death, Thomas Hood published a poem titled "The Dream of Eugene Aram," and wrote of him, "The remarkable name of Eugene Aram, belonging to a man of unusual talents and acquirements, is unhappily associated with a deed of blood as extraordinary in its details as any recorded in our calendar of crime. . . . The brow that learning might have made illustrious was stamped ignominious forever with the brand of Cain."[4] Even then the story of Eugene Aram was not put to rest. In 1873, more than a century after his death, a play titled *Eugene Aram* by W. G. Wills was produced by Henry Irving.

Despite their father's infamy, Eugene's children went on with their lives as Arams had for centuries before. His son, Joseph, became a harness maker and continued to reside in Yorkshire until his death. He was buried near York, where his tombstone describes him as a man of "deep piety, religious zeal, benevolence, and independence."

One of Joseph's sons, Mattias, followed in his father's footsteps, becoming a harness maker and saddler after serving four years in the British Army. At the age of 36, Mattias emigrated to America, leaving the notoriety of the Aram name behind. Upon his arrival in 1806, he stayed briefly in New York City. Then he bought a farm near Utica and married Elizabeth Tomkins of Cambridge, New York. In the 1830s Mattias moved his family to Newark, Licking County, Ohio. There he lived out his life.

Mattias and Elizabeth had five sons and four daughters. The daughters disappeared into history, but the sons—Joseph, James, John, Thomas, and William—became participants in the great westward expansion of our nation. Their lives were documented by historians and succeeding generations.

James Aram started the family's westward migration in 1840 when he and his wife Susan traveled by wagon and horse team to Delavan in Wisconsin Territory. There they settled and established a sheep and grain farm on the east shore of Lake Delavan. James soon became one of Delavan's most successful farmers. He expanded into other businesses, first a general store and then a successful real estate venture. In 1863 he built a large mansion in town.

While his business life was marked with success, his personal life was marred by tragedy. Each of James and Susan's three daughters died of childhood illnesses—Mary at 13, Eveline at 7, and Marion at 15. For many years James served in both county and town offices and on many governing boards. He was known as an honest and upright man.

When James died in 1897, he left $20,000 to build a home for retired Methodist ministers. This was done in memory of his parents, Mattias and Elizabeth, English Wesleyan Methodists who at one time shared their home with a Methodist bishop. He gave another $20,000 to build the Aram Public Library and established a variety of other bequests to various churches and the local cemetery. When Susan died in 1905, the balance of their estate was divided among some thirty nieces and nephews.

The same year James settled in Wisconsin, his brother Joseph moved his family from Ohio to Illinois. However, the expanding West beckoned and in 1846 the family sold out, packed their belongings and joined a wagon train bound for California. En route, Joseph Aram's wagon train encountered the Donner party near Fort Bridger. There they were encouraged to try a shorter route discovered by Lansford Hastings. The Donner party chose the Hastings Cut-off, but the Aram party followed their guide along the Fort Hall Road. At a fork in the road many of the immigrants headed for Oregon, while the Arams and 11 other wagons continued to California.

Near the summit of the Sierras, the travelers were met by two men from Sutter's Fort who bore news of the Mexican uprising against the American occupation of California. Aware that hostilities with the Mexicans threatened their own safety, the party pushed on. When they reached the Yuba River they stopped for a day of rest. There, while washing her family's clothes, Joseph's wife, Sarah Ann, brought up a handful of sand from the riverbed. In it she discovered a gold nugget, which she quietly tucked in her daughter's sock.

Reluctant to share the secret with the rest of the party, for fear they would want to remain at the river instead of moving to the safety of Sutter's Fort, Joseph and Sarah took the nugget with them. Had they not kept their secret, Sarah Aram might have been credited with the discovery of California gold. As it was, the Arams did not have their nugget assayed until after James Marshall's discovery on the American River in 1848. It was only then they knew for certain Sarah's nugget was real.

Commissioned a captain in the Volunteers by Col. John C. Frémont, Joseph left Sutter's Fort with his party to command the defense of northern California from a mission at Santa Clara. Throughout the winter of 1846-47, Aram led the defense of the mission against Francisco Sanchez and 150 well-armed Mexicans. While the Americans successfully defended the mission throughout the Mexican-American

War, the civilians suffered during the long, wet winter. Fourteen died, including 8-year-old George Aram.

The year 1848 found Captain Aram and his family in Monterey, where Sarah gave birth to a son, the first child born of immigrant overland settlers in the new state. The baby was named Eugene in honor of his great-great-grandfather, an indication that Mattias had taught his children there was no shame in the name of Eugene Aram.

Joseph eventually settled his family in San Jose. While living there he was a delegate to the California Constitutional Convention and the first person to sign the California Constitution on September 9, 1849. In December of that year he was elected a member of the new state legislature. Later, he established the first nursery in the state and helped organize schools and the Methodist church in San Jose.

Joseph's brother, Thomas Aram, followed him to the West Coast in 1848. He, however, traveled to Oregon Territory. Upon reaching The Dalles on the Columbia River, his wagon was attacked by Indians. Thomas and nine other young men escaped over the Barlow Trail to Sauvie Island where, in August, he was killed in a gunfight by a man named Dan Leonard. No motive for the killing is known.

Four years after Thomas's death, William Aram and his wife, Mary, left their home in Ohio and sailed to California on the Nicaragua Route, arriving on August 2, 1852. They stayed temporarily with Captain Joseph Aram and his family in San Jose. After locating property in the San Jose Valley, William and Mary settled into ranch life.

In those early days bands of outlaws plagued the new state. Mary was often left alone on the ranch while William rode for days with a sheriff's posse searching for thieves. The couple raised two sons and three daughters during their years on the ranch. In 1886 they moved to Oregon, where they lived in Portland and Enterprise. William died at Enterprise in 1895 and Mary in 1905.

The fifth brother, John, caught gold fever and left the East aboard an English steamer, the *Sara Sands*, with 600 other gold seekers bound for San Francisco in 1849. On the long journey the ship lost its rudder and drifted for nearly six weeks, coming ashore in lower California in early May. As compensation for not reaching their destination, the captain reimbursed his passengers $30 each. Young John, with 50 other men, walked the 600 miles to San Francisco, purchasing cattle from the Indians along the way and making beef jerky for sustenance.

After three years of gold mining, John returned to Ohio, where he married Sarah Amelia Barr. Shortly after the birth of their first child, Sarah Elizabeth, or "Libby," on August 1, 1854, the young couple decided to return to California. Sarah and the baby traveled by steamer to Panama. Carrying 6-week-old Libby, Sarah crossed the Isthmus on foot and boarded another steamer for San Francisco.

While Sarah and the baby made their way by sea, John left the East and joined a group of men herding sheep from Iowa to California. Their combined bands totaled 3,000 head. Along the way John acted as a scout for the party, riding in advance on his horse, Old Charley. Few sheep were lost on the trail because any tired, injured, or sick animals were hauled in one of the 12 wagons. Game and fish were abundant on the six-month journey, and one day the travelers were halted for several hours while a large herd of buffalo passed.

Shortly after their arrival in California, John and Sarah sold their sheep and went to mine in the Sierra Nevada. While tending Libby and living the rough life of a miner's wife, Sarah bore two more children—Mary Frances, "Frankie," born on March 9, 1856, in Amador County, California, and John Thomas, "Tom," born in Calaveras County, California, on May 28, 1858.

With their growing family, John and Sarah left California in 1859 for the rich soil of the Willamette Valley of Oregon. Little is known about the next five years, but it is surmised that the Arams spent those years farming and developing fruit orchards. It is known that a third daughter, Amelia Jane, "Delia" or "Dee," was born on April 16, 1860, in Yamhill County, Oregon.

Sometime after Delia's birth the family moved to Portland in Multnomah County. There on February 15, 1863, 8-year-old Libby died of diphtheria. The following summer, on July 7, Sarah delivered a second son, James Henry Aram.

Shortly after James Henry's birth, the family decided to leave Oregon. Markets for Oregon farmers had dried up with the end of the California gold rush, and times were hard. Gold had been discovered in the newly formed territory of Idaho, and many young men from the Willamette Valley had already left for the gold fields along the Clearwater and Salmon rivers.

Packing up their household goods and four young children, John and Sarah headed into one of the last wildernesses of the American

West. Little did they realize, as they entered that uncharted land, that the pioneering spirit of their branch of the Aram family would make its own indelible mark on the history of central Idaho for more than 100 years.

Chapter 1

EDEN FOUND

❧

This is crazy country. In places the Snake River cuts through gorges a mile deep, but up on the plateau on both sides of it, there isn't a drop of water and the land is as as dry as a moose bone. The Salmon and Clearwater Rivers cut through mountains that only a goat could visit, but no goat in his right mind would want to risk his neck on those cliffs.[5]—Andrew Henry, *Missouri Fur Company*, 1810

IT WAS DIRECTLY into the heart of this formidable wilderness that 37-year-old John Aram traveled with his young family on a late April day in 1864.[6] The family's heavy wagon, pulled by four strong horses, creaked and groaned as it lumbered along a rough stage route freshly carved into the Craig Mountains.

From her place on the hard wagon seat next to John, 33-year-old Sarah Aram kept an eye on 8-year-old Mary Frances, 6-year-old Tom, and 4-year-old Delia, who rode in the wagon bed amidst a conglomeration of provisions. She held 8-month-old James.

A sense of anticipation enveloped the little family, for they knew this was the final stretch of their arduous journey. It was a journey that had started in Portland, Oregon, nearly two weeks before when they boarded a steamship headed up the Columbia River. After several days, the Arams disembarked near the Walla Walla River. John then hired a pack train to carry his family and their few possessions overland some 75 miles to Lewiston, a trading town founded just three years earlier at the confluence of the Clearwater and Snake rivers.

It was a difficult horseback trip for three energetic young children and a baby, but eventually Lewiston came into sight. The new town bustled with miners and trappers outfitting themselves for wilderness life. While resting briefly at the little outpost, John and Sarah purchased a wagon, farm implements, household supplies, and food staples. They loaded the wagon and left early one morning, heading alone into the Craig Mountains southeast of Lewiston.

Hour after hour, the wagon lurched over the primitive road, jarring everyone on board. Instinctively, the children clung to anything fastened securely, while Sarah held tightly to the baby and the wagon seat. They toiled upward on the trail that rose into the mountains, traversing streams and steep canyons. At times they enjoyed the dappled shade of mountain pine and fir; at other times they felt the warmth of the sun as they crossed rocky, barren ravines. Suddenly, at an elevation of 3,390 feet, they found themselves on a broad and open plateau—a virtual Eden known as Camas Prairie.

Natural bunchgrass stood so tall it brushed the bellies of their horses. Early wildflowers dotted the prairie, hinting at a rainbow of hues yet to come. Rich black soil, capable of supporting a variety of crops, covered the plateau; snowcapped mountains emphasized every horizon. Tired after their trip from Lewiston, the family made camp for the night just off the wagon trail in a spot where they could watch the sun set behind distant mountains.

The next morning the Arams continued, traveling a deeply rutted trail leading to Mount Idaho, a tiny settlement at the base of the eastern stretch of mountains. From there a pack trail led to the Florence mines where gold had been discovered in 1861. But as they made their way across Camas Prairie, John and Sarah began to visualize another gold—vast fields of wheat rising from the fertile plain. Three miles from Mount Idaho, and 65 from Lewiston, their travels ended. There they staked a claim on 160 acres of prime farmland on Three Mile Creek, a tributary of the south fork of the Clearwater River.

Camas Prairie, some 30 miles long by 25 wide, is the only large section of fertile farmland in what now comprises Idaho County.[7] Most of the county is made up of mountain ranges, canyons, and higher, less fertile plateaus. Entire ranges of the Bitterroot Mountains, stretching to Montana, lie within Idaho County just beyond the south fork of the Clearwater River. These form a wide barrier to the east of Camas Prairie. The Snake River and Hells Canyon create a border to the west with the high peaks of the Seven Devils Mountains rising in the southwest corner. The Salmon River cuts a deep canyon between the Snake and the Clearwater until it veers east at Riggins and, with its mountains to the south, forms the southern border. The Craig Mountains and spurs of Oregon's Blue Mountains create a boundary to the north and northwest.

At Hells Canyon the Snake forms a cut a mile deep, making it the deepest gorge in North America, while the third deepest, after the Grand Canyon of the Colorado, is formed by the Salmon River. With these two tumultuous rivers and their canyons guarding Idaho County's borders, it is little wonder that after the first white men, Lewis and Clark, entered the area in 1805, it was 26 years before representatives of the Hudson's Bay Company followed their route and nearly 60 before the first settlers, including John and Sarah Aram, arrived.[8]

The Nez Perce Indians, whose tribal lands these parties of whites crossed, welcomed the strangers as friends. They were a peaceful nation made up of several seminomadic bands who moved with the seasons, but considered certain regions homeland to their people. Each of these bands revered the earth as their mother and believed everyone had an individual responsibility to leave the land as pristine as it was on the day of their birth. An intelligent and industrious people, the Nez Perce did not consider the whites a threat to their lands or way of life. They quickly saw the advantage of trading with their new friends. Always open to new ideas, the tribe allowed white missionaries to settle in their midst in 1836, and many became converts to Christianity.

In 1855 the Nez Perce and other northwestern tribes signed a treaty with the Americans. Since there was little interest in the remote Nez Perce lands, most of it was retained within the borders of their reservation. The Indians continued their isolated lives until gold was discovered on the Clearwater River and its tributaries in 1860.

It was at this time that many old California miners first heard of this new frontier. In their rush to stake a claim they ignored the fact that the gold fields lay within the borders of the Indian reservation. Most of the Nez Perce greeted them in peace, asking only that the whites not build permanent homes or settlements. By 1861 the town of Lewiston had sprung up on Indian land, and white settlers, intent on opening stores and growing crops to prosper from the miners, were edging onto their reservation.

The Nez Perce leaders complained to government officials, but little was done to halt the flow. In 1863 the Indians were called to another council at Fort Lapwai where the Americans proposed to take away most of the Nez Perce lands, reducing their original reservation by 75 percent.

By this time the tribe had been severed into two factions, the treaty and/or Christian bands and the non-treaty and/or non-Christian bands. Chiefs of the non-treaty bands refused to sign the new treaty and returned to their homes. In their absence the Christian chiefs, who lived on land remaining within the reservation, signed away the ancient lands of the non-treaty chiefs. Their signatures were accepted by the Americans as being representative of the entire Nez Perce nation.

John and Sarah Aram arrived on Camas Prairie a scant year after the signing of this treaty. They knew little of the politics of the region and saw only a pristine wilderness with no buildings or fences. According to their government, the rich land of Camas Prairie was theirs for the taking. Others had already settled on the prairie. Most were single men who had tired of mining and lived on homesteads scattered across the region. Only three other families lived in the area when the Arams arrived. Homesteading nearby on claims taken in 1863 were the families of Aurora Shumway and Seth Jones; L. P. Brown and his family lived at Mount Idaho, where they had settled in 1862.

Looking over their claim, John and Sarah chose as their homesite a draw fed by seven springs that opened into a natural pond. John constructed a foundation and large stone fireplace from rocks gathered at the many streams crossing the prairie. He dug a shallow well near one of the springs and directed the cold spring water into it, creating a cooler for perishables. In the nearby mountains, he cut trees for their cabin. His lean and muscular body supplied all the necessary manpower.

Once his family had shelter, John began to plow the bunchgrass under, making room for his own crops of oats, barley, and wheat. Like his neighbor, Seth Jones, who had turned over the first sod on the prairie the summer before, John saw his future in small grains. Jones also ran a small herd of cattle, and John eventually did the same. However, the first real stockman of the prairie was John Aram's other neighbor, Aurora Shumway, who with his partner, John Crooks, had trailed in 1,000 head of cattle from Oregon the summer before.[9]

To the new country, John and Sarah brought stock from their Oregon fruit trees that they used to start a nursery and plant the first orchards on the prairie. In the early years the couple spent many cool evenings before their open fireplace grafting scions from their nursery stock.

Their few neighbors welcomed these horticultural efforts and purchased apple, pear, plum, and cherry trees, which thrived in the rich black soil. The Arams provided all of the fruit trees planted along the Salmon River by later settlers. Many orchards cultivated by John and Sarah Aram exist even today.

The rich land nourishing the Aram trees took its name from the native camas plant. In June the camas flower blossomed, creating a sea of blue as far as the eye could see. The bulb of the plant, an onionlike button with a sweet taste, was a principal food for the Nez Perce Indians, who steamed them, pounded them flat, and baked them in a kiln, producing a sort of bread.

Each summer as they went from winter homes on the Clearwater River to summer hunting and fishing grounds on the Salmon, the Nez Perce stopped on the prairie—land that for centuries had provided grazing for their large herds of Cayuse ponies. Many of the Nez Perce felt the whites were illegally on their land, but they were friendly, trading cattle and ponies and staying near their farms for as long as six weeks while the women gathered wood and dug for camas roots. Sarah Aram often invited the Indians to meals and treated them as she would any traveler. Once seated, the guests ate with relish, then returned to their camps carrying any leftovers pressed upon them by Sarah.

For a time, the people lived in relative harmony—the Indian and the white man, the cattleman and the farmer. It seemed there was room enough for everyone. Camas Prairie was a bountiful oasis in the midst of a largely uninhabitable territory. Cattle and horses grazed freely on the natural bunchgrass. Hogs fed easily for months on the camas root. The freshly turned sod nourished crops of grain and a variety of young fruit trees. John and Sarah Aram had found their "Little Eden."

Chapter 2

TAMING THE LAND

∾

Most of the first settlers of Idaho were poor in purse but . . . rich in muscle and energy and most all possessed a good moral character. The rule that was in common practice was for each person to attend his own private business and to have affectionate regard for his neighbor and his neighbor's rights, and to extend a helping hand to the unfortunate that needed help . . . the early settlers were as noble . . . a people as were ever assembled . . . for the reclamation and development of an unsettled country. . . ." —John Hailey, *The History of Idaho*, 1910

EVEN AS THE Arams earned the trust of the local Indians, they were gaining the respect of their small, but growing, pioneer community. Although quiet and retiring in nature, John quickly became known as a hardworking, honest man. Sarah, whose head barely reached her husband's chest, had a natural ability to nurse the sick and injured. With no doctor in residence on the prairie, Sarah was in constant demand and often traveled through cold and stormy nights to reach someone in need.

The rich soil of the prairie yielded generous crops, but because of its isolation farmers found a sparse market for their goods. The heavily populated mining camps, located at the end of treacherous pack trails far in the mountains, were their only outlets. Most of the crops raised were used by the pioneers for personal consumption or for fattening livestock. During the first dozen years, until a flour mill was built, they hauled wheat by wagon to Walla Walla, Washington, where it was ground into flour then brought back to the prairie for the settlers.

Out of necessity everyone at the Aram farm helped with the chores, particularly those that brought food to the table. The children rose at five o'clock to milk the cows before riding their horses to school. Even the youngest helped churn butter, which was kept in a bucket and left hanging in the well. Ripe cabbages from the garden were turned into the ground with their roots exposed in order to preserve them until they were dug up in the fall. Apples were kept fresh by placing them in pits lined with hay or straw and then covering them with more straw and a foot of dirt.

The family went once a year to Lewiston for supplies. The 130-mile round-trip took a day each way and sometimes two, depending on the swiftness of the team pulling their wagon. Anything needed in the intervening months was ordered from one of the freighters who hauled goods constantly from Lewiston to the mining camps. Women ordered shoes, thread, cloth, and other household goods by describing what they wanted or showing the freighter something similar. When he returned, he brought the item with him. However, money was scarce even for necessities, and the pioneers often made do or borrowed from a neighbor. For many, a lantern was considered a luxury. To light their cabins, they used a pan of grease with cloth for a wick.[10]

This community of settlers had little to offer a thief, but a lawless element existed on the fringes and robbers often lay in wait along the 45-mile trail from Mount Idaho to the mining camps at Florence. Miners were robbed and sometimes murdered; however, farmers packing in produce were never molested. On the prairie, disputes between young men were settled by fist or gun. With no sheriff and the closest army post 60 miles away at Fort Lapwai, the pioneers were forced to become their own lawmakers.

The summer of 1869 found the Camas Prairie community faced with the dilemma of what to do with an Indian named Shumway Jim. It was believed he had committed several murders, but proof of his involvement had never been brought forward. That spring several Nez Perce women reported to the settlers the discovery of human bones under a rock at the mouth of Three Mile Creek. They indicated that Shumway Jim probably knew something about the bones.

The suspected murderer was devoted to John and Sarah's neighbor, Aurora Shumway, who had befriended him. It was from this stockman that Jim derived his name. Hearing of the murder, Shumway and his partner, John Crooks, interrogated Jim, who confessed to the murder of a French prospector—a murder that gained him $10, a horse, weapons, and a blanket. The citizens of the prairie decided then and there to end Jim's criminal activities. He was taken to Ward Girton's ranch near Three Mile Creek where three poles were erected to form a tripod. There, with all the settlers present, Shumway Jim was hanged.[11]

Most of the citizens of Camas Prairie were law-abiding and vigilante trials in Lewiston usually deterred those who weren't. Consequently, the settlers were able to devote their full attention to building their homes, farming their claims, and educating their children.

An unusually well-educated group, the pioneers of Camas Prairie established schools and literary societies even before there were buildings to house them. In the spring of 1867, Miss Biancia Reed of Wilbur, Oregon, arrived to open a school in an old log cabin at Mount Idaho. The Aram children, along with the offspring of Loyal P. Brown, F. B. King, James Odle, and Seth Jones, attended the school.

In 1868 the pioneers erected the first schoolhouse near King's home in Mount Idaho. During the same year, a log schoolhouse was built with volunteer labor on John and Sarah Aram's farm on the banks of Whiskey Bill Creek. All the Aram children attended this school. Their first teacher was a miner named McLaughlin, who was wintering on the prairie. Their second teacher was an Aram neighbor, James H. Robinson.

The Aram schoolhouse, equipped with rustic furnishings, soon became the center of social activity. Literary societies held meetings with orations and debates. Dances were particularly popular, even though the bachelors found no dancing partners as the few females present were married women or their young daughters.

Pioneer families observed the Sabbath as a day of rest and spent it in leisure activities outdoors where they enjoyed the beauty of their prairie and the surrounding mountains. There were no churches or clergy, and in the first ten years of settlement only one visiting preacher passed through.[12]

By 1866 the population of Camas Prairie had grown to 75. Over the next four years, John and Sarah's "Little Eden" drew other families and the population doubled.[13] Adding to the growth in those intervening years were the babies born on the prairie, babies who were often helped into the world by Sarah Aram. Among the new pioneers was John and Sarah's last child, Clara Helen Aram, who arrived on September 28, 1869.

A federal census in 1870 listed John and Sarah's real estate value at $800 and their personal property value at $700—considerably less than their neighbors. Seth Jones's real estate value was $2,500 and personal property, $3,000. Loyal Brown listed real estate at $5,000 and personal property at $20,000, whereas John Crooks listed his real estate at $6,000 and his personal property at $16,000.[14]

Being "poorer in purse" than the others did not diminish the Arams in the eyes of their neighbors. James Robinson noted this in reference to the early pioneers many years later when he said, "in the meetings of these early settlers . . . their greetings were as cordial, their kindness and friendship genuine. . . . Their eyes were closed and their tongues silent in regard to the cheap dress of a poorer neighbor."[15]

John's lack of wealth was not due to any lack of industry. He willingly tried entrepreneurial ventures beyond farming. Leading pack trains into the remote mining camps brought in extra cash, as did serving as a justice of the peace at Mount Idaho in the 1870s. By then, he had help with the farm from a hired hand named Isaac McDaniel, a Nova Scotian in his 50s.

A fraternal association of local farmers, known as Charity Grange #15, Patrons of Husbandry, was organized in Mount Idaho in 1874. Members elected a committee to find land for a grange hall. The group approached Loyal Brown, founder and main landholder in Mount Idaho, with a request for land. Brown refused, so they turned to John and Sarah's neighbor, John Crooks, who owned 600 acres on Three Mile Creek. Crooks deeded the grangers not only the land requested but also an additional 5 acres and water rights for a mill.

In 1876 the grangers constructed a flour mill on the land and built a grange hall. That same year a post office was established, while a small hotel, four homes, a store, a blacksmith shop, and a drugstore were built nearby—Grangeville started to grow on the prairie just a mile from John and Sarah's log cabin.

A dozen years wrought great changes. Camas Prairie was no longer the virgin wilderness the Arams first saw in 1864. Supply wagons constantly lumbered across the prairie; sawmills on Three Mile Creek turned out fresh lumber to construct new buildings and replace log homes; and a new town stood proudly near their farm, rivaling the established community of Mount Idaho.

Settlers continued to trickle in. They built homes, enclosed the land with fences, plowed the natural vegetation under, and planted crops. The friendly Nez Perce, who had for centuries roamed the open and unbroken prairie, gradually withdrew to the river banks. Few noted their plight.

Chapter 3

WAR

The Nez Perce War ought not to have occurred and would not had our government used a little more diplomacy. The Indians owned the country and had a right to it by reason of possession. One very old Indian asked me in regard to the government's order to compel all Indians to evacuate their homes and move to the reservation. I told him it was true. He said where he lived was his only home . . . he had lived there a great many years . . . his wife and child were buried there . . . he wanted to be buried there also . . . he shed tears of genuine sorrow. I do not justify the Indians going on the war path, but I sometimes wonder what their paleface brothers would have done under similar circumstances.[16]—Henry Clay Johnson, Member of the "Brave Seventeen" Mount Idaho Volunteers, Nez Perce Indian War 1877

LATE IN 1876 the government notified the non-treaty Nez Perce Indians that they must go to reservations as they had agreed in the treaty of 1863. The Christian bands whose chiefs had signed the treaty complied with it from the beginning, remaining on their homelands, which were within the reservation. The non-treaty Indians, including those who befriended the Arams, ignored the treaty for 13 uneasy years.

The pressure to make more land available increased as settlers poured into the Northwest. Tensions between the two cultures escalated. A few white agitators accused the Indians of stealing and threatening white settlers. Headlines in local papers fanned the flames of fear creeping across white settlements. One or two aggressive whites murdered Indians in disputes over property, and the Indians quickly learned there was no justice for them in the white man's court. Youthful warriors, realizing their way of life was slipping away, cried for vengeance while Nez Perce leaders, long friends of the whites, counseled for peace.

Much of the attention was focused on the largest Nez Perce band, who dwelt in the Wallowa Valley on the western side of the Snake River far from the Aram home on Camas Prairie. Those residing in this "Valley of the Winding Water" were the most prosperous of the tribe. In 1876 the Wallowa band was led by Hin-mah-too-yah-lat-kekht (Thunder Traveling to Loftier Mountain Heights) or Young Chief Joseph, as he was known to the settlers, and his younger brother Ollokot (Frog or Little Frog).[17]

The two chiefs, then in their mid-30s, were the sons of Tuekakas who had been one of the first converts to Christianity. He was named Joseph, or Old Joseph, by the whites. His eldest son, Young Joseph, was often at the mission during his first seven years and gained some of his early education there. Eventually Old Joseph came to distrust the Americans and he returned to his Wallowa Valley and the ancient ways. He foresaw the coming of hordes of white men and counseled his people to never trade anything for their ancestral lands. Upon hearing of the treaty of 1863, he destroyed his cherished Bible and declared the new agreement was no more than a "thief treaty."

When Old Joseph died in 1871 his sons inherited leadership of the Wallowa band of Nez Perce. Young Chief Joseph, an eloquent and gentle man, was a diplomat and civil leader who was in charge of the welfare of his people. Ollokot was a leader of the hunters and warriors. Both wanted peace with the white man and worked tirelessly to control their young, impetuous men.

When told over and over that his people were bound by the treaty of 1863 and must come to the reservations in Idaho, Joseph argued, "I believe the old treaty has never been correctly reported. If we ever owned the land, we own it still for we never sold it. In the treaty councils the commissioners have claimed that our country has been sold to the government. Suppose a white man should come to me and say, 'Joseph, I like your horses and I want to buy them.' I say to him, 'No, my horses suit me, I will not sell them.' Then he goes to my neighbor and says to him, 'Joseph has some good horses. I want to buy them, but he refuses to sell.' My neighbor answers, 'Pay me the money and I will sell you Joseph's horses.' The white man returns to me and says, 'Joseph, I have bought your horses and you must let me have them.' If we sold our lands to the government, this is the way they were bought."

In 1873 President Grant put a moratorium on white settlement in the Wallowa Valley in an attempt to pacify the Nez Perce, but in 1875 this order was rescinded. The Indians were embittered at this turn-about and passions flared. Gen. Oliver Howard, commander of the Department of the Columbia at Fort Vancouver, sent two companies of cavalry into the valley to keep peace during the summer.

One of the officers with those troops, Capt. Stephen C. Whipple, sent Howard a report that was sympathetic to Chief Joseph and his claim to the Wallowa. He stated that many of the whites were willing to leave if the government bought them out and added that the land was only good for stock grazing. Whipple also stated, "This band of Indians are by no means a vagabond set. They are proud-spirited, self-supporting and intelligent. . . ."[18]

Howard was impressed with Whipple's report and sent it to the War Department. He also included his own comments on the situation, stating, "I think it is a great mistake to take from Joseph and his band of Nez Perce Indians that valley. The white people really do not want it. They wished to be bought out . . . possibly Congress can be induced to let these really peaceable Indians have this poor valley for their own."[19]

However, pressure from the white community eventually forced Howard's hand and when he notified Joseph at a council meeting in the fall of 1876 that it was time to move, there was little room for negotiation. Joseph, intent on saving his homeland, tried once again to convince the whites of his claim to the Wallowa saying, "The Creative Power, when he made the earth, made no marks, no lines of division or separation on it." The Americans lost patience with Joseph's calm reasoning and asked what he would do if armed men came to remove his people from the valley. With quiet strength he replied, "We will not sell the land. We will not give up the land. We love the land. It is our home."

Joseph returned to his valley, but in early 1877 the Indian agent at Lapwai sent four treaty Nez Perce to Joseph's winter camp to demand he comply with the treaty of 1863. The four pleaded with Joseph to bring his people to the reservation at Lapwai, but he refused, saying, "I have been talking to the whites for many years about the land in question, and it is strange they cannot understand me. The country they claim belonged to my father, and when he died it was given to me and my people, and I will not leave it until I am compelled to."

In early May Joseph and Ollokot again attended a council at Lapwai. Other non-treaty chiefs, including White Bird of the Salmon River Bands, Toohoolhoolzote from the plateaus between the Snake and the Salmon rivers, and Looking Glass of the Middle Fork of the Clearwater, were also summoned. For the last time the chiefs tried to convince the whites to leave them free to roam, but fiery speeches by old Toohoolhoolzote led to his arrest. Eventually the other three, realizing they would have to relinquish their land or go to war, left with General Howard to select land on the reservation for their people.

The Indians were given a month to resettle. A heartbroken Joseph asked for a reasonable delay until his people could round up their herds and cross the rivers safely after the spring deluge down the Snake and Salmon had subsided. His request was denied. When he returned to the Wallowa, soldiers were already present to ensure his compliance with the orders.

Embittered young men called for war, but Joseph and Ollokot still talked peace. In early June, pressed by the troops, Joseph's band left their beloved Wallowa Valley with what possessions they could carry and as much of their vast herds of cattle and horses as they had gathered. The Snake River was swollen and treacherous. Women, children, and old people were safely guided across on rafts fashioned from buffalo hides, but the raging river took a huge toll on the tribes' herds. Many of the cattle and horses, particularly the wobbly colts and newborn calves, perished in the river.

Joseph and Ollokot led their people on to the Salmon where they once again crossed a turbulent river. They joined White Bird's band at Tepahlewam—Split Rocks—an ancient meeting site on Camas Prairie in the Rocky Canyon near Tolo Lake just six miles from John and Sarah Aram's homestead. The camp grew as Toohoolhoolzote's people and members of Looking Glass's band arrived. In a ten-day grand council, the Indians aired their grievances against the white man. Impassioned appeals for bloodshed caused many young men to clamor for war and the mood of the young Indians turned ugly. Many dressed in war regalia and paraded through the camp.

During this grand council, signs of discontent among the Indians were present in the settlements. Warriors arrived in Grangeville and Mount Idaho to purchase guns and ammunition. Rumors of war spread across the prairie. Refusing to believe the Nez Perce would go to war, John and Sarah along with most of their neighbors continued their daily routines. Some of the settlers were so confident they even traded their own rifles to the Indians for good Cayuse ponies.

By June 9 many of the settlers became increasingly alarmed at the Indians' activities. Friendly Nez Perce warned them to leave their isolated homes for the relative safety of town. Cyrus Overman and his wife, Melinda, who had been married by John Aram when he was serving as justice of the peace at Mount Idaho in 1874, arrived at the Aram homestead with their baby. Because their farm near Tolo Lake was uncomfortably close to the Indian encampment, they believed their family would be safer with John and Sarah near Grangeville and Mount Idaho.

On the afternoon of June 13, Mr. Overman, who had returned to his farm, was helping Henry C. Johnson at Johnson's place overlooking Rocky Canyon. The two men watched as several young warriors mounted their horses and galloped toward the Salmon River. Cyrus decided to return to his farm, sack up some wheat, and retreat to the settlement. That same day John Aram discovered two unfamiliar Indians lingering on his farm smoking a pipe in a fence corner. Concerned about the rumors of an Indian uprising, he sent his son, Tom, on horseback to Mount Idaho to learn what was happening.

Groups of Indians roamed the prairie that afternoon. The Arams' closest neighbor, Seth Jones, passed two bands in full war dress. But Jones, who had refused to sign a petition to force the Indians onto the reservation, continued unharmed. In the meantime, John Crooks, who was convinced his Indian friends would not start a war, rode out to the Indian camp to gain their assurance peace would continue. He was threatened and warned to leave, one outraged warrior pursuing him all the way to the outskirts of Grangeville. Crooks then turned in a general alarm and couriers were sent out to all the settlers.[20]

Tom Aram returned, bearing the news that everyone was going to Mount Idaho for safety. Sarah gathered a few belongings and packed the family's supper into two milk cans. Around half past four a courier told them of Crooks's ejection from the Indian camp, and they hastened their departure. The friendly Nez Perce, many of whom they knew by name, had suddenly become their enemy.

John and his sons quickly hitched a team to the wagon, saddled horses, and turned their 30 milk cows out to pasture with the calves. Sarah, Mrs. Overman, and the children crowded into the wagon for the three-mile trip. Fearful that the Indians might detect their flight, Sarah hushed the children while the heavy wagon lumbered noisily across the prairie. It was only when the family reached the safety of Mount Idaho that she realized their beefsteak supper had been left behind.

Although volunteer riders had not reached all settlers in the outlying areas, by midnight the little settlement sheltered most of the residents of Camas Prairie. Cyrus Overman arrived with his neighbors, Mr. and Mrs. Watson, and was reunited with his family. The pioneers prepared to defend themselves. Women set about molding bullets, while the men gathered arms of pitchforks, butcher knives, and guns.

That very evening three Indians, who had left the Rocky Canyon camp earlier in the day, were conducting a series of revenge killings along the Salmon River. One of these, a fierce warrior named Wahlitits, had been taunted the day before by an older Indian for not avenging his father's death at the hands of a white settler named Larry Ott. Wahlitits, who had promised his dying father he would not seek revenge, was hurt and incensed by the words. After a night of brooding, Wahlitits enlisted the aid of two friends and left to find Ott, who had long since been set free by the white man's courts.

Ott had fled, but the warriors found and killed four settlers known to be unfriendly to Indians and wounded another. The next day when one of the Indians rode into the camp at Rocky Canyon to report their murderous deeds, some 16 additional warriors rode out to join the three in a war of vengeance. Of these, only one was of the Wallowa band. The rest were from White Bird's band who lived along the Salmon and who had chronicled a list of many wrongs to avenge.

Joseph and Ollokot were away from Rocky Canyon when the warriors left on their mission. They returned to find the camp in disarray because the Indians, shocked by the violence initiated by their young men, determined to flee the wrath of the whites. Joseph and Ollokot begged their people to stay until they could explain to General Howard what had happened, but most of their people were now tired of the talk of peace.

White Bird and Toohoolhoolzote's bands, along with most of the Wallowa band, left for White Bird Canyon to prepare for the inevitable. Joseph, Ollokot, and their families reluctantly followed. Of that time Joseph later said, "I was deeply grieved . . . I knew that their acts would involve all my people. I saw that the war could not be prevented. . . . We had many grievances, but I knew that war would bring more. . . . I would have given my own life if I could have undone the killing of white men by my people."

As the Indian camp was dismantled at Rocky Canyon, the refugees at Mount Idaho started their first day in exile. To cheer themselves they sang a song. L. P. Brown dispatched a messenger to General Howard and Colonel Perry at Fort Lapwai, notifying them that the Nez Perce were ready for war. The courier reached the fort in the afternoon.

That same morning Henry Johnson, who had stayed hidden in the fields at his ranch overnight, awoke to find the Indian camp nearly deserted. He rode into Mount Idaho just as word reached town that settlers living along the Salmon River had been attacked and killed. Again, Loyal Brown called for a volunteer to carry another message to Lapwai. Lew Day, known to be one of the best shots in the territory, volunteered for the job.

After traveling over 20 of the 62 miles to Lapwai, Day was overtaken by two Indians and shot through the shoulder. Although Day was bleeding profusely, he returned the few miles to Cottonwood House, a way station on the road between Lewiston and Mount Idaho. There he joined the proprietor, B. B. Norton, his wife, and son, Hill, Miss Lynn Bowers, John Chamberlain with his wife and two small children, and Joseph Moore. The little group decided to attempt a dash to Mount Idaho. As they prepared for their flight the warrior band was pursuing two freighters across Camas Prairie. The freight drivers escaped, but their wagon full of whiskey was captured.

Near midnight, just as the party from Cottonwood came within three miles of Grangeville, the warriors swooped down on them. The Indians were loaded with whiskey and in their drunken state had long forgotten their mission of vengeance against bad whites. In the ensuing melee Miss Bowers and young Hill Norton escaped into the darkness. The Chamberlains attempted to run, but were captured. The Indians killed Mr. Chamberlain and his 7-year-old son, slashed his little daughter with knives, and attacked Mrs. Chamberlain repeatedly. The warriors' gunfire killed Mr. Norton and critically wounded Mrs. Norton, Lew Day, and Joseph Moore. The three huddled behind their dead horses, while the wounded men's gunfire held off the Indians. At daybreak the warriors rode away.

Hill Norton and Miss Bowers, who had become separated, were discovered early that morning by civilian scouts, who formed a rescue party and rode out to the scene of the massacre. Using some of their own saddle horses for a team, the rescuers brought the casualties back to Mount Idaho in the Norton wagon.

The wounded were taken to a hospital set up in the front offices of Brown's Hotel. Dr. J. B. Morris, who had crossed Camas Prairie alone upon hearing of the hostilities, was in charge of the patients. With the help of Sarah Aram, Dr. Morris amputated Lew Day's leg in an attempt to save his life, but Day succumbed to his injuries, as did Mr. Moore. Mrs. Norton, Mrs. Chamberlain, and her daughter were nursed back to health.

The arrival at Mount Idaho of the dead and dying Norton party shocked the settlers. Immediately they organized a company of volunteers. Every male old enough to carry a rifle enlisted, including John and Tom Aram. A fort was hastily constructed on a hill north of town. Using two rail fences built parallel to each other and filled with rocks and timbers, the pioneers created a 4- to 5-foot-high wall in a circle measuring 150 feet in diameter. One side was built entirely from sacks of flour. Should the Indians attack, the 200 settlers and 100 residents of Mount Idaho would make their stand behind those walls.

Over the next few days the small band of Indians, without the sanction of their leaders, continued their rampage across the prairie and along the Salmon. All whites became targets and more orphaned, injured, or dead were brought into Mount Idaho. Twenty citizens were murdered and many others wounded during the first days of the war. Ten dwellings, three stores, a number of miners' cabins, and seven barns and shops were burned. Two freight wagons left behind by fleeing freighters were plundered and several hundred head of cattle and horses belonging to the settlers were stolen.[21]

Loyal Brown sent dispatches by rider to the *Lewiston Teller* reporting the progress of the war. One report dated June 19 stated, "Scouts have found the following houses on the prairie pillaged and plundered of everything valuable, to wit: H. Johnson, Jarrett, Overman, Byrom, Hashagan, Redman, Remington, Chapman, Benoy, and Croasdale. Watson's house and Johnson's barn burned."[22]

U.S. troops, under the leadership of Colonel Perry arrived in Grangeville on June 16. The terrified citizens urged Perry to follow the Indians into White Bird Canyon, some 20 miles away. There, on the morning of the seventeenth, Perry's forces—90 troopers, 11 volunteers from Mount Idaho, and 2 Indian scouts—descended into the rugged canyon. Even as their warriors took battle positions, the Nez Perce made one last attempt at peace by sending representatives bearing a white flag to meet the troops. A jumpy volunteer took aim and fired. Suddenly, Nez Perce warriors were everywhere. Soldiers fell from their mounts as bullets and arrows filled the air.

Retreating in disorder, Perry's troops fought their way back over two miles to Henry Johnson's abandoned ranch. Perry hoped to hold that position until dark, but the Indians overran it. By then, 33 soldiers and 1 officer lay dead or dying in White Bird Canyon. With one-third of his force gone, Perry retreated, halted, and fired as the warriors pursued them to within four miles of Mount Idaho. Then, when citizen reinforcements rode out to join the soldiers, the Indians retreated. The Battle of White Bird Canyon became known as the second most disastrous defeat ever dealt to the U.S. Army by the Indians, the first being the Custer massacre of 1876.[23]

Mount Idaho became a center of activity during the dark days of the war. Sarah Aram cared for the sick and injured. She, Mary Frances, and Delia helped cook for and feed the many volunteers and soldiers. Thirteen-year-old James hauled water from a nearby spring for the community, while 8-year-old Clara carried soup to the injured. Sarah's calm and cheerful presence eased the tension for many. One day, after overhearing two volunteers from Dayton arguing loudly, she grabbed a bucket of water and interrupted the disagreement by calmly offering the men a drink. By the time she left, their quarrel was forgotten.

Two days after the battle at White Bird Canyon, the Indians moved down the Salmon River, crossed it, and took a position on the high plateau now known as Joseph Plains. In the twilight days of June, General Howard and his 400 men pursued the Indians across the Salmon. They searched the rocky terrain on the other side, camping briefly on today's Camp Howard Mountain. As the troops followed Chief Joseph's trail, the Nez Perce swung around behind them and returned to Camas Prairie.

In the meantime cavalry units under the command of Captain

Whipple—the same captain who had written a report in favor of the Indians remaining in Wallowa—and a unit of volunteers from Mount Idaho—incensed by the massacres on Camas Prairie—launched a senseless attack on Looking Glass's village along the Clearwater. Looking Glass had remained aloof from the hostilities, but rumors that he was supplying the main band of Nez Perce with warriors led to action. Many of the Indians were wounded; a woman and her baby drowned while trying to escape; their homes and gardens were destroyed and their livestock driven away.

Angered by the attack on a peaceful village, the Indians took the offensive. On July 3, a scouting party from Colonel Perry's command at Cottonwood was attacked. All 12 members of the party were killed. The next day the warriors besieged the troops at Cottonwood almost overrunning their rifle pits. On July 5 the Indian leaders decided to move their people across Camas Prairie to the Clearwater River on a trail that would take them between Grangeville and Cottonwood. Simultaneously, 17 volunteers under the command of Capt. D. B. Randall rode out from Mount Idaho to relieve Perry's troops. Five of the volunteers, including Henry Johnson, were known as the best rifle shots on the frontier.

Just two miles from Cottonwood, a war party intercepted the volunteers.[24] Henry Johnson, who had been tracking the Indians' approach through his field glasses, took the first shot at the warriors when Captain Randall ordered his men to charge the Indian lines so they would not be cut off from Cottonwood.[25] Henry dismounted and fired. His frightened horse nearly broke away, but he controlled the animal and remounted.

By then, the rest of the volunteers had ridden some distance beyond him. Henry kicked his horse into a run to catch up. A short distance away he came upon volunteer Frank Vansise whose horse had been shot out from under him. Slowing his pace only momentarily, Henry swung Vansise up behind him. The two joined the rest of the volunteers as they broke through the Indian lines. Randall and volunteer B. F. Evans fell mortally wounded. The remaining 15 took a defensive position. The Indians were to their right and rear, but the route to Cottonwood remained open.

Perry's men listened to the sound of battle from their Cottonwood post. Perry, believing the volunteers were doomed, refused to allow his men to go to their aid. For an hour the volunteers, who were later known as the Brave Seventeen, fought off their attackers. With determined fire they forced the Indians back and held their position.

Finally, a volunteer with Perry's troops mounted his horse and shouted that it was a shame and an outrage to allow the embattled men to perish without attempting to go to their aid. He dashed across the prairie to help. A sergeant who was building an earthen fortification around Cottonwood threw down his shovel and announced he would lead the troops if his officers wouldn't. When Perry saw most of his men readying their mounts, he ordered Captain Whipple to accompany them. The Indians retreated and the troops brought in the volunteers, their two dead and three injured.

Six days later General Howard and 400 men engaged some 250 to 300 Nez Perce in battle near the Indians' camp on the South Fork of the Clearwater River. At this time the tribe numbered, in addition to the warriors, some 450 noncombatants, their baggage, and 2,000 horses. It took two days for the army and volunteers to break through the Indian defenses. The Nez Perce, with their families and animals, fled toward the centuries-old Lolo Trail leading into Montana. In their haste, they left their tepees and many ancient treasures behind, but took with them most of their horses and many captured rifles and ammunition.

Once in the Bitterroots the Nez Perce retreated in an orderly manner, clearing the narrow trail of brush and rocks and replacing the debris after their people and horses passed. Howard, in the meantime, waited on Camas Prairie for fresh troops and telegraphed ahead to army units in Montana to intercept the Nez Perce. But the Nez Perce outwitted the troops and reached the Bitterroot Valley before Howard and his men had even started on the Lolo Trail.

The Indians moved leisurely through the region, assuring whites they were passing in peace. Lulled into a relaxed mood, the tribe was shocked back to reality on August 9 while camped at Big Hole. In the early morning hours some 200 troops under the command of Col. John Gibbon swept into the unsuspecting camp, killing indiscriminately. When it was over, 50 women and children and some 30 warriors were dead. Among them was Wahlitits, the young warrior whose vengeful attacks along the Salmon started the war.

The disheartened Indians retreated while their braves held off Gibbon's men. From that point on their attitude toward Americans encountered on the trail changed. They did not harm women or children, but most white men unlucky enough to cross their path were killed. By this time Howard had nearly caught up and was often detected close to the fleeing Indians as they passed through Yellowstone. The Nez Perce pressed on and continued to outmaneuver and elude Howard. Upon reaching the Bear Paw Mountains, just a day's march from their destination beyond the Canadian border, Joseph and his chiefs believed they were safe. In a beautiful valley, abundant with game, they paused to rest.

Meanwhile, Col. Nelson A. Miles, on orders from General Howard, left his headquarters southeast of the Bear Paws with 375 men. Their mission was to intercept the Nez Perce before the tribe realized there were two armies in the field. After 12 days of marching, Miles's forces engaged the Indians in a surprise attack in the early morning hours of September 30. The Nez Perce quickly formed a strong defensive position. From bluffs, ravines, and gullies, the warriors directed a devastating rifle fire on the troops.

Throughout the day the battle raged, with the combatants often fighting at close range. Miles's superior forces took dramatic losses, but soldiers who fell within the Nez Perce lines were left unharmed. The fighting stopped at nightfall. That night a fierce blizzard engulfed the battlefield, compounding the misery of the war-weary men on both sides.

Even though they were surrounded by Miles's troops and were receiving shell fire from the artillery, the Nez Perce at first refused to surrender. But by October 4, when General Howard and his staff arrived at the battleground, the outlook for the Nez Perce was bleak. Ollokot, Looking Glass, and old Toohoolhoolzote were dead. White Bird, along with many of his people and horses, had escaped toward Canada. On October 5, General Howard's two Nez Perce scouts rode into the Indian camp and negotiated with Joseph. That afternoon, on the snow-covered battlefield, Chief Joseph turned his rifle over to Colonel Miles as General Howard watched.

News of Chief Joseph's surrender was a welcome relief to the residents of Camas Prairie. Most had remained at Mount Idaho for several weeks after the Nez Perce fled over the Lolo Trail, fearing the warriors might return. Initially the settlers sent volunteers out across the prairie to assess the damage. While inspecting the surrounding area, the men discovered caches of goods on the south side of the Salmon River. One of the volunteers presented a delighted Clara Aram with an unclaimed gold breast pin he found along the river.

Drawn back to their farms by the need to harvest crops, Camas Prairie residents began to venture out of Mount Idaho in mid-August. But the fear engraved in their minds by the events of the summer did not ease until they were assured the Nez Perce had been captured. By then, the Indians had fled over 1,800 miles. This included the distance over which they had cleverly doubled back to confuse the army.[26] They were hungry, cold and tired. Many of John and Sarah's Nez Perce friends had perished on the long flight toward Canada.

In his surrender speech Chief Joseph said, "I am tired of fighting. Our chiefs are dead. . . . It is cold and we have no blankets. The little children are freezing to death. My people, some of them, have run away to the hills, and have no blankets, no food; no one knows where they are—perhaps freezing to death. I want to have time to look for my children and see how many of them I can find. Maybe I shall find them among the dead. Hear me, my chiefs. I am tired; my heart is sick and sad. From where the sun now stands I will fight no more forever."

Chapter 4

CHANGES

∾

After the close of the Nez Perce . . . hostilities, the country settled down to steady development. . . . The old placers had become so thoroughly worked out that all but a comparatively few [miners] had left. . . . The result was no local market. The lack of cheap and speedy transportation rendered outside markets unavailable, consequently there was a local monetary stringency. The increase in the population in the entire decade between 1880 and 1890 was only 964, yet at no time was there any stagnation. Cattle and horse raising increased, and slowly the rich soil of the prairie was subdued by the plow of the agriculturalist, and compelled to yield bountiful harvests.—History of North Idaho Western Historical Publishing 1903

AFTER TWO MONTHS at Mount Idaho, John, Sarah, Mary Frances, Thomas, Delia, James, and Clara arrived at their farm to discover little had changed over the summer. The Indians had not touched their home or livestock and their crops still stood in the fields. Gradually the family resumed the familiar tempo of their lives.

That fall of 1877 arrived with its busy days of harvest, but on September 23 the Arams again left their homestead for Mount Idaho. This time the occasion was a happy one. Seventeen-year-old Delia married John M. Auchinvole, a miner and member of the Mount Idaho Volunteers. Meanwhile, 21-year-old Mary Frances caught the eye of Henry Clay Johnson, the dashing frontiersman who had survived the Battle of the Brave Seventeen. The two were married on January 20, 1878. Henry took his bride to his farm near Tolo Lake where, just six months before, Colonel Perry's soldiers had fought the Nez Perce while retreating from the battle of White Bird Canyon.

By 1880 both Tom, age 22, and James, age 16, were working as full-time farm laborers for their father. Only 11-year-old Clara was attending school. A dozen years earlier, a Methodist church and academy had been established in Grangeville. To further education, the private academy worked in cooperation with the public school on the Aram ranch. When the public school ran out of funds, its students could attend the academy for a small fee.

Early in the new decade, John and Sarah abandoned their log home for a new, two-story house built on a rise just above the draw sheltering their cabin. The new farmhouse was plain and square, but from its shiny glass windows the view was breathtaking. On a clear day the family could see across Camas Prairie to the Clearwater Valley some 50 miles away. Snowcapped mountain peaks were constantly within their view. Prevailing winds from the Salmon kept the temperature at the homesite four to five degrees warmer than in Grangeville. John and his sons planted elms, poplars, and black walnuts around the house to provide shade. For Sarah's convenience, they also planted several apple and pear trees nearby.

The young Arams were never idle. For entertainment they joined other young people in taffy pulls and popcorn parties, riding their own horses to the various gatherings. Occasionally they took long horseback trips to explore old mines in the mountains. Barn raisings were always special social events. The men and boys provided the labor, while the women and girls cooked the food. When the barn was finished, a dance was held, with everyone attending.

As the 1880s unfolded, John Aram expanded his business ventures with son, Tom, under the name of Aram and Son. Together they started Excelsior, a livery stable that stabled horses, pastured stock, and hired out teams, drivers, and saddle horses. They also sold hay and grain.

The first issue of the *Idaho County Free Press*—run off on a hand press in Grangeville on June 18, 1886, to the music of a brass band and the cheers of a crowd—heralded the construction of a new stable by Aram and Son. The notice read, "Aram and Son will have lumber on the ground in a day or two for the erection of their new livery stable which will materially add to the appearance of main street by closing the gap between the post office and the Greer and Roberts building. . . . Grangeville has a boom this summer."

Throughout the summer the newspaper followed the progress of the livery. On July 23 it reported, "Aram's new stable looms up grandly and greatly improves the business appearance of the town." On August 6 the paper stated, "The elegant and spacious barn belonging to Aram and Son is rapidly approaching completion under the direction of Frank Vansise and will rank with the other solid improvements lately added to Grangeville."

Coincidentally, the builder, Vansise, was the man rescued by John's son-in-law, Henry Johnson, after his horse was shot during the Battle of the Brave Seventeen nine years earlier. Vansise completed construction of the livery early in the fall and the September 10 *Free Press* noted briefly, "Aram's new livery stable was completed and opened on Wednesday of this week."

A sign, painted by artist W. E. McCready, adorned the front of the livery. A work of art in its own right, the sign pictured a thoroughbred grazing peacefully in a lush green meadow crossed by a sparkling stream and surrounded by snowcapped mountains. Arching over the picture in a rainbow were the words Aram and Son.[27]

John Aram was frequently asked to serve in various public offices for the county. He never consented, but in October of 1886, his son, Tom, accepted the nomination as Republican candidate for sheriff. Tom ran against the Democratic nominee, A. W. Talkington. On November 12, 1886, the *Free Press* noted the election returns, with Talkington receiving 410 votes to Tom Aram's 276.

As their business holdings increased in the years after the Indian War, so did the Aram family. On February 12, 1879, Mary Frances presented John and Sarah with a granddaughter, Clara Johnson. The young mother did not fare well after the birth. For two days Henry Johnson worried about his young wife, but on February 14, Mary Frances went into labor again. To everyone's surprise and delight, she delivered another daughter, Edna. The new Johnson babies held the distinction of being the first white twins born on Camas Prairie.

Clara and Edna were followed in rapid succession by Charles, born in 1880, John T., born in 1882, Perry, born in 1883, Amelia, born in 1887, and Mina, born in 1889. In the meantime, Delia and John Auchinvole added two grandsons to the growing clan.

In the fall of 1887, John decided to raise fish in three ponds created on his farm. He traveled to a fish pond in Lewiston and returned with a supply of carp. Two years later, on July 2, 1889, the *Free Press* reported, "Mr. Aram's three carp ponds are full of young carp and some very large ones have been seen. The ponds will be drained in September and then look out for the fish stories."

The year 1888 was one in which the Arams enjoyed the fruits of their labors. The July 13 issue of the *Free Press* reported, "Mr. Aram and party, who have been rusticating at Medical Lake, are home again and are loud in their praises of the curative properties of the waters. Mr. Aram in particular has reason to be thankful since he has been cured of his lameness and now walks erect without the aid of his walking stick."

On Friday, July 27, the paper noted, "The new barn on Mr. Aram's ranch, being built by Frank Vansise, was raised Tuesday afternoon. The boys all agree that the beer was fine." The August 3 issue stated, "Mr. Aram's ranch produced this year the heaviest crop of hay ever raised on the home place south of town, which is generally conceded to be the best and most highly productive hay ranch on Camas Prairie." And again on December 14, "Mr. Aram brought us a bag of very fine pears as a sample product from his orchard adjoining town. The old residents used to think the prairie was too cold to raise fruit, but the idea has long since exploded."

The following summer of 1889 was an extremely dry year. By midsummer forest fires were burning in the mountains and heavily timbered foothills. The prairie was shrouded daily in a haze of smoke. By October fires had spread and threatened Camas Prairie residents.

At one time, along the west side of a stretch of Three Mile Creek, flames rose 40 to 50 feet. The air was full of flying cinders, which a stiff wind carried away to ignite more fires. Volunteers from Grangeville and Mount Idaho helped the farmers and ranchers start backfires. Finally, after their long struggle, a rainstorm doused the flames. No homes were lost, but acres of timber were destroyed and the ranchers' winter ranges devastated.

As the decade ended, John entered a number of business ventures with his sons and sons-in-law. Under the name Aram and Son and Johnson, a full-blooded Cleveland Bay stallion, Pilgrim, was purchased for stud and brought to Grangeville. A classified ad in the June 28 issue of the *Free Press* noted Pilgrim would "make the season of '89 at their respective places as follows. At Johnsons, Mondays and Thursdays; balance of week at Aram and Son. Terms for insurance, single mare $25, club of six $125."

Pilgrim, however, became desperately ill. By February of 1890 the partnership felt some recourse was necessary. Letters were sent to the previous owner and copied into a ledger kept by J. P. Fitzgerald, brand inspector and Grangeville blacksmith. The first letter reads as follows:

Grangeville, February 14, 1890

Mr. Hollinshead,

The horse we got of you was taken to running at the nose shortly after we got him and about December last commenced discharging matter properly and still discharges from the nose. We suppose that we were getting a sound horse, but think it is an old disease in the head of some kind. Perhaps glanders. [a disease of the respiratory system in horses] Can't tell. Don't think he will be of any use this coming season if at all. Hope you will do what is just in the matter.

Please write.

Aram & Son & Johnson

About a week later, they evidently felt Mr. Hollinshead needed further information for they wrote another letter describing Pilgrim's symptoms in detail. They explained that right after they bought Pilgrim, in addition to the discharge from his nostrils, his right eye was mattering and the glands above it were swollen. The horse had gotten worse over the course of the winter. There was a swelling in his throat, he couldn't get his head down to drink, he had lost nearly two gallons of blood from his nostrils and was growing very thin from loss of appetite. The Arams then went on to note that they had tried to cure Pilgrim by "smoking" him—exposing him to a heavy smoke—and smearing his head with salt and fat. In addition, they had provided Pilgrim with a warm stall, good hay, carrots, potatoes, bran, and flax seed.

Following their detailed letter to Mr. Hollinshead, the Aram and Johnson partnership must not have received any satisfaction for in May they wrote:

Grangeville, May 26, 1890

Mr. Hollinshead,

Since we have had a veterinary to exam Pilgrim and think we have very good reason to believe horse was diseased when we bought him. As we bought him for a sound horse, we do not feel like paying any more money on him til better satisfied in the case. Hoping you will do what is right. We remain yours.

Aram & Sons & Johnson

It is not known what happened to Pilgrim or if Aram and Son and Johnson ever received a settlement from Mr. Hollinshead for the sick horse.

Excelsior Livery was sold by John and Tom in the fall of 1888 to the Sherwin brothers. John, Tom, and James then became dealers in agricultural implements under the name of Aram and Sons. They sold wagons, plows, harrows, buggies, seeders, threshing machines, farm implements of all types, bobsleds and cutters, as well as fruit trees and shrubbery from their home nursery.

Other business interests were evident from a classified ad in the *Free Press* on May 1, 1891, which stated, "Auchinvole and Aram begs to announce to the public that they will carry a full stock of binding twine during the coming harvest season which they will sell cheap for cash."

The winter of 1891 brought a snowstorm unlike any the settlers had witnessed. Starting on the afternoon of February 28 the snow came down steadily, continuing through the next day and ending at dawn on the third day. Twenty-six inches of new snow covered the prairie, and the temperature dropped to zero. Cattle weathered the storm well because of the abundance of food and the heavy, wet flakes were welcomed by the farmers who remembered the dry season of 1889.

An epidemic of measles, scarlet fever, and la grippe, a type of flu, followed the snowstorm. Prairie residents of all ages fell prey to the grippe, while children suffered from all three. Disease took its toll on the Aram grandchildren, relentlessly attacking the family of Mary Frances and Henry Johnson. The *Idaho County Free Press* told their story under the headline "A Sorely Afflicted Family" on May 13. It read in part:

> For the fourth time in almost as many weeks, it is our sad and painful duty to chronicle another death in the family of our friend, Henry C. Johnson of Lake District. Such a lamentable record of mortality is, we believe, without precedent in the history of the state and it is certainly without a parallel in Idaho County.

March 30, 1891, Perry Calvin Johnson, age seven years, three months and twenty days; April 19, 1891, Mina Johnson, age two years, one month; April 22, 1891, Charles Virgil Johnson, age ten years, eleven months and thirteen days; May 9, 1891, John Thomas Johnson, age nine years, three months and nineteen days.

Thus out of a family of seven promising children, four are taken in quick succession by that dread disease, scarlet fever. While other families escaped its ravages, its wrath seemed confined to and concentrated on the Johnson household. In the presence of such stern realities as these, earthly honors seem empty, earthly enjoyments hollow and earthly ambitions insignificant. For when the presence death might, with reason, have been least expected, the dark-winged messenger near, and in quick succession, bore away to the spirit land four of the lambs of this sorely stricken family. And the hopes the fond parents had entertained of the future of these promising children vanished like chaff before a driving wind.

In the midst of their losses, a time span of a mere six weeks, a fire nearly claimed the Johnson home. Fortunately, most of the structure was saved by several neighbors who happened to be nearby when the blaze started. The Johnsons rebuilt their home and began to reconstruct their shattered lives. In the spring of 1892 Mary Frances gave birth to another daughter, but the child died in infancy. Eventually one more child, Helen, was born to the Johnsons. She and her older sisters—Clara, Edna, and Amelia, who had escaped the epidemic—survived to adulthood.

A much happier event highlighted the Arams' lives on March, 29, 1892 when 34-year-old Tom married Carrie E. Moore. They had two children, Chester and Vivian. 25-year-old Clara followed Tom to the altar two years later when on March 25, 1894, she married Grangeville businessman John Fitzgerald. They had one son, Oren Aram Fitzgerald.

In the late 1880s citizens started to clamor for the dissolution of the Indian reservation on Camas Prairie. They felt the more than 750,000 acres set aside for the Indians were largely unused. It was also believed that the reservation cut Lewiston off from the interior mountain regions, creating a barrier to progress. Opening the reservation would ensure the construction of a railroad from Lewiston to Camas Prairie since it would no longer have to pass through Indian land. In 1893 a final treaty was signed, under which the reservation would be opened for settlement, but only after each Indian was allotted his own farm.

In November 1895, 32-year-old James Aram was one of the many young men lined up on the border waiting to stake a claim: 160 acres could be acquired with no cash payment as long as the property was occupied and improved. Additional land could be purchased for $3.75 per acre. When trumpet blared and cannon boomed, mounted riders rushed into the new land. James, an expert horseman who knew the prairie well, rode through the crush of land seekers and staked a claim.

During the '90s the younger Arams gradually took over the operation of the family businesses and land holdings. Their father suffered from rheumatism and rarely ventured from the home farm. Their mother, Sarah, continued to enjoy good health and remained involved in her community. Stepping with ease into the positions of high esteem held by their parents in the community, Tom and James were respected in their business and private dealings. In 1893, the community honored Tom for his leadership by appointing him the marshal of the annual Fourth of July parade.

Tom and James, who were more inclined to be cattlemen than Grangeville businessmen, eventually sold the implement dealership and expanded their cattle operations, buying and selling cattle throughout Idaho County. In early 1897 they started a cattle ranch along Getta Creek just a mile from the Snake River. This acquisition provided good winter grazing land on rolling bench lands below the Doumecq and Joseph Plains plateaus.

Shortly after their purchase of the Getta Creek property, on May 20, 1897, Tom was crossing cattle at the Silcott Ferry on the Clearwater River at Lewiston. The river was at flood stage and a terrific downpour began just as he started across with his last load. The cattle panicked, stampeding to the end of the ferry. It sank and tossed Tom, who could not swim, into the water. He disappeared in the swollen river, as did his load of cattle. Some 300 people witnessed the accident, but no boat was available to attempt a rescue.[28]

Devastated by the news, the family began a search for Tom's body, offering a $200 reward for its recovery. The July 2, 1897, edition of the *Idaho County Free Press* featured an article detailing the search. It read in part:

> The banks of the Clearwater and Snake rivers were closely watched in order that the body might be recovered, and hope had been practically abandoned, when a body was found far down the Columbia river, about four miles above the Cascade Locks on May 28th, which proved to be that of our dead friend. The entire distance of over three hundred miles was traversed in seven days—an almost incredible story, but a true one. Divested of all clothing and the features mutilated and disfigured beyond recognition, identification was made through a ring on the finger and a spur and strap which remained attached to the foot. Thus through all its melancholy wanderings, through the waste of waters, a kind Providence safely guided the body to a point where it could be recovered by anxious friends. It had washed ashore on a sand bar at a wild and desolate spot on the Washington shore where there are no roads and no way of access save by the river. The settlers are few and far between and the discovery of the body was the merest accident.
>
> Such are the details of the most lamentable fatality which has occurred to a citizen of this community since the dark days of '77. We knew Tom Aram well. He had a sunny disposition, and always a smile and cheery word for all who he met. He was a useful member of this isolated community; in his business capacity he bought and sold cattle and thus helped the markets for those who could not trade themselves. He was widely known and the whole circle of his acquaintance will miss him and grieve over his early and untimely demise.

Ironically, Tom's remains were discovered on what would have been his thirty-ninth birthday. At the request of his widow, the body was taken to his parents' home where it rested for one night before burial. On the day of the funeral, the family gathered for a portrait. It was a solemn picture with Tom's wife and children, parents, brothers, and sisters clustered around his casket. Nearby, on an easel, stood a portrait of his sister, Libby, who had died in Oregon 34 years before.

With the death of his older brother and the ill health of his aging father, James became the official head of the family. By then, Idaho County was in a boom. Mineral finds along the Salmon River brought more people into the region. The prospect of a railway to replace the freight wagons, which still hauled goods in and out of Camas Prairie over a 5,000-foot high mountain range, increased interest in the area. Real estate values and housing shortages skyrocketed. The old settlers looked to the 1900s, confident they would be prosperous years, but James faced the new century alone.

Chapter 5

A HOME ON JOSEPH PLAINS

Joseph and Doumecq lie on two plateaus between the Snake and Salmon rivers. Rice Creek cuts a deep canyon between them. In the late 1800's homesteaders arrived. They built cabins, cleared land, dug wells, built fences and schools. They planted crops, fruit trees and gardens; but they found it difficult living off the land. Transportation [to the outside] was most difficult. Winters were harsh with frequent blizzards . . . the homesteaders became disillusioned and one by one they sold their land and moved on.—Narcie Aram See 1988

JOHN ARAM LIVED only long enough to share the dawn of the new century with Sarah and their son James at the old homestead south of Grangeville. There on September 30, 1901, at the age of 74, he died. His obituary in the October 3 issue of the *Idaho County Free Press* read in part:

> Thus one by one pass to the great beyond the men who first redeemed this garden spot of the wilderness and made it habitable for those of us who follow the footsteps of the pioneers. It is said that death is the great enemy of our race, but under certain circumstances this is not true. When the young, vigorous, ambitious and hopeful are stricken down we stand shocked, as if before some unfinished painting or statue where the pencil or chisel has fallen from the nerveless hand of a great artist. But when life's work is done, when the task is finished and we simply await the inevitable end, death is sometimes a friend. Mr. Aram lived a

long, honorable and useful life and now sleeps the last long sleep in Prairie View Cemetery overlooking the beautiful land he loved so well.

The country settled by the Arams 37 years before was rapidly changing. Farms prospered, but cattle ranches dwindled as ranchers looked for less populated regions to graze their herds. In 1904 Sarah sold her homestead to the Spencer family and moved to Grangeville to live with her divorced daughter, Clara Fitzgerald. James leased his farm on the old Indian reservation and, for a time, conducted his cattle business from the Getta Creek ranch. Recognizing a need to expand his land holdings in the area between the Salmon and the Snake, James started buying homesteads from disillusioned farmers on the high plateau known as Joseph Plains.

He chose as his new home ranch a farm originally homesteaded by the Key family. It was a section of land made up of rolling hills and meadows, deep canyons with rugged cliffs, and higher timbered hills. The ranch stretched along the south side of Joseph Plains, just above Rice Creek's steep canyon walls, at an elevation of approximately 4,000 feet.

From his cabin James could see Doumecq Plains on the other side of the creek. In the near distance, Camp Howard, a 5,000- to 6,000-foot mountain used as a base camp by General Howard during the Indian War, dominated the southern horizon. At night, along the far northeastern horizon, the lights of Grangeville twinkled a warm reminder of home.

In 1906 James was introduced to Phebe Lucinda Smith, the new schoolteacher at the Yellow Pines School some ten miles from his ranch. Phebe, at 26, was a striking young woman, tall and slender with dark hair drawn into a bun. She arrived on Joseph not only to teach but also to homestead her own 320-acre stone and timber claim. With the help of her father and two brothers, she built a cabin, dug a well, and hauled in provisions.

Undoubtedly, James was drawn immediately to the optimistic and competent young lady who had been raised on a farm near Garfield, Washington. When Phebe was eight her mother, Narcissus Jameson Smith, died 14 days after giving birth to another healthy daughter. Phebe was left to help her father raise two younger brothers, Harry and Henry, while baby Minnie was cared for by nearby relatives.

At 16, Phebe took a teaching position at a country school near her home. Many of the students were her cousins and some were bigger than she. It was a difficult time for Phebe; however, she persisted. Eventually, she left to attend the Teachers' College at Moscow, Idaho. She was one of the first students to receive a teaching certificate from the school. After completing her course of study, Phebe learned of the opportunity to teach and simultaneously take a claim on Joseph. She ventured forth on her own.

Although 16 years her senior and rather shy and retiring, James courted Phebe. Eventually they became engaged, but he insisted on waiting for marriage until his business affairs were in order and a home built. The years slipped by. Phebe was called back home to tend her ill father until his death on July 29, 1909. The couple corresponded often, and finally Phebe wrote James telling him she wanted to get married, even if they had to live in a tent.

When Phebe returned to Joseph that fall, James still would not rush the wedding. Instead, he continued to concentrate on his vision of a large cattle ranch. He had little formal education, but was a self-taught man who readily grasped the knowledge necessary to run a business. James didn't worry about money and never minded borrowing to expand his holdings.

By 1910 he held title to 1,600 acres and owned outright 75 cattle valued at $750, 4 saddle horses at $80, 8 work horses, at $280, and 12 swine at $30. In addition, under the name Aram and Co.—possibly a partnership with relatives—he owned 18 stock cattle valued at $180, 25 milk cows at $500, and 8 swine, $200.[29]

By the end of 1910, James decided he could finally marry. On February 4, 1911, he and Phebe said their vows in a ceremony at Moscow, surrounded by Phebe's relations. Several female relatives, meeting the groom for the first time, noted his tall, slender frame, Theodore Roosevelt mustache, and receding hairline emphasized by a fringe of dark hair. "Why," they asked Phebe, "did you keep that handsome man hidden for so long?"

After the wedding, the newlyweds took a train to Seattle where they boarded a ship and traveled down the coast to southern California. Phebe became terribly seasick and was relieved to arrive in San Diego where they had reservations for several days at a fine hotel. Fun-loving Phebe convinced James to spend one of those days at an amusement park where they unwittingly rode down a slide that landed them fully clothed in a pool of water.

From San Diego they traveled by train up the coast to San Francisco. There they enjoyed an elegant hotel, fine restaurants, and the ambiance of the city. One day they attended an auction where James, feeling he should bid on something, bought a huge vase they didn't want and couldn't transport home. The vase was left behind when they returned to the Northwest by train.

Arriving back at Joseph, James and Phebe settled in with the Peters family whose frame house was located just a quarter mile from the Aram ranch. These arrangements had been made by James who didn't want Phebe to take up housekeeping in his own rough log cabin. Their new house was still under construction. It was built on four-by-four-inch braces set on a flat rock foundation to compensate for the slope of the land. Lumber from a local mill was used for the construction, while siding was hauled in by wagon over a rough trail from White Bird.

When completed the house stood two stories high, except the kitchen, which was one story and ran across the entire back of the structure. A narrow porch stretched across the front of the house. From this porch two separate doors provided entrances. One opened into a dining room where a wood-burning stove was installed near the center. This would become the main gathering place for the family.

Beyond the stove a door opened into the kitchen where a huge Monarch cookstove was placed in the center of the back wall. The wood-burning stove had a large hot water reservoir, warming ovens, and four burners. Along the south wall another door opened into a one-story mud room, which jutted out from the main house. It had an entrance on the east opening out to the farm buildings. Nails were pounded into the wall to hold coats and hats, and a pantry was built along one wall. A hand pump dominated the center of the room and provided water from a shallow well under the floor. On the west side of this room a door opened into a woodshed built to hold six or seven cords of wood.

The second door at the front of the house opened into the parlor. An archway connected the parlor to the dining room on the south wall; on the north a door led to an adjoining bedroom. At the far end of the dining room, in a corner near the kitchen, an enclosed stairway provided access to three upstairs bedrooms. James and Phebe chose the room over the warming stove where the stovepipe running through the center of the room provided additional heat.

When the house was finished, Phebe ordered wallpaper for most of the rooms from the Sears, Roebuck catalog. She mixed her own paste and hung the paper herself, covering walls and ceilings. The kitchen walls were covered with oilcloth, the downstairs floors with linoleum, and, for a final touch, all the interior wood was painted a cherry red.

The house was furnished with sturdy furniture—a long wooden table flanked by a bench and several chairs for the dining room; an assortment of comfortable chairs to gather around the stove; pine cupboards for the kitchen; simple beds and pine bureaus for the bedrooms; an oak bookcase; studio sofa; a new sewing machine in a gleaming oak cabinet; and Phebe's new piano for the parlor.

The piano arrived after an arduous journey from White Bird by buckboard on a route that was not more than a trail. After a ferry trip across the Salmon outside of White Bird, the sturdy team toiled up a hillside to a rocky ravine ascending to Doumecq Plains. From southern Doumecq the team and drivers hauled the heavily laden buckboard up one ridge, over the top of Camp Howard Mountain, and down another ridge to Joseph Plains on the other side. By taking this trail, which ran between the headwaters of Rice and Getta Creeks, Rice Creek's steep canyon was avoided.

The Arams were settled into their house in time for the birth of their first child, John Lorenzo. When John was born on September 19, 1912, James was 49 and Phebe 33. With a newborn in the household, James suggested they move to Cottonwood or Grangeville in order to be closer to doctors, schools, and neighbors. Phebe, who loved the wild beauty of Joseph Plains, vetoed the idea saying, "Let's just stay here for a few more years."

Phebe had always wanted two girls and two boys and they arrived, as if by special order. After John's birth in 1912, a daughter, Rosamond, was born on August 9, 1914; a son, James or Jim Jr., April 11, 1916; and another daughter, Narcie, on January 5, 1918.

Dr. Wilson Foskett of White Bird attended Phebe in childbirth. He rode his horse overland through all kinds of weather to reach his patient. The only painkiller he provided was chloroform on a sponge. Phebe sniffed the sponge each time she had a severe pain. Fortunately, there were no complications during any of the deliveries. When it was time for Jim Jr.'s birth in 1916, the good doctor arrived too early. Instead of returning to White Bird, Dr. Foskett helped James brand cattle for two days until it was time to tend Phebe.

Often, when returning home from calls to outlying regions, the doctor fell asleep while his surefooted horse took him safely home. But in April 1924, when the horse had been traded for an automobile, Dr. Foskett fell asleep at the wheel. His car plunged into the Salmon and the beloved doctor drowned. A monument in his memory still stands at the point on the Salmon where his car entered the river.

By 1918, James and Phebe's family was complete. The Arams settled into the busy rhythm of ranch life. Paths appeared in the prairie grass: one from the side door to the barnyard where farm animals were fed and cared for, another to the blacksmith shop, once James's cabin, where equipment was repaired and horses shod. A third stretched 200 feet from the back door to the double-seated outhouse where sheets of paper torn from catalogs awaited the user. Rough wagon tracks led away from the ranch toward other trails to neighbors, the schoolhouse, or the "outside."

Phebe added her own touches to the ranch house. Hop vines, planted around the front porch, flourished on strings stretched to the roof and provided a shady summer retreat. Flower boxes, set near the front door, overflowed with nasturtiums. During the winter, wind and snow howled around the uninsulated home, but a warm fire burned constantly, and hot food and coffee greeted the men when they came in from the range. The soft glow of coal-oil lamps spilled from the windows in the evenings, a welcoming beacon for night travelers. James's suggestion that the family return to Camas Prairie was forgotten. The ranch would remain their home for 30 years.

Chapter 6

A FAMILY OF WORKERS

Our lives were committed to work. Just as soon as we were big enough to do a task we were assigned to do it. . . . Our parents taught us by the influence and power of example. Life on Joseph enabled us—by its isolation—to be responsive to our parents' leadership rather than conflicting forces. —John L. Aram 1992

I N THE FIRST decade after their marriage, as the Aram family grew, so did their ranching operation. James bought more old homesteads scattered across the region, which he referred to by the name of their original owners: the Peters place, located one-quarter mile north of his home; the Kerlee ranch and Miller place, southwest and across the canyon; the Briddle place across Rice Creek to the southeast; the Lacey place tucked away along Rice Creek; the Rosey, Sculley, Wiley, Bessie, Hackett, and Dewey places; the Billy and Thomas property; and Totem Pole, known by that name after the former owner trimmed the branches off all the trees.

James also leased as much available land as he could. Two properties, which he rented continually for more than 30 years, were those belonging to the Canfield family and a portion of land known as the School Section. Each year Mrs. Eva Canfield negotiated terms for the Canfield ranch, which was made up largely of meadows originally planted in timothy and harvested by James. The School Section was a small piece of state-owned land surrounded by his other holdings, for which he paid a small yearly fee.

By the end of the decade, James controlled over 12,000 acres, owning much of an area known then as the "Little Empire".[30] The Aram ranch became the largest employer in the area, hiring neighbors for branding, herding, grain and hay harvests, and other ranch chores. In the years Phebe's hands were full of toddlers and babies, James hired neighbor women to help in the house. When the children grew older, they became the helpers. Their father taught them how to work and take responsibility. His attitude was, "If they are big enough to do a job, they are old enough." Each of the children learned to handle a horse by the age of 6 or 7. The boys rode off to work with their father on the range, while the girls stayed at home to help their mother.

Ranch work was never-ending. There were cattle to herd and brand; fences to build or repair; grain to plant and harvest; horses to break; cattle to drive to market; wood to cut, split, and stack; sick livestock to tend; farm equipment to repair; cattle and hogs to butcher; cows to milk; and orchards and gardens to maintain. Long, hard hours were necessary to keep the operation afloat, even with two or three full-time hired men.

At the ranch house the women tackled their chores without electricity or running water. Making food was the biggest chore, because they not only cooked for the family but also fed the permanent ranch hands and the crews hired at harvest time. The women cooked, canned, and baked on the wood-burning stove, they washed clothes by hand in an old washtub, mended, cleaned, tended the garden and harvested the fruits and vegetables.

There was little leisure for the women; however, when the girls were small, they did find time to build a playhouse under a tree in the yard. A faded piece of linoleum served as a floor for the house, which was furnished with an old cupboard and couch, along with a makeshift table and chairs constructed of crates and bits and pieces of wood. Whenever possible, the girls carried their dolls out under the tree for a brief interlude of make-believe.

Phebe worked from early morning until nine or ten at night. Then she took time to read from her magazines, either the *Saturday Evening Post, Literary Digest, American Home, Collier's,* or *Woman's Home Companion.* Long after everyone was asleep, Phebe sat by the coal-oil lamp writing long descriptive letters about ranch life to her friends and family or stories she hoped to publish—stories she never had the time to finish.

"I wish the children had more time to play," Phebe often said and brought what fun she could to their day by reading to them, telling stories, and encouraging imaginations. On the mornings when she did not have to prepare breakfast for a crew, she woke the children by playing the rousing tune "Solomon Levi" on the parlor piano. On rare summer Sundays when the family could sneak away from ranch chores, she packed a lunch and they rode into the cool shadows of Rice Creek Canyon for a picnic.

One beautiful summer day, when Jim was 6 and John 10, James took the boys out to the summer range on Center Ridge to look after the cattle. Phebe, determined to make this day more than a workday for the boys, packed a lunch and rode along. They stopped at Rice Creek for a picnic. The boys discovered many little fish in the creek and spent most of the lunch hour trying to catch them in their hands.

Phebe's desire for the children to have fun was part of her nature. She was liberal with hugs, kisses, and smiles; a sharp contrast to James, who was never demonstrative. He was 55 by the time Narcie was born. Distracted and overburdened with work, he rarely smiled or laughed and confined his conversations to the business of running the ranch. The children regarded him as stern and gruff. Consequently, he never once laid a punishing hand on any of them, for if they misbehaved a stern look or word brought them quickly into line.

The Arams were known well in their far-flung community on Joseph Plains—James for his honest and forthright business dealings and Phebe for her outgoing and kind personality. Many of the neighbors looked to the Arams for leadership, and both became active participants in the community, serving on the school board and highway commission, registering voters, and counting ballots at the election polls. But not everyone on Joseph appreciated the leadership of the Arams, and occasionally rivalries and jealousies flared.

Phebe was considered by many to be knowledgeable about almost everything because she was unusually well educated. One neighbor, intent on proving she couldn't know everything, liked to test her by educating himself on a subject, then questioning her about his topic. Others turned to Phebe in time of need. She was often asked to preside at funerals, help the sick, and deliver babies. The latter was not her favorite duty and she avoided it whenever possible (once taking so long to prepare and leave her own home that she arrived after the baby).

During the flu epidemic of 1919, James and Phebe took their children, then ranging in age from infant Narcie to 6-year-old John, to the isolated Getta Creek ranch. They left the children with the hired hand when they returned to Joseph to help their sick neighbors. There were no undertakers or ministers, so James helped embalm the dead and Phebe gave the memorial services. They wore flannel masks for protection when away from Getta Creek. Upon their return, the masks were burned and clothes and bodies washed before they rejoined the children. Fortunately, no one at Getta Creek got so much as a sniffle.

Her own devout Christianity made Phebe the perfect stand-in for a minister at funerals. She willingly took on this task even though some Joseph residents made fun of her because they were not religious and didn't appreciate her outspoken devoutness. After one funeral, an agnostic neighbor was heard to comment, "Phebe's prayers won't rise any higher than her head." Raised as a Methodist, she deeply regretted the absence of churches on Joseph and longed to take her children to Sunday school. Still, every spring she planted a row of potatoes for the preacher, a custom practiced to help support pastors in rural communities.

Whenever an itinerant minister visited the region, Phebe dressed in her Sunday best and attended services held at the schoolhouse. At one such service the presenters spoke in tongues. The Joseph residents snickered; Narcie stole a look at her mother; Phebe wasn't smiling. The little girl held her breath, fearing her mother might join in, breathing a sigh of relief when she didn't.

The family's source of religious inspiration was through a subscription to the *Weekly Unity*. This connected them to the Unity School of Christianity of Kansas City, Missouri. Each family member read it, and, although they rarely said a blessing at the dinner table or set a time aside for worship, faith was present in all they did. Phebe prayed regularly and believed in the power of positive affirmations. She lectured the children constantly on faith and shared her beliefs with all who touched her life.

In later years she wrote in a note to an unidentified friend, "Affirm silently or orally *over* and *over* and *over*, impressing your sub-conscious. 'The spirit of the Lord goes before me, making plain, easy and truly successful all my way,' and 'God is my immediate and abundant supply.' They work if you keep up your part."

As part of her strong religious beliefs, Phebe neither drank, smoked, nor took the Lord's name in vain. She abhorred the use of alcohol, tobacco, and foul language by anyone else. However, James smoked an occasional pipe or cigarette and indulged in a rare drink, but never in her presence. When James was angry and his usually quiet voice boomed curses at the cows in the barnyard, she would say to the children, "I wish your father wouldn't swear like that." If a curse so much as slipped from their childish lips, they were threatened with a thorough soapy mouth washing.

Both parents were anxious for the children to be brought up properly and have an education. Good manners were stressed, as was the proper use of English. When they were taken out of school to help with ranch work, the children were expected to take their books with them and continue their studies. Phebe helped with their homework, if necessary, and she encouraged each one to read. They were all taught to take responsibility for themselves, their possessions, and their actions. She told her children, "If you can't take care of something, then you don't deserve to have it."

As much as possible, the children's interests were nurtured. John, who was awed by the violin player at community dances, expressed a desire to play the violin. His parents bought one for him, and, although he attempted to play it, he never had the opportunity to take lessons until he moved to Grangeville to attend high school and found a teacher. However, when his father received the first bill, the lessons were quickly canceled.

But James did pay for piano lessons for Rosamond when she attended high school, and a teacher was found to give Narcie piano lessons at the ranch. Jim Jr. asked for, and received, a harmonica. The boy played by ear and taught himself quite well. By the time he was in his late teens, he could occasionally give the violin player at community dances a break while he played the tune on his harmonica.

Although the four young Arams shared an interest in music, in many ways they were a study in contrasts. The two oldest, John and Rosamond, looked like Phebe's side of the family with sturdy builds and prominent noses. However, John had olive skin, straight dark hair, and brown eyes, whereas Rosamond had a flawless and fair complexion, curly blond hair, and bright blue eyes like her father. Jim Jr. and Narcie looked like the Aram branch of the family—fair skin, slender builds, and green-blue eyes. Jim Jr. had auburn-tinged hair; Narcie's was a light brown.

John was outgoing and assertive. As the oldest, he had been idolized by his parents since birth. In the wake of the arrival of three siblings, the boy attempted to maintain his position in the family in the only way he knew—teasing and badgering Rosamond, Jim Jr., and Narcie at every opportunity. When the younger ones were engrossed in play, he approached like a whirlwind, punching and hitting until all three were in tears. As he got older, he preferred to boss them around. Arriving at the gate to the ranch after a day on the range, John sat on his mount and hollered until one of the others left their chores to open and shut the gate for him.

Jim Jr. on the other hand was a pleasant companion for his sisters. He was much more reserved than his older brother. His gentle disposition and quiet mannerisms belied a dry sense of humor, which brought many laughs to the household, but he was committed to the ranch and was diligent with his chores, never neglecting his assigned duties.

Rosamond was more like John in personality, assertive and outgoing, but like Jim Jr. she displayed a commitment to the family, always carrying her share of the work even if others didn't. She was serious and a worrier, but was outwardly cheerful and pleasant. Rosamond preferred homemaking to ranch work and was an excellent student: bright, ambitious, and determined. Although Rosamond tended toward plumpness, she was considered pretty by everyone, including her brothers.

In contrast to her sister, Narcie was a tomboy. Her father often referred to her as "Spike" or "Slim," names she found unflattering for she longed to be pretty and feminine. Narcie preferred to be outdoors, spending time with the horses, kittens, dogs, and lambs, her greatest pleasure. She also delighted in the early spring wildflowers that bloomed in a pasture near the house. When it was colored with a profusion of buttercups, yellowbells, birdie bills, and bluebells, Jim Jr. referred to the field as Narcie's flower garden. Narcie eased her everyday chores by talking to an imaginary companion and spinning fanciful daydreams.

By the age of 8, both boys carried a workload far beyond their years. There was little time for playing or roughhousing with other boys. Occasionally John and Jim Jr. rounded up a couple of yearling calves and rode them around the barnyard, whooping and hollering like rodeo riders. Their father ignored their antics and allowed them their little bit of fun, saying "boys will be boys."

Both John and Jim Jr. were responsible and carried out their father's orders daily. John, however, sometimes rebelled and his attention-getting pranks took on a serious tone. One time, when he was about 7, he piled wood and grass alongside the house and started a fire while his parents were entertaining neighbors in the parlor. The fire was put out and John was told sternly that what he had done was wrong. Neither Phebe nor James punished him in any other way, viewing his behavior as mischievous rather than mean-spirited and recognizing their environment offered little opportunity for the boy to let off steam in positive ways such as sports, club activities, or playing with a friend.

Shortly after that, when his parents were again entertaining, John set fire to a pile of straw mounded around the outdoor well to protect it from the winter freeze. Again the fire was put out and he was admonished. His real punishment came when his older cousin, Oren Fitzgerald, whom he greatly admired, teased him about being a pyromaniac. Shamed, John never again started a fire.

John never challenged his father openly on the rare occasions when he disobeyed. Instead, he quietly avoided a chore. Once during John's eighth year, his father asked him to help look after the hogs early in the morning. The boy got up and saddled his horse, but when his father rode off John didn't follow. Later, an angry James returned, got a long switch, and took his son out behind the house. But, instead of switching John, James rebuked him and extracted a promise that he would never again be so irresponsible.

John thought he was pretty smart avoiding the whipping and bragged to Jim Shillam, an Englishman who was working for James at the time. Shillam, who had his own ranch at the head of Rice Creek some eight miles away, didn't think little John was very funny. "Don't ever treat your father that way again," Shillam said. "You respect your father. It's not smart to make a joke of him for not disciplining you with a whipping."

Shillam's tongue-lashing embarrassed John enough that it was four years before he disappointed his father in such a manner again. At that time he had been asked to mow and rake a field about two miles from the house. He completed the mowing and was sent out on Sunday to rake the hay, but the field was sparse and had lots of weeds—to John's young mind hardly worth the effort. When he grew tired of raking, he walked out on the tongue of the rake and stood on it, jumping up and down until it broke. He then unhitched the horses and went home, never admitting to his father what had happened. His only punishment that time was a guilty conscience.

Despite their different personalities, a strong sense of family bound the Aram children. Dependent on one another for survival, they became helpers, playmates, rivals, and friends. In the early years, the younger Arams did not like John very much. Gradually, they learned to stand up for themselves in the face of his aggressiveness and, as they grew, allowed him little opportunity to push them around. John outgrew his devilish ways and expended his energy on ranch work, declaring throughout his youth, "All I ever want to be is a cowboy."

Phebe harbored a dream that her oldest son would become educated and successful in the "outside" world. She sometimes even said, "John's smart enough to be president." Still, in her usually calm manner, she supported her son in his desire. "I have great hopes that John will be an outstanding leading citizen," she wrote relatives, "but all he wants to be is a cowboy. If that's the case, then I want him to be the best cowboy he can be."

Chapter 7

KEEPING IN TOUCH

One deterrent to travel to town was the primitive road system. The people in those early years didn't have money, time, equipment, manpower or know-how, to build a road with a uniform, gentle grade of 5 percent or even 10 percent slope. As the country became more settled . . . a great hue and cry went up for better roads and also telephone service.—Jim Aram 1991

WHEN PHEBE WAS lonely she often sighed, "I wish someone would come today." Sometimes she admitted to "feeling blue" and other mornings she proclaimed, "Something good is going to happen today." The absence of the large family she had grown up with left a tremendous gap in her life, and she talked often of her sister, brothers, cousins, aunts, and uncles. Keeping in touch with them across great distances was difficult, but for Phebe it was a priority. Writing letters after a long day of work was a joy, not a task.

A telephone line, connecting Joseph to White Bird, was built across Rice Creek shortly after Phebe's marriage. Residents of Joseph volunteered money and labor to construct the line. The battery-operated, crank phone installed in the Aram dining room, however, was not used to chat with relatives living in other parts of the country. Instead, the line served the local people in emergencies and linked the Arams to their neighbors and their Getta Creek ranch.

In later years, when the line to White Bird fell into disrepair, the Arams connected into a telephone line that ran from Boles, down the Hogback Ridge, across the Salmon River, and on to Cottonwood. Joseph residents, including James, then helped themselves to the wire from the White Bird line, using it for repairing machinery, wiring cream can lids and making gate latches. The Arams continued to maintain their own line to the Getta Creek ranch.

Thirty families shared the Cottonwood line, limiting the use of the phone to brief conversations and short messages. Each family had a different ring to signal their calls; the Arams was four short rings. Eavesdropping on another family's conversation was a favorite pastime for many Joseph residents, and Narcie and Rosamond did their share, but they were in for a scolding if Phebe caught them.

The restrictions on the telephone meant Phebe's main communication line remained the long, descriptive letters she wrote and the responses she received from relatives. She looked forward to the mail, which was delivered three times a week via a route established in 1907 from White Bird. The original route ran across Doumecq Plains, stopped at the Canfield post office, and then went on to Joseph Plains, ending at the McDougall homestead, where a little outbuilding served as a post office. This was Joseph, Idaho, not a town, just a place where letters and packages could be mailed and stamps purchased from Mrs. McDougall, postmistress. Incoming mail was sorted and placed in boxes to be picked up by residents who did not live along the mail route.

By 1911 this route extended to Boles in the northern reaches of Joseph Plains, where another post office was established. Over the years several different men held private contracts with the postal service to deliver mail including Ross Zehner, Charlie Miller, H. P. Twogood, Ern Bentley and, later, Muggs Bentley.

When the mailman came across Doumecq from White Bird, he stopped to hitch up a fresh team of horses for the trip across Rice Creek Canyon. This Doumecq-Joseph mail route was difficult, especially in the spring and fall when a wagon was required at the lower elevations where the snow had melted and a bobsled was needed at the upper elevations where several feet of snow remained.

Those living along the mail route received their letters in pouches placed in mailboxes constructed of wood with a small compartment for the pouch on the top. A bigger compartment, with a three-foot door for larger packages, was on the bottom. The parcel post system was used for delivering all types of items ordered from catalogs or out of the stores in White Bird and Grangeville, and the wagon was often heavily laden with such purchases. Deliveries were made on Monday, Wednesday, and Friday. If the weather was very severe, the mailman delivered letters only, bringing them to Joseph by saddle horse and pack train.

Mail day was anticipated by the entire family. Jim Jr. often met the mail stage as it stopped at the Aram box en route from the Joseph post office to Boles. "I'll never forget the sight of those four sweating horses pulling that heavy wagon down the narrow road," recalled Jim. "There were bells on the harness that jingled as they came. It was quite a stirring sight for a little boy."

After spending the night at Boles, the mailman made the return trip to White Bird on Tuesdays, Thursdays, and Saturdays with a stop at the Joseph post office for outgoing mail. Additional stops were made at mailboxes where he collected mail, packages, and even items destined for market such as cream or wool. The driver returned the cream cans on his next trip and the rancher received his check from the creamery by mail.

Beyond letters, contact with relatives was infrequent. However, when it was necessary to travel out of Joseph for any reason, the trip was combined with pleasure. Phebe's severe sinus problems necessitated a few trips alone to Spokane, Washington, where she consulted a physician. These occasions afforded her the rare opportunity to visit her family.

On one such trip, she took Jim Jr. along. The toddler had been refusing to use one arm and Phebe wanted her doctor to see if he could detect what was wrong. Much to Phebe's surprise, the doctor discovered that Jim's arm was broken. To her knowledge there had been no accident or fall dramatic enough for a broken limb. After the arm was set, Phebe stopped to visit relatives. It was her first chance to show off one of her children to her large family.

Travels out of Idaho County were a rare event; trips to White Bird, Grangeville, and Cottonwood were more common. Phebe kept a list of needed items, and when it was time to market livestock, buy farm equipment, pay taxes, purchase land, acquire a team of horses, or borrow money, her list was filled. Items were selected and brought back in the buckboard or sent later by parcel post.

The Salmon River lay between Joseph and any large settlement. Whether traveling north to Cottonwood or south to White Bird, Joseph residents had to cross the river, which had ferry services at crossing points. The terrain from the Salmon to the Joseph plateau created the greatest obstacle, and routes up mountains, through canyons, down ravines, and across creeks were difficult to build and maintain.

Southeast of the Aram ranch a rugged wagon road was constructed shortly after young John's birth. This was the well-traveled route used by the mail stage. To the northeast, only a horse and cattle trail led to the Salmon and then a nearly impassable wagon route led on to Cottonwood, so White Bird became the main trading center for the Salmon River cattle country in the early years.

The little town had a population of about 400. Along its one street were two stores, two hotels, two saloons, a barber shop, drugstore, jewelry store, and a cigar and confectionery shop. There was no law, and when cowboys from outlying ranches came to the frontier town, they often took over. One story, related to an impressionable Jim Jr., was of two hard-drinking cowhands who raced their horses back and forth along the street one night shouting, "I'm a wild man, on a wild coyote on a windy day."

The young Arams rarely saw such displays, since they were usually in town on weekdays when they could shop at the Salmon River General Store. It supplied them with every practical item needed—tools, barbed wire, plows, food staples, fabric, and durable clothing. It even stocked a small amount of fashionable items from New York, many of which were two or three years old. On rare occasions oranges and bananas were available.

Once or twice a year the family piled into the surrey for the long trip to Grangeville where they could shop, conduct family business, and visit relatives. Drawn by a team of sturdy horses, the buggy made its way into Rice Creek Canyon inching down the narrow road with its 30 percent grade, then climbed out again at the same angle until reaching Doumecq Plains. After crossing Doumecq, the route took them down a shallow but steep rock-strewn ravine, which led them off the plateau. From there the road paralleled the river and clung to the contours of the hills, dropping gradually to the banks of the Salmon.

At the river, the family, surrey, and team were loaded onto a ferry that deposited them on the opposite shore. Then it was just a mile to White Bird, where they usually spent the night with friends or at one of the hotels. The next day they completed the final lap of the 50-mile journey. When it was extremely hot, James stopped at the Salmon River General Store and purchased lemons and oranges, which were squeezed into a can of water for a refreshing drink or sliced to eat on the dry, dusty trip.

Sometimes they stopped on White Bird Creek for a picnic before starting up the mountain to Camas Prairie. On one stop in 1918, the family shared their shady rest spot with two young cowboys who watered their horses, adjusted their saddles, and rode on. "I wonder," said Phebe, "if those young men are on their way to join the army." Her spoken thought brought the terrible conflict half a world away momentarily to the serene canyon where they rested.

The entire family looked forward to arriving in Grangeville where they stayed with Clara Fitzgerald, James's younger sister, her son, Oren, and their grandmother, Sarah Aram. Two vacant lots next to Clara's house provided pasture for the team, while Clara's excellent meals, tidy house, and indoor bathroom awaited the travelers.

These rare visits allowed the children little chance to become acquainted with their grandmother and they grew up with only dim memories of her. On January 11, 1921, while the children were still very young, Sarah died at the age of 88. She was eulogized in an article in the January 20 issue of the *Grangeville Globe*, with the following words:

> Silently, but ceaselessly, the ranks of the pioneers are growing thinner. The passage of each widens the gaps between the remaining few. Little attention does the world in general pay to the passing of one of these lives and but so few so much as stop momentarily to realize that the answering of this last call means one more who was instrumental in making the present day civilization possible has crossed the horizon of life and started on the long journey.
>
> Last week Grangeville recorded the loss of one of these few remaining pioneers, Mrs. Sarah A. Aram. . . . Although the body has ceased to move and the lips are still, the soul continues to shed its benediction, an ever present guardian angel over the many to whom in this world she was affectionately known as Grandma Aram . . . as always with lives so lived, those who know her best can not believe she is dead. Easing the pain in their heart with the thought that she has wrapped herself in her mantle and laid down to pleasant dreams.

John, who attended the funeral with his parents, remembers it well, although he was only 8. "Her funeral is one of my saddest childhood memories. The body was on display in Aunt Clara's bedroom for a couple of days. We were staying at her house and my parents took me to the service, which was held right at Aunt Clara's. Then we all rode in surreys behind a horse-drawn hearse to the cemetery."

Most of John, Rosamond, Jim, and Narcie's memories of visiting Grangeville centered on the years following their grandmother's death. The children were treated to picture shows and church services. Shopping at Grangeville's department store—Alexander Freidenrich— was exciting for the children, particularly for the girls, who loved pretty things. Once, while shopping with Phebe, Narcie eyed the silk lingerie displayed in a glass case. Thinking of the ugly, homemade khaki bloomers she wore, the little girl asked, "Do rich kids always wear silk underwear?"

While at Aunt Clara's, the children played with the Geary children who lived next door. The Gearys—Estaline, James, and Verna—were the children of Edna Geary, daughter of their father's oldest sister, Mary Frances, and her husband, Henry Clay Johnson. Narcie thought the Geary children were exceptionally good-looking and well dressed. She enjoyed their large house with big rooms. Glass French doors separated the dining room and parlor and a winding staircase led upstairs. Most of all, she loved the grapevine-covered gazebo at the side of the Geary home. Narcie longed to live in a pretty house with a lawn surrounding it. Yet, when it was time to leave she was always glad to return to Joseph and her beloved animals.

Trips home were sometimes treacherous, particularly in late fall. On one occasion, in early November of 1920, James took the family from Grangeville out to the ranch he owned on the former Nez Perce Reservation. His friends, Charlie and Essie Miller, ran a wheat farm on the acreage. After spending the night, the Arams set out for Joseph at 4:00 A.M. James drove the surrey and young John followed on a saddle horse.

It started to snow, but the surrey top and side curtains kept the family dry. By the time they reached the mountains bordering the Salmon River and White Bird Creek, snow was coming down hard and fast. They started down a series of switchbacks to White Bird, but six to eight inches of snow slowed down the loaded buggy, and it took several hours to reach the little town, where they spent the night. They left for Joseph early the next morning.

The snow continued to delay them. Finally, they stopped at the Twogood ranch on Doumecq, a point about halfway between White Bird and their home. From there James called ahead to his ranch and asked one of his hired hands to meet the family the next day with a fresh team and bobsled. Early the next morning the surrey started out again in the storm, crossed Rice Creek Canyon, but bogged down in the snow before reaching Joseph Plains. The bobsled arrived and the family and goods were transferred to it for the trip home. The surrey was abandoned until spring and the weary team led home.

Most journeys to Grangeville were planned when weather would not be a threat—many were taken by James alone, who rode overland 20 miles to Cottonwood where he put his horse in a stable and took the train to Grangeville. He always returned with treats for the kids, usually candy and oranges.

On a rare occasion Phebe, who was eager for her children to have a variety of experiences, took them to a circus in Cottonwood. The day before they selected the horses they would ride and staked them out near the house. Eager to arrive in time to see the circus parade at 11:00 A.M., Phebe woke the children at 2:00 A.M. and fixed a quick breakfast. The horses were saddled and bridled, and mother and children were on their way.

They arrived in Cottonwood by late morning and checked into a hotel, only to discover the parade had been canceled. Disappointed, they ate lunch and went to the circus. They were dazzled by the clowns, trapeze artists, and animal trainers. After the performance, the girls enjoyed a merry-go-round ride. That evening they returned to their hotel and the outing provided an exciting topic of conversation for many days.

These long horseback trips to Cottonwood always reminded Joseph residents of the need for an additional road. A decent route would open up new markets for the Joseph farmers and ranchers because Cottonwood was on the railway line but White Bird wasn't. Eventually the Joseph Highway District was established with James Aram, Joe Keener, and Bill Abercrombie as commissioners. County taxes were levied and by the mid-1920s a new road was started, with Abercrombie in charge of construction.

Progress was slow because roads were built with picks, shovels, dynamite, and teams of horses dragging dirt scrapers. Many of the Joseph men, recognizing an opportunity to make extra money, gladly accepted jobs with the road crew. Even young John Aram worked one summer for $.15 an hour. He saved $12 and then went to a rodeo in Grangeville, where he was enticed into a carnival game. In a matter of minutes, he lost every penny.

After several seasons, the dirt road was completed. It ran from Cottonwood along Graves Creek, across the Salmon River by ferry, and then along Rice Creek. The creek routes were the path of least resistance, but whenever the road crew encountered a bluff, which would make the road too narrow, they switched it to the opposite side of the creek and constructed wooden bridges. Consequently, the road crossed Graves Creek nearly a dozen times and Rice Creek about four times.

When the road left Rice Creek it was necessary to build a series of steep switchbacks to gain elevation. These switchbacks—four hairpin turns known as the Box Flats switchbacks and five others at a higher elevation—were carved into the side of the mountain. Eventually, the narrow road "topped out" on Joseph Plains and blended into the well-traveled wagon roads crisscrossing the plateau.

From the beginning, an all-encompassing rift developed over the route, and divided the Joseph community. Some residents opposed the road, felt it was unnecessary, and resented the taxes levied for it. Adults took sides and children fought with each other at school over the issue. For the first time, James Aram had enemies. Aggressive opponents continually tried to slow the road work and sabotage it. Others claimed funds were misused and leveled a lawsuit at the commissioners.

James, who had managed the money for the road, was required to travel to Grangeville several times during a seven-year court battle, but nothing ever came of the accusations. Still, for years afterward many families against the road avoided the Arams and the Arams avoided them.

With the advent of the Cottonwood road, travel in and out of Joseph improved. A few cars and trucks were able to negotiate the narrow route from top to bottom and back again, but most Joseph residents stuck to their steady horses and wagons. When riding horseback, the Arams continued to use the much faster trail to the Salmon River and then followed the road into town. Either way, the trip was much easier. Cottonwood became the main trading center for Joseph, and the route to White Bird was relegated to history.

Chapter 8

VISITORS

A few of the relatives braved it to visit us, but once having arrived they worried all the time about how they would manage to get out over that steep, tortuous road. My aunt and uncle came once in their Ford. Aunt Margretta was a gentle, lovely looking lady of Welsh ancestry. She had come from a rather well-to-do, refined background. She wore beautiful clothes and was used to gracious living. Our way of life must have been absolute culture shock.—Narcie Aram See 1988

OVER THE YEARS a few of Phebe's relatives risked the trip to Joseph. In the early 1920s her youngest brother, Henry Smith, traveled to the Aram ranch from his home in Dryden, Washington, where he owned an apple orchard. He brought with him his wife, Margretta. At that time the road from Cottonwood did not exist, so the Smiths drove their car along the route from White Bird, although this was not much more than a wagon trail. Henry and his wife bumped along the road across Doumecq and headed into Rice Creek Canyon. They must have shuddered when they stared at the 30 percent downgrade ahead of them, still, Uncle Henry eased the car into the canyon, crossed the creek, and started up the other side. A mile beyond the creek the car gave up.

Henry and Margretta abandoned their vehicle, struggled up the steep grade to Joseph, and walked on to the ranch, a distance of some three miles. Later, neighbors managed to get the car back out of the canyon and on to Doumecq. Uncle Henry and his wife never returned to Joseph. A few years later, they met the Arams in Grangeville instead.

One relative who tackled the trip more than once was Phebe's younger sister, Minnie. For several years Minnie, who was well educated and spoke Spanish, French, and Greek, taught high school in Kalispell, Montana. Later, she accepted a position at Salem College, a girls' school in Winston-Salem, North Carolina.

Aunt Minnie was unmarried and free to spend her summer months traveling. Nearly every summer she came to Joseph and stayed for six weeks, but even while Minnie visited, ranch chores took precedence. Since she had grown up on a Palouse Country farm, she understood and cheerfully helped. Still, Minnie took time to play with the children, sometimes packing a picnic lunch and riding off with them into the surrounding countryside. Her visits were one of the children's great joys.

Minnie arrived with a pile of baggage from which she pulled books, games, and toys. In the days to follow, her lively imagination joined Phebe's and created a special atmosphere of make-believe. The two women wove a continuous story for the children, which they made up as they went along. The lively narrative of the Gump family—Mr. and Mrs. Gump and 12 children— was intertwined with daily chores. Mr. Gump started each day with a dozen eggs for breakfast, and his 12 children encountered many mishaps and adventures. After telling part of the story, Minnie and Phebe sent the children off to pick raspberries or gooseberries for an hour before they were allowed to return and hear more about the Gumps.

Usually Aunt Minnie arrived in Cottonwood on the train and then caught the mail stage to Joseph. One summer before she moved to North Carolina, she came with her brother Harry's wife, Hannah, and their son, Norman. The three travelers attempted a car trip through Rice Creek Canyon only to end up abandoning their car not far from where brother Henry had left his. Later a team of horses pulled the car out of the canyon and back up to Doumecq.

When the Cottonwood road was complete, Minnie decided once again to drive to Joseph. She left the East in a Model T Ford with a friend and the friend's two young daughters. From Cottonwood the women traveled the narrow dirt road down Graves Creek, across the Salmon River on a ferry, and along Rice Creek without incident.

As the one-track road rose from the creek to Joseph, the women encountered their first problems. Minnie managed to negotiate the initial hairpin turn on the Box Flats switchbacks. On the second, which was steeper and more treacherous, the car stalled because it simply didn't have enough power to go up the incline. From their seats the passengers could see the canyon at the edge of the turn. Just below the road a steep slope led to a 50-foot bluff.

The women and children carefully eased their way out of the vehicle, fearing it would roll over the edge. They tried in vain to push it up and around the curve; then they found a large rock and wedged it under the back tire. Suddenly, the Ford began to roll. It rolled over the rock, off the end of the curve, and down the slope toward the bluff. Fortunately, a farsighted rancher had erected fences along the ends of each switchback and the Ford hit the fence and held.

Shaken, Minnie and her party walked back to a house near the Salmon River and rang Phebe on the telephone. James and a hired hand rode out with four saddle horses to collect the women. After a brief stop to retrieve their belongings from the car, the travelers returned to their surefooted mounts and were delivered to Phebe. Later, James, his ranch hands, several neighbors, and a team of workhorses pulled the car back onto the road where it was driven down to the Salmon River to await Minnie's departure. In subsequent years, even when she owned a more powerful car, Minnie never again drove farther than Cottonwood.

The only other aunt who visited Joseph was Aunt Delia Auchinvole, James's older sister, who was widowed and had two grown sons. Sometimes, Delia came to Joseph to stay while Phebe visited her doctor in Spokane. James brought her to Joseph after seeing Phebe off on the train from Grangeville and returned her when he picked Phebe up. Delia wasn't used to four lively children and often did things they didn't understand, such as putting Narcie to bed each evening right after an early dinner and well before dark.

Aunt Delia was talkative and cheerful, and the kids genuinely liked her, but they weren't always cooperative. One time, when John was 10 and Jim Jr. 6, Delia decided the boys needed baths, so she filled the round washtub with warm water from the cookstove's reservoir. When she told the boys to undress and hop into the tub, they ran away. Dashing across the front yard, both scurried up a pine tree and out of their aunt's reach, where they stayed, even though Delia begged them to come down. "We'll come down," they finally told her, "when you promise not to give us a bath." Frustrated and nearly in tears, Delia agreed.

James's younger sister, Clara Fitzgerald, never came to Joseph, but her son Oren arrived every summer to work and earn money toward college. Oren was older than the Aram children, and they all idolized him. He in turn was fond of his younger cousins and enjoyed teasing them. Oren was very dependable and always carried his share of the work, but the summer before his senior year at the University of Idaho in Pocatello, Oren made it known that he didn't like ranch work and wouldn't be back.

Instead, he went on to a career in journalism at the *Salt Lake Tribune*. Later, he moved to the University of Idaho at Moscow where he held prominent positions in the editorial and publicity departments and was an assistant to the president of the university. His years on Joseph, however, created a special bond with his Aram cousins, and as each of them came to the university he extended a helping hand. When John told Oren he intended to major in business, instead of Oren's suggested major in forestry, Oren counseled him, saying, "With your kicked cow complex [feeling sorry for himself], you'll never make it in business."

The only other regular "outside" visitor to the Joseph ranch was a worker who arrived in 1935. Early that year, Aunt Minnie wrote James and Phebe to ask if a nephew of a good friend of hers could spend the summer at the ranch. The young man, 15-year-old Hilton "Hilt" Thrapp, lived with his parents in West Chicago, Illinois. There wasn't much to do there during the summer months and Hilt's parents wanted their son in a different environment. After corresponding with the Thrapps, James and Phebe agreed and that spring they received a card announcing Hilt would arrive sometime in June.

The young Chicagoan hitchhiked across the country and walked the last eight miles from Doumecq down the old Rice Creek road and up to Joseph, where he asked directions to the Aram ranch. When he came down the hill toward the ranch house, Hilt spied a handsome, lean yet muscular young man splitting cookstove wood in the wood-shed. For a moment Hilt thought he was seeing Li'l Abner in person. Just then the young man noticed the stranger approaching and put his ax aside. With a grin of welcome he strode toward Hilt, extended his hand and said, "Hi. You must be Hilton Thrapp. I'm Jim Aram, Jr." Thus began a friendship that was to last a lifetime.

Hilton arrived with his own preconceived notions of the West, garnered from Zane Grey novels. If life on Joseph was different than he expected, he never let on. He readily accepted the primitive conditions and didn't compare the ranch to his city home with its indoor plumbing, oil heat system, and lights. Joseph residents took to the likable young man and promptly nicknamed him "Chicago." Although he was a real greenhorn, Hilt was anxious to fit into their very different lifestyle and was particularly excited about learning to ride a horse.

Already an early riser, Hilt didn't find getting up at 5:00 A.M. a bother. He readily took to feeding the livestock, harnessing work teams, letting the hogs out, and, reluctantly, milking the cows. That summer he didn't participate too much in the heavier work involved in haying, but one day in late August he went with Jim Jr. to load some stray shocks of hay. Having observed the frenzy of the haying season and the heavy workload carried by his new friend, Hilt looked at Jim Jr. and asked, "Why do you want to work?"

Jim Jr., then 18, was dedicated to the ranch and had never questioned the work ethic. He was surprised by Hilt's question, but tried to explain how hard work and sacrifice were necessary to develop a larger stock ranch, and since the ranch was his future he needed to put in the time and effort to achieve that goal.

Shortly after, Hilt returned to Chicago. When he left, Phebe wrote his parents the following letter dated September 26, 1935.

> Dear Mr. and Mrs. Thrapp,
>
> Mr. Aram asked me to write and tell you that Hilton left here yesterday on his way home. He will probably get there as soon or before this letter.
>
> He expected to leave about the first of the month, but when he found there was a possibility of getting a ride through to Chicago on a sheep train, he decided to wait.
>
> He left yesterday for Grangeville, Idaho, about fifty miles from here by stage, and if he gets a ride may not leave there for a few days. The train will probably leave about Sept. 30.
>
> We hated to see him go, especially that way, and will be anxious to know that he gets home safely.

We all like Hilton and feel like another one of the family had gone. He certainly took to the ranch and the West and I think he learned to do most everything about the farm but milk.

We found him very dependable and he took an interest in everything, quite unusual for a young boy. One thing I admire about him is that he has ideas of his own on every subject. He may be wrong sometimes, but he is thinking at least.

I hope he likes school better than he expects to, for he has a good mind. Your ambitions for your family remind me of our own. We have a senior and a freshman in college this year. Rosamond is through [college] and James Jr. has only finished high school.

I hope this summer has been a real benefit to Hilton. He will tell you all about it.

Very truly yours,
Mrs. James Aram

With James and Phebe's approval, Hilt returned to the ranch the following summer. He arrived at their door declaring, "I came to work." That summer he was no longer a greenhorn and he took on additional duties, including shocking hay. When September came he again returned to Chicago, requesting only that he be allowed to come back the following summer as soon as he graduated from high school. "Next time," he asked, "may I stay for a year?"

He arrived in early August 1937 after sightseeing along the way with two friends. A local paper described their arrival that summer:

Hilton Thrapp of Chicago, accompanied by two young men friends from the same city arrived on Joseph Monday afternoon. The boys left Chicago two weeks ago and drove to Los Angeles and up the coast to Seattle, taking in many points of interest en route. This is Hilton's third summer as a Joseph cowboy and he is a seasoned westerner, but the other boys gasped with horror when they dared to peep over the brink of the Rice Creek road.

In a letter to his parents on August 7, 1937, Hilton wrote:

> Dear folks,
>
> I suppose Mike and Hass [Hilt's traveling companions] are home by now. Have you seen them? We arrived here Monday at about 2 P.M. I worked Tuesday and Wednesday in the hay and it sure made me stiff. My hands had blisters and sore places all over them. We finished up Wednesday and Arams went to town Thursday. Mainly to get a binder. Anyway they got one and the binding starts today. They have lots of grain this year and that means lots of work. We have a new corral and several new gates, fence and so on. This fall we're scheduled to build a new barn. We may buy a few head of horses this winter. About the middle of July they had a cold snap here and one morning the temperature got down to twenty-seven. . . . I hope you sent my long underwear and the red sweater.

Three days later, on August 10, 1937, Phebe sent her own letter to Mrs. Thrapp.

> Hilton arrived at last, looking the same as when he left. He never seems to get hurried or flurried and takes life as it comes. You'd be interested to know the various tasks he has had a hand in since he came.
>
> His hardest job was pitching hay in the field. His hands were soft and were all blistered before the job was done, but he stayed with it. We left him and a man who works here while we went to town for two days. They had to cook and wash dishes and I asked Hilton if some woman had been doing the work as everything was so orderly.
>
> He and Jimmy set up a binder which we had brought in piece meal and it works, so I guess the pieces are put together right.
>
> Hilton is to go up and herd some cattle in the field this morning while Mr. Aram comes to

breakfast. He and Jimmy have a horse to break to ride as soon as they get a little time.

I must finish this to get it on the mail.

Sincerely yours,

Mrs. Aram

Hilt got a real education that year at the ranch. After harvest he helped brand a bunch of new cattle and move the stock from summer pasture down to winter pastures at lower elevations. When winter set in at the lower elevations, he helped move them all back up to the home ranch. In the spring he helped Jim tend pigs and cows giving birth; plowed and planted grain fields; and helped repair fences, brand calves, and build watering troughs from hollowed-out logs. Summer brought the familiar chores of summers past. After harvest it was time for Hilt to say a final goodbye to Joseph. He left like a true cowboy, trailing cattle with Jim Jr. as far as Cottonwood, where he caught a train for home.

Unlike Oren Fitzgerald, who had disliked the ranch work, young Hilton thrived on it. His months on Joseph left a deep impression on him. Within a short time he returned and enrolled at the University of Idaho at Moscow, left to serve in World War II, and returned again to complete his education. He married and raised a family, living in Idaho for a number of years. Later, the Thrapps moved to Missouri, but when it was time for retirement they returned and settled near Lewiston. The friendship between a Joseph cowboy and a greenhorn from Chicago, forged during hours of backbreaking labor, lasted until Hilt's death in 1992.

Chapter 9

NEIGHBORS

The fact that Joseph was remote didn't prevent us having association with other people. When we were very young, up until the Depression, we had men working all year and large crews during haying and harvest. We occasionally visited neighbors, went to most of the school functions and to town. For those reasons we didn't feel isolated.—Jim Aram 1992

THE POPULATION OF Joseph Plains was a transient one. Many families, after struggling to maintain a living on their small homesteads, gave up and moved on. Others took possession of the farms only to face the same future, and eventually, they, too, walked away. Those who stayed found that "making ends meet" was difficult. The poor land yielded little income, and there was sparse opportunity for outside employment.

The Arams helped by hiring neighbors when extra hands were needed, loaning supplies and equipment, and, on occasion, even money. One family almost starved during their first winter in the area. James, after learning of their plight, lent them $500. The family saved their homestead but never attempted to pay back their benefactor.

When James bought the home ranch from the Key family in the early 1900s his closest neighbors were the Peters, the family he and Phebe stayed with while their own house was built. After the Arams settled into their home, the Peters sold out to James and moved away.

James then used the Peters' house as a home for his married hired hands, offering it as part of a man's wages. The first family to live there under this arrangement was the Shearer family, who had children similar in age to the Aram children. Then, in the early 20s, Bill and Ester Coltman, along with Ester's mother, Mrs. Unzicker, lived in the house while Bill worked for James. They were followed by Al Graham, his wife, and children, who arrived in the mid-1920s.

The next closest neighbors, Russell and Minnie Dodge, lived south of the Aram ranch and across a small canyon. The Dodges homesteaded 80 acres surrounded almost entirely by Aram-held land. Most of their property was timber, brush, and rough grazing land; only about 15 acres was tillable. There were six Dodge children, the youngest the same age as John Aram. Russell took outside jobs in order to support his large family. His cheerful and industrious wife kept her own small house immaculate and worked for Phebe, first when the children were young and then during many harvests.

Relations with these neighbors sometimes became strained when the Aram cattle or hogs wandered onto Dodge property. Most of the time, however, the families were friendly and treated each other to a yearly dinner. Minnie delighted in sharing her collection of postcards with her guests. Eventually, the Dodges sold their land and bought a cafe in Cottonwood.

Closer friends of Phebe and James were Essie and Charlie Miller whose only child, Charlotte, was John's age. They homesteaded southeast of the Dodges on land running along the road through Rice Creek Canyon. The Millers left Joseph for a few years to manage the Aram wheat farm on Camas Prairie, but returned and settled on the Christian homestead just four miles from Phebe and James. While living there in the '30s, Charlie had the contract for the mail run from Cottonwood to Joseph.

The Aram and Miller houses were relatively close, but the four friends had little time to visit. It was a special treat to go to the Millers', particularly when they acquired one of the first radios on Joseph and shared their favorite programs with friends. Little Narcie loved visiting. To her the Millers' white house was large and beautiful and it had her much-wished-for lawn and an inviting wraparound porch.

To the west, beyond the Peters' place, was the Kidder homestead. As soon as Mr. Kidder "proved up" on the land and received title, he sold out to James. A mile beyond the Kidder's was the William "Bill" Reed family. Although their two children, William Jr. and Vivian, were much older than the Aram offspring, the Reeds were good friends of James and Phebe and often came to the ranch when Phebe invited neighbors in for an evening of singing at her parlor piano.

The Reeds eventually leased their homestead to Coral and Mary Wright who lived there briefly before moving to Boles, where they ran the post office for a number of years. The Marion Lyda family then moved in with their seven children—Bill, Nola, Jettie, Leta, Cecil, and twins Earl and Pearl. All attended the Sunset School with the Arams until moving to another ranch on Doumecq. Later, when Earl and Pearl were in ninth grade they lived with James and Phebe during the week, because the Sunset School had a special provision to teach one year beyond the eighth-grade level. Eventually, the Lydas returned to Joseph and started a cattle ranch.

After the Lydas moved to Doumecq, Bob and Margaret Dobbins occupied the Reed house. Bob and his brother, George, were raised on a small ranch near Getta Creek. During one extremely hard winter in their youth, the family ran out of hay for their cattle. By gathering cactus and singeing off the spines, they managed to keep the herd from starving.

Bob was progressive and, after living at the Reed house, put together a ranch of his own and a nice cattle herd. Narcie Aram and Bob's daughter, Mirabel, became fast friends, and Bob proved to be a kind and considerate neighbor. Once, when James was riding home from Cottonwood in the midst of a blizzard, Bob met him as he came out of Rice Creek Canyon onto the snow-laden plateau near the Reed house. Realizing how tired James and his horse were, Bob insisted on escorting them home through the deep drifts and driving snow.

George Dobbins drifted from place to place for a while, hiring out for work wherever he could. He eventually settled on 40 acres near Charlie Miller's ranch with his wife, Oma, and two children. George was a good neighbor, the first to offer help whenever it was needed. Over the years James, and later Jim Jr., relied on him many times, and they could count on George to hitch up his strong team of horses and help with a difficult job even on short notice.

After Bob Dobbins moved, Price Keener, his wife, Adeline, and their five children settled on the Reed homestead. Price and his brother, Joe, had operated a ranch on south Joseph for many years where they had a pond from which they cut ice in the winter. The ice was stored in sawdust in an icehouse and sold to the neighbors who owned iceboxes. The Keeners raised pigs, a few cattle, and kept a herd of milk cows. They traded work with the Arams during harvest, but since the Arams had more acreage, the Keeners were paid a cash difference.

Joe and Price were originally from Missouri, and their southern drawls and colorful expressions were unique on Joseph. Both were honest and stalwart friends, never backing down or running from anybody or anything. This trait served Joe Keener well when he worked with James as a road commissioner and controversy erupted over the financing and building of the Cottonwood Road.

Neighbors on Joseph were not just those living near the home ranch. Others, including the Qualeys, McDougalls, and Brusts, were scattered across the plateau or owned property adjacent to the Getta Creek ranch. The Arams often crossed land homesteaded by the Qualey family while on their way to Getta Creek. Frequently, James drove cattle across their land, which was not always appreciated by the Qualeys, but they tolerated it since they also had to cross Aram land to leave their own ranch by wagon or buggy.

Mr. and Mrs. Qualey, their four boys, and two girls were from Sweden. They had large gardens, cattle, hogs, and sheep and kept their ranch extremely neat and tidy. The boys—Nelse, Tom, Olaf, and Therwald—added to their livelihood by hunting, fishing, trapping, and making and selling beautifully crafted silver-mounted spurs, bridle bits, and saddle decorations.

The McDougalls were longtime Aram neighbors and lived about five miles away. They had homesteaded 160 acres early in the century, planting crops and starting a small dairy herd. When Mrs. McDougall was appointed postmistress, she kept the post office boxes in her home, but eventually a 16-by-20-foot building was erected about 100 feet from her house.

She didn't sit in her little office all day, for customers were few and far between. Instead, she kept the building locked. When someone needed her services, she bustled from house to office, her dog barking a warning when a customer arrived. If the dog wasn't present, a shout of "hello" brought her out. Activity at the post office increased when Mrs. McDougall began to offer gum, candy, and cigarettes. She remained postmistress until 1944, when the Joseph post office was officially closed.

Not far from the McDougalls, along Wolf Creek, was a spread owned by Lou Brust, another large cattle rancher. Mr. Brust, who was one of the first pioneers on Joseph, donated a small plot of his land for the Joseph cemetery where some 15 to 20 people are buried. His home was some distance from the Aram ranch, but Brust also owned summer range on Center Ridge adjoining James's rangelands. In later years,

Brust bought a threshing machine that he shared with all his neighbors, including James; everyone helped each other with the harvest.

Over the years, James hired a variety of Joseph neighbors or their sons, but a few of his hands were young cowboys who drifted through, men with nicknames like "Shotgun" or "Ramrod." Their conversation at the dinner table was of horses, guns and the fistfight at the last community dance, but all were polite and never used rough language near Phebe. These men were all-around ranch hands who helped with cattle roundups, vaccinations, brandings, and farm work. James and Phebe never knew where many of them came from, or where they went.

Some of the more colorful characters who touched the Arams' lives were the bachelors of the region. One was an Irishman—an eccentric who lived in a shack on the Salmon and who ordered a bride from England. When the young girl arrived, some of the neighbors gave the couple a shivaree, but the girl soon packed her bags and left. Another single homesteader along the Snake River who had a long-running feud with a neighbor whose cattle kept wandering onto his property confided to James one day about the offending neighbor, "If it wasn't for this here hereafter, I would have killed him a long time ago."

Mr. Maples, who lived on the Salmon River below Rice Creek, was an occasional visitor to the ranch house. He usually arrived on foot about dinnertime, claiming his horse was on loan to someone. A slender little man with bright blue eyes and a pointed nose, Maples was quite a talker and he spit a lot. Because he appeared to be quite old, the children called him Mr. Maples to his face and "Daddy" Maples behind his back. They enjoyed his unique way of giving directions, for he always used the mailbox of Ed Knorr, who lived on Fall Creek, as a point of reference. He would say, "Well, before you get to Ed Knorr's mailbox, turn off to the north" or "From Ed Knorr's mailbox you keep going until. . . ."

On his homestead Mr. Maples kept three or four horses and a few cows. He, too, had a running feud with his neighbor over straying cattle and he continually accused the rancher of stealing grass from his 160-acre claim. When Maples needed summer grass for his horses he took them up to the Arams' pasture, never riding but always leading them. To work out his pasture bill and earn a grubstake for the winter months, Maples worked for the Aram haying crew. He was a hard worker, but like many other bachelors was careless about his cleanliness. When he was at the ranch, Phebe insisted he bathe and wash his hair even when he protested that his balding head was hardly worth the effort.

One summer Mr. Maples brought a large, old horse up to the ranch. Jim Jr. decided to take the horse to another pasture. Securing the lead rope to the saddle horn on his own mount, he urged both horses to trot. The old horse followed Jim into a canyon and partway up the other side. Suddenly, Jim felt his rope go taut and his own horse pulled up short. Looking back he saw Maples's horse lying dead by the side of the trail. Jim felt terrible, but when he told Mr. Maples, the bachelor just shrugged and said, "Well, he was pretty old."

Another bachelor was a local trapper who often stopped to visit the Arams when he was out checking his lines. After spending several days skinning all sorts of animals, he could be pretty smelly when he warmed up by the fire. Still, he was always welcome and usually spent the night, going back to his traps in the morning.

In addition to his fur business, the man had a small ranch on Graves Creek en route to Cottonwood. A few times, when James was driving cattle to town, he rented a pasture from him to contain his cattle for the night. James then slept in the trapper's house where he was once taken to an upstairs bedroom, handed a pot, and told, "Here's a chamber if you have to get up in the night, but the boys usually jest use the winder."

The most frequent bachelor visitor to the Aram ranch was Billy Rankin. He was working a copper mine on the Snake River's Oregon side right across from the mouth of Getta Creek, and he had a homestead adjoining the Aram Getta Creek ranch. Billy hailed from Oregon, where he once attended a Bible school in Portland. He was a brilliant mathematician who had been schooled as a surveyor, although he never received his license. Instead, he chose to herd sheep on the steep and dangerous terrain of the Imnaha, Grande Ronde, and Snake rivers.

On one of his herding jobs, Billy found himself in the Snake River Canyon across from Idaho staring at a rock with green coloring. Deciding it was copper, he staked a claim and named the area Copper Mountain. In order to keep his claim, he was required to work it. He made the mine his winter quarters and built two tent buildings with wooden floors and hired a man to help him work the claim every winter. Although Billy believed deeply in his mine, he worked it for most of his life but no copper vein was ever found.

The entire Aram family liked Billy. His cheerful presence was always welcome, and when he came to visit he stayed with the family for several days. Much of his talk was of his mine and the assaying of his ore, but he also told tales of his sheepherding days in steep terrain where in the winter he often clung to clumps of bunchgrass to keep from tumbling into a canyon. Billy had more education than most of the Joseph residents and was often viewed as a little eccentric because of the contrast between his scholarly demeanor and his lifestyle.

In the 1930s Billy operated a sawmill south of Camp Howard Mountain that provided lumber for many residents. He wanted to move some of his lumber down to Copper Mountain, so he hauled it around Camp Howard to a road from the Salmon River bridge to Pittsburg Landing. At the Snake he bound the lumber together with chain and cable borrowed from James. His intent was to float it like a raft down the river. Instead, the swift current spun the lumber raft away, crashing it into the first bend. Billy lost most of his lumber to the river and residents who lived along its banks; James lost all his chains and cable.

James and Billy became loyal friends. When James helped Billy out by buying a quarter interest in the mine, he gave the interest back to Billy when no buyer was found. Billy in turn staked claims for James and Phebe on a power site and other government land along the river. Billy helped James when he needed extra ranch hands, and James almost always had a team of horses on loan to Billy. When John needed a horse one summer, while working on Sourdough lookout for the U.S. Forest Service, Billy loaned him his own horse, Baldy.

Jim Jr. worked side by side with Billy for many years and came to know him well. When Billy spent two seasons herding sheep for James in the early '30s, Jim Jr. often stopped by the camp to share Billy's company and cooking. The boy enjoyed the simple fare of beans, camp stove bread, and a tin of fruit or vegetables. "Billy didn't feel the need to restrain himself with me, like he did with Dad," said Jim in later years, "so I got to know him real well. Sometimes in the winter I went down to the Snake and yelled across the river a few times. If Billy was at his camp, he climbed in his old boat and rowed over to get me. I staked my horse out and went over to Copper Mountain to spend the night with him."

But not all relationships on Joseph were as friendly. Occasionally ranchers, including James, became embroiled in feuds over land rights and missing livestock; hard feelings erupted at dances or in the schoolyards. Despite these arguments many ranchers preferred to overlook the minor transgressions of their neighbors—it was not worth stirring up a mess of trouble over one missing cow or a trampled pasture.

In this land of no organized law, working together developed deep friendships. Even a seasoned bachelor like Maples sometimes revealed these special feelings. Jim Jr. witnessed this when Maples learned that James was going to Chicago with a trainload of cattle. Convinced his employer and friend would never return from that great distance, Mr. Maples shed tears of genuine sorrow.

Although this softer side of these 20th-century pioneers was often hidden, similar bonds were forged between many other neighbors over the years. The ruggedness of the land and the strength of the men and women who worked it could not diminish the depth of feeling these people held for each other.

Chapter 10

GETTA CREEK

❧

I loved Getta Creek. It had a special smell about it, presumably from the plants growing along its banks. Our cabin was about 200 yards from the creek. We loved playing and wading in it. There was an abundance of fruit trees—apples, peaches, apricots, and plums.—Narcie Aram See 1988

JAMES ARAM PURCHASED his Getta Creek ranch in partnership with his brother, Tom, in 1897, just before Tom's death. The land around the ranch was excellent winter range, with temperatures much warmer than on the heights of Joseph Plains. Snow was rare and the cattle grazed easily on the long, low benches of land that rose gently from the creek for some distance before joining the steeper ridges below the Joseph plateau.

There were four routes to Getta Creek from the Joseph ranch, but the one most often used was the Fir Gulch Trail—the steepest, most direct route that crossed Aram land. It started six miles from the home ranch at the top of a hill with a panoramic view of Copper Mountain in Oregon on the far side of the Snake River and the Seven Devils Mountains of Idaho to the south. The path descended approximately three rugged miles to the benches along Getta Creek, where it followed the gentler contours of land for approximately a mile to the cabin.

"That Fir Gulch Trail was hell for a little kid," remembered Jim Aram 70 years later. Narcie echoed her brother's sentiments, adding, "It was a frightening trip for a small child on a horse. I especially remember one trip when Mother was with the four of us. My brothers were on their horses, and Rosamond and I were riding another horse. In the very steep places it seemed that we would all be crying, and she would take us off the horses and lead us down the trail until we came to a more level spot."

In her preschool years Narcie often rode behind her mother on Old Flax. She felt secure with her arms wrapped around Phebe and her face pressed against her mother's back as they traversed the steep terrain. However, one winter while on the trail Narcie fell asleep. Her grip on her mother loosened and she slid off the horse. Her fall was cushioned by several thick layers of winter clothing and a soft mound of snow. The little girl went right on sleeping while her mother continued on.

Phebe had gone several yards before realizing Narcie was gone. Momentarily she was paralyzed with fear, but as she turned her horse around on the narrow trail she saw a small bundle nestled in a snow-bank several yards behind her. Hurrying back, Phebe picked up her slumbering daughter and continued on her journey, this time with Narcie tucked safely in front.

The pleasure the family derived from the Getta Creek ranch compensated for the difficult trip. The cabin had become a special haven for them during the flu epidemic of 1919 and remained a retreat during other hard winters. When Jim Jr. and Narcie were still preschool age, James and Phebe took the two older children out of school for a few weeks and moved the family from the Joseph ranch, where there was four feet of snow, to the temperate climate at Getta Creek. "It was just like part of heaven to suddenly move out of all that cold to a place with warm days and nights," remembered Jim.

The cabin at Getta was constructed of lumber and had one bedroom, a kitchen, and living area. A ladder leaning against one wall led to an attic where John, Rosamond, Jim, and Narcie slept on mattresses. A lean-to off one side was used for storage or extra sleeping space. When they were small, the children spent many happy hours wading in the nearby creek or playing along its banks.

Generally, the Arams went to Getta Creek to work. In addition to grazing cattle, they raised hay and grew nearly all their fresh fruits and vegetables there. Most of the apple, peach, apricot, and plum orchards were in marshy areas created by springs. Some peach and cherry trees, located near the cabin, were irrigated with water from the creek; a large vegetable garden produced tomatoes and a variety of melons. The family spent several weeks there each spring planting the garden, returning frequently during the summer months to irrigate and harvest the produce.

In order to take the fresh produce back to the main ranch, they brought three to five packhorses down from Joseph several times during the hot months of July and August. Usually they arrived in the late afternoon and picked fruit in the cool of the evening and all the next day. In the late afternoon, they loaded the full pack boxes onto the horses. With the heavily laden pack train, they avoided the Fir Gulch Trail and took a much longer, but gentler, route through the Qualey ranch. Even after the sun set, the air was hot and stifling, so the horses were rested frequently. Often it was 10 P.M. before they arrived home, tired and miserable.

Sometimes James kept a hired man at the Getta Creek ranch to take care of the gardens and orchards, raise hay, and herd the cattle. More frequently, as the boys got older, he relied on his sons to help him with the work. Each winter, when John was in the fifth, sixth, and seventh grades, James took him out of school to look after the cattle at Getta Creek. John always packed his school books because James promised Phebe he would help his son with his lessons. However, the boy never opened a book in the weeks he spent tending the cattle. Still, he passed the county examination after eighth grade and was promoted to high school.

Phebe was not as easy on the children when it came to their studies. She expected them to keep up with their class while at Getta Creek and to take books along to read even when school was not in session. When Jim Jr. was in his first year of school he dutifully packed a little book to read at the cabin; however, shortly after they arrived, the book disappeared.

When it was time to leave, the family started out, only to be halted when Jim cried, "Wait." He scrambled off his horse and ran to a little cage that once housed a former owner's pet monkey. Reaching under the lid, he pulled out his missing book and explained to his mother, "I just remembered where I left it."

The Getta Creek ranch house was only a mile from the Snake River, which the children regarded as mysterious and wonderful. Occasionally Phebe packed a lunch and took the children for an afternoon of digging in the warm sandbars or looking for freshwater shells along the riverbanks. Often they met the weekly mail boat when it stopped at the mouth of Getta Creek on its way upriver from Lewiston, 85 miles away.

The children were cautioned about the dangers that lurked in river country—poison oak, cacti, and rattlesnakes—and became adept at recognizing the poison oak plant and dodging the spines of any cactus they encountered. Once Narcie was pushed into a cactus by the older kids, and Phebe was shocked to find the little girl's bottom covered with the tiny spines. Patiently she removed them one by one.

Rattlesnakes were uncommon on the high plateaus, although they could be found along the edges of canyons on Joseph. Only one was ever seen at the Joseph ranch, but many were confronted in the country around the cabin at Getta Creek. The children were admonished to look carefully before they stepped. It was rumored that a rattler with a head as big as a calf's had been seen near an old corral on the route between the cabin and the Snake River. Fearing the story might be true, the kids always hurried past the corral, their eyes wide with wariness.

When in his teens, Jim Jr. became adept at killing snakes. He came across some while riding after cattle, but most of his encounters occurred when he was on foot, harvesting hay or herding sheep. One August he noticed the McDougalls were having trouble getting their hay in at their ranch in the river country. He suggested to Hilt Thrapp that the two of them go down and help. The hay shocks had been in the field for a while and rattlers found them a nice retreat from the summer sun. As Jim pitched the shocks onto slips—hay boxes drawn on runners—he found 13 rattlers in a couple of days. Using his pitchfork he killed them all before they had a chance to strike.

On another occasion, he was herding sheep for a Mr. Kinney in the Getta Creek area. He came across 18 snakes in 30 days and killed them with his sheep hook. Generally, the snakes rattled a warning or attempted to slip away; however, Jim once met one on a narrow trail and it refused to give ground. Instead, the snake reared back and came down the trail with its head high and rattles whirring. Carefully, Jim backed away until he found a long stick which he used to kill the snake. His success at avoiding snakebites was displayed in a chain of rattles worn around his hat.

The snakes caused some stock losses, although most animals seemed to recover from a bite. One of the stock dogs tangled with a snake while working the Getta Creek range. It was quite ill and was laid up for three weeks, but recovered and went back to work. Cattle were wary and avoided snakes, sheep didn't seem to be bothered by them, neither were hogs who, it was rumored, were immune to snakes and capable of running them out of their own territory.

The Getta Creek ranchland encompassed some 4,000 acres and

stretched from the top of the Fir Gulch Trail to the creek far below. It ran three or four miles along Getta, crossed the creek, and extended south as far as High Range Creek. On the west it was bordered by the Snake River and ran northward almost to Wolf Creek.

Most of this acreage was relatively rugged grazing land. Some of it was considered "steeper than a cow's face" and not much good, even for grazing. This treacherously steep land lay between the south side of Getta Creek, the east side of the Snake River, and the north side of High Range Creek. Cattle sometimes wandered into this area and the men would have to ride in to round them up. The best land—long benches and meadow areas—was that near Getta Creek and running north toward Wolf Creek.

Included in the land that bordered the Snake was a section called Ragtown where a tent city, set up by miners searching the sandbars for gold, once stood. Before James bought the Ragtown land, an irrigation ditch was constructed from Getta Creek to some of the long benches of land above Ragtown for the purpose of raising hay. The ditch was about two miles long and followed the contour of the hillside. Where the land ended in deep gullies, wooden flumes carried the water to the next stretch of ditch.

John and Jim Jr. spent many days one summer trying to repair the ditch and flumes, but were not able to keep the water flowing to the benches. Consequently, they used that land for grazing cattle and limited their crop raising to the meadows along the creek which were irrigated by a local ditch flowing from Getta Creek.

All these endeavors in the river country—cattle grazing, hog raising, orchards, gardens, and hay fields—required many supplies, which had to be packed in by horse or mule. Out of necessity, they learned to pack everything from mowing machines, hay rakes, cook stoves, wire, lumber, and fence posts to steel watering tanks five feet in diameter. The tanks were not heavy, but they were bulky, and to get them down into the canyon, they were loaded on one side of a large mule. A box of rocks balanced the tank on the other side. Every time the narrow trail bordered a hill on the side the tank was on, the tank was switched to the other side in order to pass.

To secure loads on the pack animal, the Arams used the traditional diamond hitch in which packs were loaded on the horse by ropes attached to a wooden "X" frame formed on the top of a light packsaddle.

The weight was distributed evenly for balance, and an additional pack was often placed on top. Then a long rope was attached to a cinch which was thrown over the load. The rope was brought under the animal's belly and through a ring on the pack cinch on the other side. It was then thrown over the load, pulled snugly and intertwined on the top with a section of rope looped around each of the side packs. Again it was pulled tight, securing all the packs and forming a diamond shape on top.

Sometimes a load was just too big to pack, such as the time a teenage Jim Jr. and Bob Dobbins hauled a 16-foot water trough down a canyon in the Fir Gulch area. Instead a team of horses pulled it. Concerned that the trough might start moving too fast and overrun the horses, the men anchored it by cutting a young jack pine with lots of limbs and tying it behind the trough. In the steepest terrain they unhitched all but one horse, figuring one horse had a chance at getting out of the way if necessary. The trough was delivered without incident to its resting place near the bottom of the canyon and was placed so spring water ran directly into it for the grazing cattle.

Despite the difficulty of traveling in and out, the Arams loved the Getta Creek ranch as an oasis with its temperate climate, many fruit trees, vegetable gardens, gentle creek, and proximity to the Snake River. It provided the children with warm memories of sun-splashed days playing on the sandbars of the mysterious and intriguing Snake in the depths of Idaho's spectacular Hells Canyon.

Chapter 11

FOUR-LEGGED FRIENDS

I've often said that at times I didn't know a boy could walk until I was about 14, because I hadn't been off the back of a horse.—John Aram 1984

WHILE GROWING UP, the Aram children were surrounded by animals. Much of the responsibility for their care and well-being fell to the children; some of their favorites became pets. Narcie had the softest heart where the animals were concerned, particularly when it came to the kittens and puppies and later, when her father had sheep, the orphaned lambs. Phebe came up with colorful names for the milk cows often based on comic strip characters such as Tillie the Toiler, Daisy, and Maggie of "Maggie and Jiggs." In addition, there was Old Thunder, who had to be lassoed and tied down twice a day before she could be milked.

Every animal present had its place. The cats were in charge of controlling the mouse population; the dogs herded stock with the cowboys. When Narcie was two, her father brought home Major, a little gray-blue Australian shepherd mix with spots of brown and white. The puppy had one eye Phebe referred to as a glass eye because it was much lighter than the other eye and had a glassy sheen.

Major was very smart and grew into a strong, competent cattle dog—a valuable asset on many difficult roundups in all types of weather. In addition, Major was a great friend to the Arams and the only dog ever allowed inside the house. When any member of the family came down the hill toward the ranch, they could count on Major running up to greet them.

A year or so after Major arrived, James bought a black-and-white mixed breed named Colonel. He was a tough little character whose only fear was the sound of thunder. Although trained as a stock dog, he had a mean streak and was rough on the animals. He often bit the cattle, instead of gently nipping, to force them in the direction the cowboys wanted them to go. If a cow gave him a particularly difficult time, Colonel grabbed it by the nose until it headed up the trail.

John and Jim Jr. played on Colonel's quarrelsome nature and teased him mercilessly. Colonel's archenemy was Bum, a neighbor's dog who sometimes ventured onto the Aram ranch. Colonel hated Bum and fought him at the slightest provocation. Using this antagonism, John and Jim stood just inside the screen door yelling "Bum," which set Colonel to frantic barking and racing around and around the yard in a fruitless effort to find his enemy.

The boys also started fights with each other, knowing the dog would join the fray. Barking and snapping, Colonel forced his way between the two, often biting one or the other. The boys also teased Colonel when he went with them to round up cattle. Talking to the dog as they rode along, John would say, "Hey, you old dummy what were you doing chasing yourself around the house the other day?"

"Yah, you're not very smart," Jim Jr. would add. "Old Bum was probably sound asleep on his porch and there you were wearing yourself out looking for him."

The mere inflection of their voices, not to mention the name of Bum, sent the dog into a frenzy of barking, growling, and lunging. If words didn't work, the boys made a whirring noise with their tongues to get a reaction. Colonel was smart and knew just what the boys were up to, often getting even with them with a sound nip when they least expected it. But the boys continued teasing the dog, convinced Colonel enjoyed their confrontations just as much as they did.

James didn't like it when one of the boys was bitten, so twice he gave the dog to cattlemen who lived miles away. Twice the dog returned, so James gave up and kept him, for despite his faults Colonel was a good stock dog. Any time they swam cattle across the Salmon, Colonel was quick to jump in and keep them moving. One time Jim Jr. found Lou Brust's bull in one of their haystacks. He chased it to the Snake where the bull jumped in and swam for Oregon. Jim decided it would be a mean trick to let the bull go to another state so he sent Colonel after it. In no time at all, the dog turned the bull back to Idaho.

Of all the animals on the ranch, the horses were the most important, for they provided both transportation and labor. There were few hours of any given day when the men were not working with a horse. Sixteen or more horses were needed daily in the field during harvest, and at least eight were used for plowing in the spring. Backup teams were necessary in case any of the horses fell ill or were injured. A wide variety of saddle horses was kept on hand for herding cattle, branding, and travel. Some did triple duty, serving as saddle, pack-, or workhorses depending on whatever was needed.

James often bought and traded horses. One year he bought three excellent Avalons from Charlie Warnick, one of his hired hands. One, Cora, was used mostly for work, but the other two, Bluebird and Stockings, were saddle horses. Bluebird proved to be one of the best saddle horses the family ever had—strong and surefooted in all types of terrain, tackling even the steepest slopes with ease.

James also kept a range herd of unbroken mares from which he raised his own stock. For many years a beautiful Morgan stallion, which James had brought to Joseph, ran with the mares. The Morgan herded as a wild stallion would. Fences were little deterrent to him, and when he came upon a group of horses within the confines of a fence he simply jumped the fence, checked the mares over, and jumped out again.

The Arams raised many fine horses from this stallion including Mars, one of Jim Jr.'s favorites whose mother was the Avalon Cora. Like his sire, Mars was a jumper and could clear any fence in his way. One day Jim left the horse in a pasture down near Graves Creek while he went to Cottonwood. When he returned Mars was gone. The horse had cleared the pasture fence and returned to the Joseph ranch, jumping five more fences to reach his destination.

Two-year-olds from the range herd were trained as saddle or workhorses. Regardless of what its job was to be, each horse was first "broke to lead" by roping the animal and fastening a hackamore of strong half-inch rope over its head. The hackamore was like a bridle, but instead of a bit to control the animal it had a loop, or slip noose, capable of being tightened about the nose or lower jaw. The wild horse was then tied to a post or tree for a day or two until it realized there was no escape from the rope. One favorite method for acquainting the horse with the rope was to tie it to a young sapling. When the horse struggled to free itself, the sapling bent. When the horse grew tired of pulling, the sapling straightened and led the horse back toward it.

Once a horse was accustomed to the rope, it was taken out on a lead tied securely to the saddle of a reliable mount. The unbroken animal was allowed to run to a length of about 20 feet until it came to the end of the rope, where it did a flipflop and hit the ground. The trainer turned the bronc back and forth in this manner a few hours each day for several days until it learned to stop when the rope ran out. The animal could then be led without struggle, and the process of gentling it was on its way.

The men continued to work with the horse each day, leading it around the corral, rubbing its nose and back, and eventually placing a saddle on it. Once the horse was used to the weight of the saddle, it was snubbed up tightly to the saddle horn of another well-trained horse so it couldn't buck and was led around the corral with a man on its back. When it seemed the horse was accepting its rider, the lead rope was untied and the cowboy was on his own. Sometimes he was bucked off; other times he was grudgingly allowed to remain in his seat.

After the bronc could be ridden, there were still many more hours of teaching it to respond to commands within the confines of the corral. When the trainer felt confident, he took the horse out on open land. Even after this first outing there was still a long training period before the horse was considered completely broken and trustworthy.

The process of breaking a horse to pull farm equipment was similar, except once broken to lead it was put in a harness and hitched with a strong, gentle work horse to a light conveyance. The young horse was tied to the neck yoke in front and hitched to the singletree behind. The hackamore was tied across to the other horse so there was very little slack.

One of the best animals James had to team with a new horse was a mule named Molly. Molly had come to the ranch with five other mules trained as teams for heavy farm work. Her teammate died and Molly became a favorite of the Arams, serving them for many years as a work and pack mule. When she teamed with a horse, her size and strength served her well. The young horses couldn't push her around when hitched at her side and, if necessary, she pulled the conveyance, other horse and all. If a horse lunged and fought, Molly brought it back in line with a sound bite.

The children learned to handle horses at an early age—from infancy they were on horseback, either in front or behind one of their parents.

Phebe L. Smith (Aram), an early graduate of Idaho Teacher's College at Moscow, taught at the Yellow Pines School on Joseph Plains from 1906 until 1910.

In late 1912 James H. Aram, early settler of Camas Prairie and Joseph Plains, posed with his first-born son, John Lorenzo.

In 1916 Phebe Aram posed with her first three children, (L to R) Rosamond, Jim Jr., and John.

Sarah Barr Aram, the matriarch of the Aram family, was an early settler of Camas Prairie. She was known to help anyone in need—miner, pioneer, or Indian. In her later years prairie residents fondly called her "Grandma" Aram.

Minnie J. Smith, "Aunt Minnie," was Phebe Aram's younger sister. Her visits to the ranch on Joseph provided the Aram children with many fond memories.

Ruth Lightfield (Aram) as a senior at the University of Idaho (circa 1943-44).

Jim Jr. after his accident and the acquisition of a prosthesis (circa 1940).

Jim Jr. as a high school senior in 1935.

James and Phebe Aram in their Lewiston home with their adult children. Back (L to R): Jim Jr., James, and John. Front (L to R): Rosamond, Phebe, and Narcie (circa 1943).

Al Graham watches John ride a bucking horse.

An outing with friends in a buckboard (Idaho County, Idaho, circa 1920).

The Sunset School on Joseph Plains. The Aram children attended classes here from 1918 into the early 1930s.

Ranch hands with the hay wagon and team at the James Aram ranch (Joseph Plains, Idaho, circa 1930).

Jim Jr. and Ruth Lightfield married on November 24, 1946. Their wedding party consisted of: (L to R) Robert Lightfield, Ruth's brother; John L. Aram, Jim's brother; Jim and Ruth; B. Mae Lightfield, Ruth's relative; and Narcie Aram, Jim's sister. The flower girl and ring bearer are John's children, Janie and Johnny Aram.

James and Phebe Aram on the back steps of their Joseph ranch house (circa mid-1930s).

The abandoned James H. Aram ranch on Joseph Plains as it looks today. The house is on the right. Part of the barn built by Jim Jr. is visible just to the left of the pine tree.

By the time they were 6 each was riding alone. John's first ride on his own was taken on Old Dutch, a large bay with a dramatic white streak down his face. James took his son out into the pasture directly in front of the house. When the two riders came to a cluster of pine trees with low scraggly boughs, Old Dutch headed toward one of them, in order to scrape his inexperienced rider off.

"What do I do now? What do I do now?" John yelled at his father.

"Well," James responded laughing, "just bend over the saddle horn and keep going."

A couple years later Rosamond learned to ride and then Jim Jr., who was anxious to catch up with his father and big brother. Shortly after his first ride, Jim went to mount his horse from a rock at the Getta Creek ranch. With great confidence the little cowboy hoisted himself into the saddle, only to find he was facing the horse's tail. Hoping no one had noticed, he squirmed around and faced front.

Narcie soon wanted to ride like her siblings and by the age of 6 was on her own and ready for her first solo trip to Getta Creek. Her horse, Old Shorty, refused to walk and ignored Narcie's commands. Instead, he jogged the entire terrifying distance with the little girl bouncing along in the saddle.

John loved to run his horses, racing them along the wagon roads or across the fields. During his tenth year he decided he was going to ride bareback all summer on a little bay mare named Delta. As he went about his chores, he raced the horse from place to place. Delta possessed a mind of her own, occasionally tossing John off during a sudden turn, but always pulling up coyly down the road to wait for her rider.

One afternoon James sent John to round up cattle that had gotten into the wheat field. John took Delta at a dead run. On a curve in the old wagon road, the horse turned abruptly, tossing John over her neck into a fence, where he hit his head on the top of a fence post and landed stunned on the ground. He was not injured and rode on to finish his task.

On another occasion, with another horse, John wasn't as lucky. It was June and he was helping his father round up and brand the cattle. The men had come in for a lunch cooked by Rosamond. As they rode the mile back to the branding corral, young John lagged behind and stopped at a barn in a field along the way. By the time he was ready to remount, the others were out of sight. As he swung up the saddle slipped because he hadn't tightened the cinch. The horse bucked and threw him headfirst into a pile of fence rails.

The boy was briefly unconscious and woke to find he was bleeding profusely from a cut on his upper lip. Dazed, he eased himself up, recinched his saddle, and mounted the horse. The world was still reeling, and thinking his horse wasn't acting right, John got off and led it home. Rosamond, the only person at the ranch house, was terrified when her semiconscious and bloodied brother arrived at the door. She quickly called neighbors for help and then, after seeing to John's immediate needs, rode out to find their father.

When James returned to the house, his greatest fear was that some permanent damage had been done. Phebe, who had been notified by the neighbors of John's plight, arrived in the late evening after a prayerful trip from Getta Creek where she had been picking fruit. The cut on John's lip had been tended to, but there was little she or a physician could do for his dazed state. She continued to pray.

By morning her prayers were answered; John was completely coherent and alert. Remarkably he suffered no brain damage and bore only a tiny scar on his upper lip. However, as an adult he suffered for years from sinus trouble. He was in his 70s before a specialist surmised the root of his problem by noting John had crushed his nose in an accident decades before. Memories of that June day when he was 11 came rushing back.

Jim Jr. also had his share of escapades with the horses. When he was in the eighth grade, he rode a horse he was breaking to school every day. While in school he kept it in a barn nearby. In the mornings the horse did not like leaving the home barn and fought Jim all the way.

Jim had pretty good control with the hackamore and usually won, but one day the horse ignored Jim and "took its head," running in a direction of its own choosing along a row of trees and suddenly swerving under a tree. A branch caught Jim full in the chest, and he fell to the ground with a thud, the wind knocked out of him. After he caught his breath, Jim walked back to where the horse had stopped. Grabbing a length of rope he hit the horse, venting his anger with several resounding smacks that continued even after he remounted and turned the horse back toward the school.

Jim had two other harrowing experiences in later years. Once a spirited animal lost its footing while galloping along an old road track and fell with Jim firmly in the saddle. He was saved from a broken leg by a deep rut that cradled his leg and held the horse's weight. Another time a partially broken saddle horse started bucking at the steep edge of a canyon and stopped only when a terrified Jim grabbed a fence post in an attempt to save himself.

However, Jim's most unnerving accident happened when he was in his midteens and he and John were rounding up cattle after the first frost of the year. The horses had not yet been sharp-shod—fitted with their spiked horseshoes designed for slippery winter travel. As the boys wound up a steep trail, they encountered a 2-foot-high rock ledge. John's horse navigated the ledge, but Jim's horse, Midnight, lost his footing and plunged over the edge into a steep 50-foot ravine.

The momentum threw Jim headlong over the horse into some wild rose bushes. The horse somersaulted two or three times and rolled to a stop at the bottom. After a moment of dead silence, Midnight got to his feet, shook himself off, and nickered at the boys. Jim was shaken, scratched, and bruised, but with John's help he slid down into the ravine and led the horse out. While John rode on, Jim returned home where Phebe tended his injuries and sent up a silent prayer of thanks that once again her son had escaped harm.

Just as taking care of their own minor illnesses and injuries was a way of life for the Arams, so was doctoring the animals, which included castrating, or gelding, the range studs, a task that fell to James. The delicate process was accomplished when the males were two and still wild, fast, and strong. A rope was tossed around the young animal's neck to hold it. Then another rope was fastened around his front feet and pulled until he fell over on his side. The bottom hind leg was tied in with the front legs while another rope was fastened around his shoulders and top hind leg. This rope was tightened until the leg was almost up to the shoulder.

Once the horse was tied securely, James swabbed the scrotum generously with disinfectant, cut it open and pulled the testicle cords out. He clamped the cords with a wood clamp and burned the length of cord off with a hot iron. Burning the cord seared the end and prevented excessive bleeding. James was careful to pull out plenty of cord, otherwise the animal would be "cut proud" and have a temperament like a stallion and be useless as a work or saddle horse. After the cord was severed, James set the animal free. Crude as the procedure was, he never lost an animal because of it.

One of the greatest hazards for the horses grazing on Aram land was the miles of barbed-wire fences crisscrossing the range. Many of their fine horses became victims of vicious wire cuts on their chests or legs when they ran into fences they couldn't see. Once entangled, the horse struggled to be free against wire that acted like a saw. The beautiful Morgan stallion jumped his last fence when he lost his footing and plunged into the wire, cutting himself and bleeding to death before he was found.

Luckier horses were freed when found by someone or occasionally by their own struggles. Their nasty cuts took a long period of doctoring. Usually the wound was washed with sheep-dip, a terrible-smelling, tar-based salve that helped the healing process and kept the flies away. Sometimes James doused a wound with potassium permanganate or cayenne pepper. After the wound healed properly it generally did not interfere with the horse's ability to carry on its duties, but a wire-cut blemish usually made it impossible to sell.

All of the animals at the ranch were treated humanely. If an animal was sick or injured, every attempt was made to save its life. But when an animal was in terrible pain or too weak to survive, it was put out of its misery with a bullet or a blow to the head. Of all the animals to come and go at the ranch, Major, the faithful Australian shepherd, survived the longest. At the age of 15, after years as a constant friend and cattle dog, Major became blind and arthritic. Phebe gently eased his final days with inhalations of chloroform.

Horses remained the main mode of transportation on Joseph even after the road to Cottonwood was finished and automobiles appeared frequently on the plateau. Horse trading was a popular "sport" for some of the ranchers in the area as late as the 30s when traders often drove herds through the area. It was said that whoever "gave the boot" (additional cash) in a horse trade was the one getting the worst of the deal. "I suppose I 'gave some boot' in those years," said Jim. "I got some good workhorses from the traders, and a little bit of cash in addition to the horse I was trading [and that] made a big difference to them."

Following the death of the Morgan stallion, the range herd dwindled. When he was 17, Jim Jr. met a man named Wilson who was grazing sheep on the Getta Creek range. He told Jim that he had a thoroughbred stallion the Arams could use for stud if Jim wanted to go over to his Oregon range and bring it back. Max Newman, a friend of Jim's, also wanted to use the stallion. Together the two boys crossed the Snake in an old wooden boat belonging to Billy Rankin.

Mr. Wilson rounded up the stallion, who was barely broke to lead, and Jim put a hackamore on him. They led the horse to the river and climbed in their boat. Jim held the rope while Wilson shooed the horse into the river and Max rowed. Although Max was rowing as hard as he could, the horse soon overtook the boat and started bumping it. Fearing the horse might try to climb in, Jim pushed him away and gave him some rope. The stallion reached the Idaho shore ahead of the boat, but remained controlled on 100 feet of rope. It wasn't until years later that it occurred to Jim he had been in a very dangerous situation—he couldn't swim a stroke.

Both Max and Jim used the stallion to breed several mares and then took him back to the river and shooed him in, letting him swim across on his own. Max got two colts; Jim got one. Still he was pleased with the effort. His colt, Ramona, was a beautiful sorrel with a good disposition who was destined to be a fine saddle horse.

Eventually, the Arams joined some of their neighbors and gave in to progress. James, who was then well into his 60s and had spent most of his life on a horse, agreed to purchase a used Dodge touring car from his friend, Bill Abercrombie, who was a salesman for Star Cars in Grangeville. He paid $480 for the car and had it delivered to Joseph where he tried his hand at driving it around the ranch. Rolling up to a gate he yelled, "Whoa." The car didn't respond and plowed through the fence. After that James let it be known that he preferred his horse.

The Dodge was not made to withstand the rigors of the road to Cottonwood or the rough Joseph roads. Its transmission bearings, clutch, and differential bearings broke down constantly. James often asked his neighbor, Bill Coltman, to drive him to Grangeville, but there the car usually had to go into the garage for repair before the trip home. Then, after the trip back to Joseph, he often had to have the Qualey boys over to the ranch to repair the car again. Finally, on one return trip from Cottonwood, the Dodge gave out on the steep grade. James took a team of horses and towed the car back to the ranch. As it came down the hill to the house, Rosamond ran out yelling, "There comes old four-eighty! There comes old four-eighty!"

Young John had his first lesson behind the wheel of the Dodge on a trip down the steep, winding Cottonwood road. A neighbor, Bill Reed, sat next to John and instructed him as he drove the route in a severe rainstorm. When Jim Jr. took his turn behind the wheel at the ranch, James rode with him. Jim drove it into a ditch and James just sat there. Finally he said, "Well . . . I'll be damned!"

During the 1930s cars were made that could actually navigate the road to Joseph. Tractors, trucks, and combines arrived to lighten farm work. Still, James never really met a motorized vehicle he preferred to his reliable four-legged helpers like old Molly the mule, Major the stock dog, the numerous sturdy horses that pulled his farm equipment, or the surefooted horses that had carried him for decades across treacherous mountain trails.

These sentiments were echoed by his sons. John left a Model T he had bought at the ranch and took Bluebird to use as his summer transportation for his Forest Service job on Sourdough Mountain, and Jim Jr. traded the same Model T Ford, which he couldn't keep running, for a good saddle horse. Both generations had difficulty moving from the back of a reliable horse into the motorized future.

Chapter 12

COWHANDS

We operated what was called a cattle ranch as opposed to a farm where various crops were raised. In contrast to the grain farmer, who only had to work a few months a year, a stockman was busy the whole year. However, to a dedicated stockman there was a greater satisfaction in the growing of animals, even though it was a daily effort and long hours.—Jim Aram 1991

GRAZING SOME 800 head of cattle on over 12,000 acres of rugged ranchland required monumental effort. In the early years on Joseph before the boys rode, James hired several cowhands to help with the work. Later the father and sons accomplished the work with the help of only one or two full-time hands. Sometimes they did it alone.

Riding out to check on the cattle was a daily task, except for a few weeks during harvest when only Sundays could be devoted to the herds. John and Jim Jr. rode with their father to oversee the cattle, carry salt to them, or move them from one pasture to another. Often the boys were given the task of counting cattle in order to update the inventory. If they came upon sick or injured animals, those were taken back to the home ranch for care.

These tasks were carried out nearly every day of the year regardless of the weather. Practical clothing, designed for the elements, was necessary. Winter clothes, purchased at the Salmon River Country Store in White Bird, consisted of several pairs of wool underwear, a woollen shirt, two pairs of Levi's, a heavy fleece-lined coat with a fleece or wool collar that could be turned up against the cold, a dozen pair of woollen socks, two pair of work boots with 6- or 8-inch tops, a pair of rubber overshoes, and a broad-brimmed hat.

The Levi's, which lasted three or four months, were paired with work boots, cotton underwear, and shirts for the summer months. The ten-gallon hat was worn all year. In the winter its wide brim could be tipped toward the wind to shelter a cowboy's face, while in the summer it provided protection from the sun.

James and his boys also wore leather chaps and gloves. The boys wore spurs on their cowboy boots, whereas James wore heavy ankle-high shoes and no spurs, preferring to prod his horse with the end of a doubled rope. When it was cold, snowy, or wet, riding after the cattle could get downright miserable. It was impossible to stay dry and warm. When their hands got cold and wet, they waved them in the air in an attempt to bring back some warmth. When their toes started to feel numb, they wiggled them inside the heavy boots.

During inclement weather the men stopped at lunch and built a fire to warm up before continuing for the afternoon. Being exposed to the cold for too long could be harmful. One winter James suffered severe frostbite on his feet, making it difficult for him to walk in later years.

From the beginning of April well into May attention was focused on the cows who were about to give birth. Daily checks on their progress were critical. Healthy cows who had calved before grazed the benches of Getta Creek and the Snake River until their calves arrived. Sometimes they were unable to deliver because a calf was turned around, had a leg back, or was too big. If a cowboy came upon a cow in distress, he helped her give birth; if a calf was born during cold weather, it was taken to shelter. Sometimes a cow wandered into steep terrain or a ditch and then couldn't get back on her feet after the birth; mother and newborn often died.

Once, when Jim Jr. was in his late teens, he was riding with Max Newman looking for strays in Lou Brust's cattle herd. The two young men spotted one of Brust's 2-year-old heifers, which had been trying to give birth. The calf's front feet and part of its head were protruding. It was dead and badly swollen, indicating the problem had existed for a day or two. Jim and Max roped the cow and threw her to the ground. Then they put a rope on the dead calf's front feet and pulled until it came out. When they took their ropes off, the cow rested awhile then got up and wandered away.

Cows bearing their first young were kept at the ranch and monitored closely, since they often had trouble delivering on their own. Most were only 2 years old and not always fully grown. Over the winter they were fed the best-quality hay to try to achieve maximum growth. In the spring they were moved from nearby pastures into the feedlot at the ranch. Then the Arams separated out those that looked as if they would calve soon and moved them into the barn or pen near the barn.

Each night, during the calving season, James or one of the boys checked on the heifers before they went to bed. About 2:00 A.M. each morning they rose and looked the cows over again. If one had started to deliver, they returned in a couple hours. By then they could usually tell if it was going to need help. If all was well, they assumed the cows would be fine until someone returned at 5:30 in the morning.

When a cow was having trouble they tied its head to keep it under control. If the calf was in a normal birth position with its front feet protruding, helping the delivery was simply a matter of force—they tied a rope to the calf's legs and pulled it out. Deliveries where one foot was back or the head was turned were more complicated. Sometimes when the foot was back, pulling worked. But if the head was turned it was necessary to push the calf back in and turn the head into a normal position. That was a difficult job with the cow straining to deliver while a man strained equally hard to force the calf back. If the situation was discovered in time, this method often succeeded.

First-year heifers were usually bred to young, small-boned bulls so the calves wouldn't be big and create extra problems. However, one year a large bull got in with the yearlings. The following spring the Arams had their hands full helping with difficult deliveries. Jim Jr. had taken on much of the responsibility for the cattle, and noted one of the heifers going into labor early one evening. By 8:00 P.M. he knew she was going to have trouble and two hours later he was assisting. He worked all night trying to deliver the calf, but it was just too big for the little heifer. The calf died during the struggle and by dawn the cow was dead. Tired and sad, young Jim walked back to the ranch house where he cleaned up and started another day.

One problem they often encountered during deliveries was cows not "cleaning," or delivering the afterbirth. James treated this with a solution of cayenne pepper, three tablespoons to a quart of water. The cow was roped and two strong men held her head high while the solution was poured down her throat. She was forced to swallow by the men pulling her tongue in and out. These treatments continued daily until the afterbirth was expelled or the cow died. In later years, they learned how to go in at arm's length and "unbutton" the afterbirth, which was held in the uterus in the same manner as a button fastens a shirt.

Once the calving season was over, the mother and new calf still faced some dangers. On the range coyotes sometimes got the young, even though the cow fought to protect it. One coyote teased the mother away from a calf's side, while a companion moved in for the kill. Poison weeds also took their toll. In the spring, when the ground was soft, cattle pulled up larkspur and ate it root and all. The root, which plagued the Arams every year, produced bloat and death; poison hemlock, which grew in marshy areas, caused instant death.

"One year we lost four calves we had just turned out on the range," recalled Jim. "They were at the age when they had started to nibble on grass. They were beautiful white-faced calves from heifers we had watched over day and night at the Joseph ranch. It was a low blow after getting them that far along. They had such a good start."

Bloat was another critical problem. Eating rich clover caused a cow's stomach to swell with gas. If the pressure wasn't relieved it could force the heart to stop. Sometimes, if the cow became severely bloated and death seemed imminent, James stuck a knife in the cow's stomach at a certain spot. This let the gas out and gave the cow a chance at survival.

One spring a herd of beef got into a field of yellow-blossomed sweet clover, but someone discovered the cattle before they had consumed too much. The herd was moved to the feedlots at the home ranch where James kept a close eye on them. Fortunately, none of the cattle needed treatment that time, but there was a continual chorus as the cattle expelled the gas.

When the calves born at Getta Creek were about three weeks old, they were moved with their mothers to greener areas on the south side of the creek. The terrain was steeper there so it was not used in the winter and by May had more grass than the winter-grazed bench lands. Because water rushed down Getta in the spring, some of the little calves had trouble fording the creek. To keep any of them from washing downstream, the men rode into the middle of the creek, prepared to catch those that lost their footing.

After a few weeks of grazing on the south side of the creek, the cows and calves were taken to Joseph. The boys often helped with these drives. "One such drive I remember well. It must have been 1925 or '26. Dad, Charley Warnick, who lived on the Getta Creek ranch looking after cattle and raising hay, and myself spent a couple days rounding up the cows and calves," recalled Jim.

"At daylight on the day of the drive we gathered the cattle and drove them through the Qualey ranch, right through their barn lot, across their pasture and through a place we called the Mexican ranch. We stopped there at lunchtime to let the cattle rest and graze. Nobody lived there, so Dad left me to herd the cattle while he and Warnick rode about a mile to Jimmy Shillam's place for the noon meal. By the time they returned I was starving. Dad hadn't forgotten me though. He brought back a bean sandwich spread with sugar—he thought. It turned out to be salt. I couldn't eat much of it, so I continued to starve."

From the Mexican ranch the trail circled around and came back across Qualey land at the top of the ridge and then ran into 40 acres of Aram land. That land was fenced and had water, so the cattle were held there overnight. The next morning Jim helped herd them onto the county road, which had fenced land on both sides and made it much easier to keep the cows together all the way to the home ranch.

"There were around 200 hundred cows with calves and of course some cows that hadn't calved yet," remembered Jim. "It was a noisy, wild scene to drive that herd of cows with young calves. Most of them took their calves and followed the trail or road, but grazed along the roadside as they went. Sometimes the little calves got under the barbed-wire fence along the road and then it was a problem getting them out and back with the rest of the herd. There was always a number of cows that bawled, chased the dogs, and created a problem. Some fought a dog all day and never gave ground until we called the dog off and forced the cow to travel!"

In early June, during rainy weather, the cattle on Joseph were rounded up and sorted. Those destined for market were put into special pasture, usually a leased area called the School Section or on an old homestead known as the Dewey place where the grass coverage was good. The cattle were held there until after harvest in August. Then they were put in the fields to fatten on the second crop of timothy, alfalfa, or clover.

After the beef cattle were moved to new pasture, the men drove the cows and calves into a corral on land James rented from the Canfields, halfway between the Sunset School and the Canfield ranch. The cows were then let out of the corral, while the calves were held back. Most of the cows hung around bawling in distress, but some wandered away and it was Jim Jr.'s job to make certain they didn't wander too far.

It was a boring job for a young boy who preferred to be part of the action in the corral. There, one cowboy on horseback roped one calf at a time and dragged it out of the bunch to a place where the men held it down. While one man branded, another earmarked, and a third castrated the young bulls. In addition, they were treated for blackleg—a disease of young cattle—by putting a piece of smooth wire through the skin on their shoulders and fastening it in a loop. The Arams were never certain what this loop of wire did, but it was an old method and seemed to work as no calf with the loop was ever lost to blackleg. Later, a vaccine became available and the men used that at branding time.

The Aram brand was a big A, but some of the calves were branded with the number 111 to signify they were part of a herd owned jointly with Clara, who loaned him money to start that herd. The cattle also were earmarked for Aram ownership by having part of one ear snipped and the other ear notched. The earmark was for quick identification, but it could be altered easily. Branding was for positive identification and was harder to alter.

As soon as John could toss a rope, his father let him serve as a roper during branding. Jim Jr., however, remained on the ground starting the fire, keeping the branding irons hot, and carrying them to the men. When he got older and stronger, he graduated to the job of throwing the calf to the ground and holding it down.

The men were fast and efficient—the entire process took about three minutes per calf. Branding lasted for three or four days from about 9:00 A.M. to late afternoon, and sometimes again later in the summer when they found calves they had missed or those born after the June branding. Once the calves were treated they were moved with their mothers into a large pasture nearby where the castrated bulls were watched.

Most healed easily and within a few days the herd was taken to the Center Ridge area, which was the Aram summer range, made up of a couple sections of land on the Doumecq Plains side of Rice Creek. Center Ridge ran along the creek and stretched south toward Camp Howard. This drive of cows and young calves meant fording the creek, often during high water, but it was managed in the same way as the earlier fording of Getta Creek.

On the first of July the bulls were turned in with the cows and heifers. If breeding started right away, calves began to arrive on April 1. However, few were actually bred in the first days, so the breeding season lasted into August and sometimes September. Late breeding created many problems, since calves born in June would not be old enough to wean before winter. A small calf's system didn't tolerate roughage, so it couldn't graze on its own and wouldn't survive the cold. A late calf was detrimental to a cow's health and had to be taken away from its mother before it was ready; consequently, it was important to monitor the length of time the bulls remained with the cows.

After the breeding season the cool crisp days of autumn arrived, bringing with them a sense of anticipation. It was time to take the cattle to market. The start of the drive was scheduled so the herd arrived at the railhead in Cottonwood the day before the shipping date, which was set to ensure their arrival in Portland on a Saturday. This gave them a day to rest and eat before the auction on Monday.

It took a few days to round up and sort the beef—3-year-olds who had reached their full growth and had fattened on the range or, in later years, 2-year-olds who had been fed premium hay mixed with grain. On the morning the drive was to start, James, John, and Jim Jr. rose at 2:00 A.M.

At daybreak they drove the cattle out onto the road and traveled as far as the fork to Boles. The cattle were then driven cross-country down the Hogback Ridge toward the Salmon River. By noon they were two-thirds of the way down the ridge at a spot where there was shade and water. They usually stopped for lunch and, if it was hot, remained until midafternoon. The cattle were then moved slowly down to the river so they wouldn't get footsore, overheated, or lose weight.

There was a ferry at the river, but it was not strong enough to carry cattle. Instead, the milling herd was held along the bank while cowboys and dogs cut 15 to 20 head out and forced them into the water. The swift, roaring current frightened and disoriented the cattle. Some swam directly to the safety of the other shore, while others headed upstream or downstream. Occasionally, a bunch swam most of the way across only to turn back. These errant cattle were often turned by the Arams' feisty dog Colonel, but if they made it back to shore it was virtually impossible to force them into the river again. However, once the first bunch of cattle arrived at the far shore it became easier to move the rest, because they could see the others grazing on the far side.

"One time we had the cattle at the river and were forcing them in when Dad's horse fell and he got soaked," remembered John. "We went to a halfway house nearby, a home that served travelers and had beds where people could rest. Dad went in the house to dry out. I know they were serving booze in there, so I'm sure he had a drink to warm up and probably something to eat. He was in there a long time while I sat out alone and waited. I wasn't very old and I was terribly worried and put upon when he stayed such a long time, leaving me out there alone with my horse. Finally he came out and we returned to the far side of the river where our hired hands were holding the cattle for the night."

Sometimes James formed joint drives with the Brusts, Lydas, or other neighbors. This gave him more manpower at the river, but the cattle were jumpier since they didn't like mixing with strangers. On one occasion a large steer spooked and started downriver in mid-stream. He was never seen again. On another the mixed herd was forced across the river and held for the night in an area between the river and a narrow passage in the road lined by fences. James and his sons agreed to take the night watch at the upper end of the road, while one of their neighbors took watch on the river side. Other cowboys guarded separate points around the herd.

It was cold and rainy, and James, John, and Jim huddled near a fire. At 3:00 A.M. the restless animals surged up the road toward the Arams, who turned them back, then the excited herd broke through the guards posted along the river and swam back to the other side. The cowboys forded the river and forced most of the cattle back in and across again, but several broke away and ran into the steep hills with some cowboys in hot pursuit. It took over an hour to round up the strays and get them back across the river, minus several pounds each. By then it was daylight, so they moved the herd on to Cottonwood.

Most times night herding was much calmer. Several cowboys were posted at various points around the herd, while others slept under the stars near a warm fire. Sometimes, they held the herd in a place called the Box Canyon, which required guarding on only one side, the sheer canyon walls forming a natural corral for the animals. Usually the weather was nice enough and the men didn't even need a blanket, but they carried jackets tied to the backs of their saddles for cooler evenings.

The second day of a cattle drive started at daylight with the cowboys forcing the cattle to move up Graves Creek until they "topped out" on Camas Prairie and drove on to Cottonwood. If they were part of a joint cattle drive, the animals were sorted by brand at the stockyards. The next day they were loaded onto a train for Portland. There was a law that after 72 hours cattle had to be unloaded and fed. If there was any delay after leaving Cottonwood and the trip was longer than normal, it was sometimes necessary to unload them at The Dalles, Oregon; then they arrived just in time for market with no day to rest and feed.

When John was 10 he accompanied his father to Portland, riding in the caboose of a train hauling five carloads of Aram cattle. "Each time the train stopped for a period of time, Dad and I walked down along the track until we came to our cattle, examining them to make sure they were all right," said John. "We stopped in Rubens, Idaho, just before going down into the canyon to Lewiston late in the afternoon. It was terribly hot and the animals must have been suffering, because we certainly were.

"As a general rule, the railroad gave the owner, or his representative, a free ride to and from Portland, even if he only shipped one carload of cattle. I was wearing my cowboy hat and boots and the train crews made a big thing out of this young cowboy getting a free ride to Portland because of the cattle shipment. The trip must have been two days and one night. When we arrived in Portland the cattle were put in stockyards and fed. Of course, my father had to pay for all of this. We stayed at the Imperial Hotel and everyone paid some attention to me—the little cowboy. Dad always had to explain why we were there and where we came from.

"At the auction the cattle sold at a horribly low price, two and a half cents per pound. Because of the arduous long trip, the hot weather, and our not feeding and watering them along the way, they had lost much of the fat and were sold as feeders in a market that was about as poor as any market could be. My father suffered a terrible loss. After that unhappy trip to the stockyards, we got on the train at night and returned to Lewiston. Dad stopped there and talked with officers at the bank where he had borrowed money for the cattle. We took another day to get back to Cottonwood and still another to get home."

The Salmon River proved the greatest obstacle on cattle drives. In the late 1920s a bridge was built that cattlemen were allowed to use, but they were cautioned to only allow 20 to 30 cattle across at one time so as not to damage it. Cattle drives became somewhat easier and the cattle lost less weight. Still, the bridge spooked the animals, and it took several men to get them started with one man riding his horse out onto the bridge so the cattle could see it was safe. One time a single frightened cow held up the drive for two hours when she balked at crossing the bridge, even when a group of men and dogs tried to force her onto it.

When the Arams purchased other cattle, they drove the herd from Camas Prairie to Joseph. One spring James bought some yearlings and cows that had been in feedlots and barnyards all winter. They were delivered to the breaks of the Salmon and with Jim Jr.'s help driven home. The cattle had soft feet and their hooves were "ground down to the quick." Two of the yearlings were in such bad shape they left them at Rice Creek to graze over the summer and returned in the fall to bring them to Joseph.

On this same drive they came upon a snowdrift just before topping out on Joseph. One cow bogged down in the snow and got on the downside of the hill. When she managed to get to her feet, she was fighting mad. The men left her and she made her way into Fall Creek Canyon where she found lush grass and water.

In midsummer, they went back, found the cow, and drove her down toward Rice Creek, rimmed around from the creek out to Box Flats, and intercepted the road leading to Joseph. On the switchbacks above Fall Creek Canyon, the cow left the road and headed down a steep slope leading back to her "home." Jim Jr. roped her and tried to get her back on the road, but she just kept plunging down the canyon. Finally he released her. In the fall, when they passed with their beef cattle, the errant cow was collected and delivered to Cottonwood for sale and shipment to Portland.

When James was asked by his bank to take over cattle owned by another rancher who had gone bankrupt, he agreed. John was only 9, but he rode with his father and several hands to round up the 500 head of perfect Herefords. They were grazing near the headwaters of Wolf Creek in the Flyblow region where the men set up camp near some corrals. At daybreak each morning they had a breakfast of bacon, eggs, and hotcakes, then fixed a lunch of hotcakes and bacon to carry with them as they rode out to round up the cattle, bringing them back to the corrals each evening. After four days they had accumulated the herd and moved them to a rented pasture nearby.

Eventually, James drove the Herefords back to his ranch, but he didn't have enough range for them. He decided to ship the herd to Montana where they were to be fed and fattened. The winter in Montana was so severe many of the cattle died. James took a train to Montana, gathered what was left of his herd, and traveled with them by train to market in Chicago. He returned in two weeks, giving his family the impression the trip had not been a terrible financial disaster, for the bank had shared some of the risk on those particular cattle.

Each year after the beef had gone to market, the men returned and started weaning the spring calves from their mothers. The animals were separated and the cows forced into rugged country in the Rice Creek Canyon where they were left to graze. The men drove the calves down the trail to Getta Creek and left them on the gently sloping bench lands where they were protected from the weather and could graze freely.

After the first snowfall the cattle in the steep Rice Creek Canyon were rounded up and taken to the home ranch where they were fed hay in the feedlots for a few weeks. Winter on Joseph was harsh and temperatures sometimes plunged to zero or below. At Getta Creek it was somewhat warmer, but could get quite cold and uncomfortable. Still, riding after the cattle continued as long as there were any out on the range.

The winter of John's 13th year started with a heavy snowfall just after Thanksgiving. The cattle were grazing the rugged Rice Creek Canyon and the breaks of Fall Creek. James was ill and there were no hired hands that winter.

"You'll have to go after those cattle," James told his oldest son. "They won't survive long in that snow."

By 8:00 A.M. John was on his horse. He signaled the faithful Major to join him. Alone he rode into the vast white wilderness stretching for miles in every direction away from the warm ranch house. Following a ridge from the Reed homestead, he made his way to the mouth of Fall Creek where it joined Rice Creek. When he turned up Fall Creek he found cattle scattered throughout the canyon. Some were along the creek, some were high up the south slopes, and others were up along the Joseph-Cottonwood Road.

John rode along the creek, sending Major up the higher slopes to round up a group and bring them down. The cattle readily responded, for they were hungry and eager to move on. Working diligently the boy and dog collected some 200 head and started for home, arriving about five o'clock.

The next day John rode out, again with Major as his only hand. He took the same trail to the mouth of Fall Creek, but turned up Rice Creek. Cattle were scattered up and down the steep slopes on both sides of the canyon. Several times he rode up the mountainside on a trail that dropped sharply to the creek a quarter mile below to bring cattle down. Continuing on he discovered a group of cattle high on the eastern mountains, almost to the top of Doumecq Plains. With Major assisting, he rode up and brought the cattle down. When he had thoroughly scouted the canyon, he started back with the herd and forged through the snow some five miles to the gates leading to the ranch.

On the third day John and Major went down a gulch to Rice Creek and followed the creek to the county road from Doumecq. From there they went on to the Bidel place where cattle were scattered across exceedingly steep country. Riding his horse out as far as he felt safe, he shouted at the animals and then sent Major in to round them up. He rode about 20 miles that day, gathering cattle and driving them back to the ranch. On the fourth day he rode out to bring in the last of the cattle foraging on the Scully place. Over the four days the 13-year-old and his dog brought in over 800 hundred head to the safety of the feedlots.

In later years James and Jim Jr. took some of the yearlings into steep land near the Fir Gulch Trail to graze until winter. Like the cattle left in Rice Creek, these yearlings were rounded up and returned to the Joseph ranch after the first sign of snow. This steep land had lots of bluffs and grassy slopes that were tipped away from the sun, making them especially dangerous once the ground was frozen.

One early winter Jim Jr. was helping his father gather cattle from this rough Fir Gulch country when a yearling heifer lost her footing on a frozen slope. "She shot down the slope and sailed over a cliff about 50 feet high," recalled Jim years later. "Dad and I went right down there and found her neck broken so we cut her throat and dressed her out. It was getting toward evening so we left the cattle in a sort of basin and went to the Joseph ranch for the night.

"The next day we took two packhorses with us to carry the meat. The heifer dressed out at about 300 pounds, which was too much for one horse. We skinned the carcass, wrapped the meat in canvas, and put two quarters on each horse. Then we rounded up our cattle and drove them up the steep Fir Gulch Trail and on to the ranch. That was a full day."

On another winter day Jim Jr. was gathering cattle alone in Fir Gulch with the help of Major, who was flushing them out of the brush and steep areas. Jim decided to take the herd up the canyon through the brush and then rim back to the Fir Gulch Trail. "We had to cross one of those grassy slopes," said Jim. "One big red cow didn't make it. She was right in front of me when she lost her footing. She shot like a bullet for over a quarter of a mile and hit some big rocks and brush at the bottom. I went down there and, although she was still alive, she was broken up so badly I had to knock her in the head with a big rock to put her out of her misery. That was one of those disheartening and gruesome experiences one never forgets."

As soon as green grass began to show at Getta in February or March, the cattle in the Joseph feedlots were taken down for the rest of the winter. Weaker cattle were separated and kept in a feedlot there, while the rest grazed the open range until after the calving season.

Thus the cycle of ranch life began once again—the triumphant births, the bustle of branding, long rides through beautiful countryside to care for the cattle, and the excitement of fall cattle drives. These were the joys of ranch life—joys that were often offset by the treachery of the rugged terrain, the elements, and a market that offered the rancher little or no return on his investment.

"Some loss was calculated," remarked Jim as he looked back across the years. "If it was not too severe, we could survive and if necessary go to the bank, borrow more money, and try again. A true stockman will not give up, but will keep at his business until he completely fails or—he wins!"

Chapter 13

FROM DAWN 'TIL . . . ?

We learned to work. In addition we learned to be self-reliant and thereby able to trust our ability to do whatever needed to be done. It followed that we formed the habit of taking the initiative in starting projects and following through.—John Aram 1992

An old adage often repeated in the Aram household declared, "He who has yet to thrive must arise at five. He who has thriven may lay a-bed 'til seven." No one "lay a-bed" at the Aram's. Each day began at five when the family left the warmth of their beds to start the morning chores.

The comfortable sound of their mother grinding coffee beans greeted the children when they came down the stairs to the kitchen. James, his sons, and the hired hands gathered in the pantry to put on boots and jackets, while the girls helped Phebe start breakfast. The aroma of the freshly ground beans followed the men into the yard as they left to milk the cows.

"We operated our milk cow herd differently than most dairy people, but then we weren't running a dairy," explained Jim. "We were milking mostly white-faced beef cows and raising the calves either for beef or as heifers to breed and increase our herd. Our system was somewhat un-orthodox, but it did raise pretty good calves, which were more valuable than the cream.

"In the summer we milked about 20 cows in the all-purpose corral. The calves were kept in what we called the barn lot, which was about fifteen acres. Next to the corral we had a small pen where the calves were held at milking time. The number of calves let into the corral with the cows depended on how many people were milking. The calves were allowed half the milk, which was two teats of the four available. When they had consumed their half, they were taken away and put back in the barn lot."

The calves were left to feed on native grass, while their mothers grazed in adjacent pastureland. The cows didn't stray too far because of their penned young. Later in the season, when grass near the barn lot became sparse and dry and the calves were older, the cows ranged farther. Often, in the evenings, they had to be brought in from distances of a mile or more.

After the August harvest the milk cows were allowed to graze in an alfalfa field west of the ranch house; however, it was necessary to be cautious about letting them into the field if the dew was still on the ground, because wet, green alfalfa caused bloat. When this happened James brought the afflicted animals into the corral, gave them a drench of soda, and tied sticks in their mouths to allow an unrestricted expulsion of the gas.

After the cows were milked, the men carried the full milk pails to the cream separator in the pantry. Phebe, Rosamond, Narcie, or one of the boys separated the cream from the milk and poured it into five-gallon milk cans. Every other day the men carried the cream on horseback to the mailbox where the parcel post service picked it up for delivery to a creamery in Cottonwood. Checks from the creamery, which were mailed back to James, provided the family with a little cash.

In addition to milking the cows, the men fed and watered the saddle horses, mules, workhorses, and pigs. Then they went in to a breakfast of oatmeal, bacon, ham or sausage, baking powder biscuits slathered in homemade butter and topped with homemade jelly, canned fruit, and fried potatoes with gravy. After breakfast they saddled their horses and harnessed teams. The main work for the day—riding after cattle, working in the fields, or building fences—started by 8:00 A.M.

The only crops raised were feed crops needed to support the cattle and pigs. "Dad was ambitious. He put together all the land he could get his rope around," remembered Jim. "He wanted to run more cattle than the winter range could support, so he made hay from the fields on Joseph Plains and fed some of his cattle there all winter. The feeding period usually extended from December to April and required a lot of hay."

This growing of hay, along with some grains, ranked second in importance only to the daily task of looking after the cattle. To start his fields James broke the land with a walking plow, often referred to as a "footburner" because it wore out the user's feet. When Jim Jr. was concentrating on expanding the ranch in the mid-30s, he plowed acres and acres of land with a 16-inch footburner.

Walking in the furrow behind the plow, the teenager turned sod just as his father had when he started the ranch—holding on to the plow handles to steer, while the reins to guide the team were knotted and thrown over his shoulder. The footburners were used mostly for breaking the sod and plowing the native grasses under. The men also used riding plows, a harrow to smooth the soil, and disk plows for rocky areas, each pulled by four horses. Once the land was prepared, seed was spread from the back of the buckboard.

"Someone drove the team," recalled Jim. "Dad filled a tub full of seed. The tub was mounted on a stand, and Dad, with his back to the driver, developed a rhythm as he threw the seed out, spreading it evenly. The biggest problem for the driver was keeping the right distance from the area already seeded. Dad broadcast the seed about ten feet in each direction. The driver had to line up right from there so seed wouldn't get too thick and grow improperly. In the middle 1930s we bought a grain drill with the Keeners. The drill was eight to ten feet long with a hopper on top to hold the seed. It was pulled by four horses and made planting much easier."

Only about 40 or 50 acres of grain were planted on the Joseph ranch. A much larger proportion of the fieldwork was dedicated to the many acres originally planted in timothy, bluegrass, or alfalfa, which reseeded annually. All three made excellent hay for winter feed during the harsh winters. Harvesting started around the first of July with the alfalfa crops and continued until mid-August when the last of the timothy and bluegrass was harvested. Small grains such as wheat and barley, which were sometimes mixed with the hay for a richer diet, were harvested in the early fall.

Haying required 12 to 14 men and several teams of horses or mules. The Arams traded work at harvest time with their neighbors, but since they ran a larger operation they often had to hire extra men and pay their neighbors additional cash. The crew usually consisted of three men mowing with sickle mowers each pulled by two horses, one man or boy raking the hay into windrows with a hay rake pulled by two horses, three men shocking or stacking the hay by hand into upright sheaves, three men driving teams and wagons, and two men pitching hay onto the wagon.

As each wagon filled with hay it was driven to barns at the home ranch, the Peters homestead, the Kerlee place, or the Canfield barn, located a half mile west of the home ranch. At these barns, all on land owned or rented by James, the hay was put in the haymows. The rest of the crop was piled in haystacks in strategic locations across the ranch.

To help put the hay in these huge loose stacks, James developed two different types of derricks. The first of these consisted of two long poles tied together at the top and spread at the bottom over the area where the haystack was to be built. The poles were held in place by cables and set so they leaned back at about a 45-degree angle. The hay was lifted from the wagon by a heavy "Jackson fork"—two hinged forks that could be latched into a cupped position like two hands closing together. It was suspended by cables and attached to a pulley hanging from a chain at the apex of the poles.

A man on the wagon pushed the fork into the hay. When it was full he pulled a rope attached to the latch and the four-tined forks closed together, holding the hay. The weight of the hay tightened a cable attached to the poles and they swung forward, pulling the fork up. As the weight came into play, the poles dropped back and pulled the fork in a wide arc from the wagon to the haystack. As soon as the fork was in the proper position, the stacker—a man designated to build the haystack properly—hollered "trip 'er."

The man on the wagon jerked the rope attached to the fork's latch and its jaws flew open, dropping the hay onto the pile. Then the person on the derrick horse (or mule) backed the horse up, and cables attached to the horse ran through the pulley, swinging the fork back to the wagon. Once the job was finished the poles were taken down and moved to the next field to start another haystack.

James's second derrick was more sophisticated. It was fashioned after the Mormon derricks many of his neighbors were buying. With the help of Al Graham he built the derrick from red fir poles, which were used for runners, cross beams, the center column, and boom. The upright was braced to the frame with four-by-six-inch timbers. In the blacksmith shop, located in a lean-to behind the old cabin, Al forged ironwork from scrap iron and used it to bolt the corners.

This derrick operated on the same principle as the first, but it was a much more substantial piece of equipment, was self-contained, and required little setup in the field. However, it was so heavy it took two good teams of horses to drag it on its runners to the fields.

Shocking the hay after it was mowed was one of the most labor-intensive aspects of haying. It was necessary to stack the hay into small piles, or sheaves, so it didn't dry too much or bleach out in the sun. The sheaves could be pitched easily onto the hay wagons or slips.

For a few years in the late 20s, James used two buckrakes during harvest. The buckrakes were unique, each consisting of two wood-framed, wood-toothed rakes with a seat set somewhat back but between the rakes. Two horses were needed to push the buckrakes, one behind each rake just to each side of the driver. These rakes cut down on labor and expense. The hay did not have to be shocked, as the buckrakes picked the hay up out of the windrows and carried it directly to the haystacks. Two men with buckrakes brought in as much hay as three drivers and wagons plus two men pitching hay onto them. Eventually, the buckrakes broke and new parts could not be found, so the men went back to the old method of shocking and pitching hay.

Harvest time was hectic—daily chores still needed tending, and everyone carried an extra load. As Narcie wrote when she reflected back on those harried summer months so long ago, "Very often we had five or six hired men for most of the summer. For Mom, Rosamond, and myself that meant fixing three full meals a day with meat, potatoes and gravy for every meal. In addition, there was always bread to be baked and desserts for dinner and supper. Besides the meals and housework, the gardens had to be tended, fruit picked and canned, and jams and jellies made.

"It seemed I was sort of an all-around helper. When I was about 10 it was my job to drive the cows into pasture. Sometimes I drove 'derrick' when they were stacking hay, riding the old mule Molly who was hitched up to a cable tied to the fork. About four o'clock, after my father relieved me, I'd go home, get my horse, and drive the cows in. The men worked until five. After that they cared for the horses and did the milking. Their days ended about 7:00 P.M. Our days were longer because after dinner we still had to separate the cream, do the dishes, straighten the house, and prepare for the next day's meals."

Soon after putting up the hay, it was time to harvest the grain crops. Some of the grain, beardless barley and oats, were cut for hay to fatten two-year-old beef steers for market. The rest was shocked and threshed to separate the grain from the straw. The Arams used the straw as long as it lasted to feed the cattle, giving them straw in the morning and hay in the afternoon. Lou Brust had a stationary threshing machine powered by a John Deere tractor. All the neighbors formed a threshing crew and, using Brust's machine, helped each other finish their crops. The machine blew the straw into a pile where one man worked to shape it like a haystack so the rain would run off. It took about 30 days to complete all the neighbors' threshing.

When snow started to fall and the men drove the cattle back to the feedlots at the home ranch or the Kerlee place the daily task of hauling feed began. On cold, windy days they spread the hay in sheltered areas, but on sunny days they tossed it into open fields where the cattle could move freely. The Kerlee place had a barn full of hay and two haystacks, but much of the hay for the cattle at the home ranch had to be brought by bobsled from distant stacks.

"The snow blew around those stacks of loose hay. The outer edges were frequently wet from rain or a thaw, so the stacks settled unevenly. The rain went into the low spots and froze, especially in stacks two or more years old. It was hard work to dig that frozen hay out," recalled Jim. "It was a continuous struggle to get the hay from stacks in various fields, some of them a mile or two from the home ranch. Dad often had two or more men hauling hay for the cattle using two double bobsleds with 16-foot hayracks and four-horse teams. They made two trips a day, hauling one and a half tons each trip. As more snow fell the sleighs gradually built up a track. Then the load went along easily, unless the road drifted full of snow and the sleigh got off the track and upset. It was a tremendous job to right it and reload the hay."

Most years the Arams successfully fed their cattle through the winter. But in 1920, after a sparse hay harvest, winter arrived unusually early. One long cold day followed another until the haystacks disappeared. James bought all the hay, grain and cottonseed cake he could get his hands on, but hundreds of cattle starved. He spent innumerable hours with the sick and dying cattle trying to nurse them through. At one time some 40 carcasses lay below the barn. It was a long, heartbreaking winter for the entire family.

Fence repair and construction was another endless year-round job necessary in all types of weather. Fence building was usually done in the spring and early summer when the ground was soft, but it always started with making posts during the winter.

One February James put Jim Jr. to work helping Bob Dobbins make fence posts. Bob was trading his labor for the use of Aram grazing lands. He went down into the Fall Creek Canyon and felled several red fir trees with a crosscut saw. After trimming off the branches, he cut the trees into six-foot lengths, which were split into posts approximately four inches in diameter.

Jim Jr. went down into the canyon with a double bobsled and four-horse team to haul the heavy green posts out. On each trip he brought out about 100 posts that he delivered to areas on the ranch where fences were to be built. Dobbins then went to each location and sharpened the posts, and Jim Jr. took several hundred back to the home ranch. He made a tripod, leaned the top of the post to be sharpened in the apex of the tripod and rested the other end on a block of wood. This held the post steady so he could use both hands to sharpen the end with an ax. The 14-year-old sharpened up to a hundred posts each day.

That spring Bob Dobbins, James, Jim Jr. and John—who helped for a time while home on spring break from high school—built about ten miles of fence, much of it along two sides of the county road that crossed Joseph where they owned or rented land. "We went down the road a quarter of a mile or so and set up three posts in the line we wanted. Then we went back and drove the other posts in between those already in line," said Jim. "Dad lined up the posts and I drove them with a 16-pound maul. Along the road section, I drove posts from the wagon. Sometimes I would drive posts all day and I couldn't get enough to eat to last from one meal to another. I was chubby when I started that spring, but with the fence building and haying I lost all my baby fat.

"Bob helped us put wire on the posts. We loosened about a quarter mile of wire from the roll, put a rope on one end, took some turns around a saddle horn, and pulled it into place with a saddle horse. Three strands of wire were usually stapled to each post. Sometimes we needed more wire, so we took it from an existing fence that was no longer needed. Then, rather than roll up the wire to move it, we dragged it down the road behind us until we reached the new fence. When we needed to drag the wire around a turn, we set a crowbar in the turn and pulled it around that. If it was dragged around a tree or fence post, the wire broke."

During the Depression the government paid ranchers to put up fences, which encouraged them to defer some of their range, allowing it to grow and go to seed so it would not be overgrazed. Under this program the Arams fenced some of their range, including acreage in the steep canyons where it was necessary to deliver the posts by pack-horse.

Since posts couldn't be driven into the hard, rocky ground, they were set in rockbucks—frames the men built at the site and set on the ground. One man held a four-foot post upright in the center, while another nailed braces from the frame to a place near the top of the pole and poured rocks into the frame to hold the base secure. If a tree happened to be in the fenceline it was used as a post instead of building another rockbuck.

Posts set in rock lasted longer than those driven into the ground. To extend the life of fir or cottonwood posts, which would last only five or six years, they sometimes charred the sharpened ends in a fire. In addition to the barbed-wire fences, the men built split-rail fences around haystacks and hog pastures. These were made from rails 12 feet long laid crisscross. Making a split-rail fence was extra work, but it was strong and considered "cattle and hog tight."

"Fencing was more or less routine, but making log water troughs was a specialty," said Jim. "I think we got paid $100 by the government in the '30s for putting in a steel tank or log trough. The log trough was more satisfactory as it could be left to freeze without damage. The wood expanded with the ice, but the steel tank split when frozen solid. Anyway, we had lots of trees for log troughs, but not much money for steel tanks."

When Hilt Thrapp was at the ranch, he helped Jim Jr. make several log water troughs. The young men picked out yellow pines with no limbs on the part they wanted to use for the trough and cut them down with a crosscut saw. They had a 2-inch-diameter auger about 18 inches long with a handle fashioned like a drill brace that Jim used to drill a hole straight down to the center of the log. Then he drilled another hole at a 90-degree angle to meet it. A series of these holes were drilled about 16 inches apart for the entire distance needed to form the interior of the trough. Jim then stuck burning pieces of pitchy wood down in the holes. The heat created a draft, and the vertical hole acted as a chimney. Soon he had all the holes on fire.

The log was left to burn all night and by morning the heartwood was burned. The interior was like a blast furnace, so Jim and Hilt plugged the holes with dirt and let it stand a few days until it cooled. They then sawed across between the end holes and split the wood between the holes along the top. The charcoal was scooped out and the interior of the log cleaned with a foot adze. The log was sawed to finished size leaving about two feet of solid wood from the hollowed-out section to each end.

Cutting wood for the two stoves at the ranch house was another annual chore done in May or June. However, because there was a lot of seasonal work at that time, wood cutting was often pushed back until September. When the wood was cut late, it was wet and hard to burn. Sometimes Phebe stuck wet logs in the oven to dry before using them in one of the fires. It took 12 to 14 cords to supply the ranch house, the heating stove for the winter season, and the cookstove year-round.

The heating stove took lots of wood because the house was drafty. It was not insulated and had air spaces around the windows and doors. Phebe used rags to plug cracks and pushed rugs up against entry doors to stop the wind from blowing under them. The upstairs bedrooms were relatively comfortable, because heat from the stoves rose up the stairs. However, by morning the fire was out, and the water bucket in the kitchen was layered with ice.

The woodshed behind the pantry held six to seven cords of wood, much of which was brought from about a mile away. Usually the men felled a yellow pine, then a neighbor who had a drag saw, either Fred Williams or Joe Keener, was hired to cut the trees into 16-inch logs for splitting. The Aram men worked right behind the saw, splitting the wood with a maul and wedge and ricking it one log deep in piles 4 feet high by 24 feet long. Each pile was considered a cord and the neighbors were paid $2.50 for each cord cut. The men hauled the wood to the woodshed when they found time. Sometimes they couldn't get to this until winter when it had to be moved by bobsled.

Relying heavily on horses and such a variety of farm equipment for their daily chores sometimes created problems. "The mule spans were spirited and had to be watched. If given the chance they ran away and broke up whatever they were pulling," remembered Jim. "We also had one horse named Buck that we rode, worked, and packed. Buck ran away with more equipment than any other horse we had. He might look like he was asleep, but if a rein brushed his legs or heels he was off like a shot.

"One time John was doing some mowing about a half mile away. I rode out to call him to dinner. When he turned out of the field across a border strip of high grass the mower hit some big rocks. He was driving a team of mules. The jarring bounced him off. The mules lurched and upset the mower. Away they went. Before I got them headed off they had torn the mower all to pieces.

"Another time John and I were fixing fence along the road just before Fall Creek. We were using the buckboard on the slope above the road. The slope finally got so steep the wagon overturned into the road. We were driving Dick and Buck, and away they went toward the Sunset School. The road had a fork in it and each horse tried to go a different way, which resulted in breaking up the harness, neck yoke, and parts of the buckboard plus spilling our supplies. We found out the buckboard would run just as well upside down. It was really a tough piece of equipment."

Such runaways delayed work until repairs were made. There was no such thing as a quick trip to town to pick up a part. In the blacksmith shop there was a forge, a blower, a drill press, old parts, and scrap iron. The men improvised and usually managed to create a part that was a passable and workable replacement for the original.

Even though he was heavily burdened with the task of keeping his huge spread running, James, much like his pioneer father, was always willing to try something new. "Dad was a risk taker," said John. "Plus he had a high degree of mechanical talent. Both traits were demonstrated in much of what he did—building the derricks, constructing a water-powered sawmill with Bert Hamilton at the Scully Place, buying a steam-driven tractor, and even providing the courage and leadership to build the road to Cottonwood."

This entrepreneurial spirit was evidenced in the fact that James diversified his investment of time, energy, and money. Although he was mostly a cattleman, he liked raising hogs and always had them at the Joseph and Getta Creek ranches. They added to the workload because it was necessary to plant and harvest grain for them. Several sows and one boar produced most of the ranch's hogs. The sows were kept in a separate pen for farrowing and watched closely until the pigs were two or three weeks old. Occasionally a sow got out of the barn lot and had her pigs somewhere in the woods. Then it was a race to find her before the coyotes, who loved young pigs, discovered them.

It took about a year to get the hogs to 250 pounds, when they were considered ready for market. Usually they were penned and fed grain, but one summer James did not have enough grain, so he decided to have the boys, then 13 and 9, herd them into the woods and nearby pastures, avoiding the hay and grain fields. John had the job first, but eventually it became Jim Jr.'s. At 6:30 each morning he took some 70 head out, returning at the end of each long day to pen the hogs and feed them a small amount of grain.

"That was the most miserable job I ever had," recalled Jim. "Hogs are so stubborn that when one or more decides to go in a certain direction it is almost impossible to head them off. Of course I had Major to help me, and I rode Shorty, a little chestnut horse."

Each fall they butchered about 10 or 15 hogs for their own use. It took several men to do the butchering. James set a metal vat full of water over a fire pit. The water was laced with a can of lye to help remove the hair. When James could just stand to run his finger through the water three times, he considered it hot enough to scald a hog. One was then shot between the eyes and its throat was slit. It was then dragged to a platform near the vat, tied with ropes, and lowered into the water to be scalded for a few minutes until the hair could be scraped off easily. After the men removed all the hair with knives, they hung the hog from a scaffold, washed it with clean water, and gutted it.

For one or two nights the hog hung on the scaffold and cooled. The carcass was taken into the pantry where it was cut into hams, shoulders, and bacon slabs. These portions were packed in table salt to draw the blood and moisture out of the meat and preserve it. The fat was cut up and rendered into lard. Lean meat, which was trimmed from hams, jowls, and other parts, was made into sausage by running it through a hand-operated meat grinder and seasoning it with black pepper and sage. When the sausage was finished, Phebe fried a batch and the family had a little party. She packed the rest into crocks, which were sealed with two inches of lard. Meat from the head was made into head cheese, while the heart and liver was eaten fresh.

After four or six weeks, the meat was removed from the salt pack.

The excess salt was cleaned off and it was hung in the smoke house about a hundred feet from the wood shed. There, with a smoky thorn wood fire burning just five feet under the meat, it was smoked every day for a week to ten days. Once the meat was smoked, nothing bothered it. It could hang in the pantry through the summer months without spoiling; however, the meat was so salty it had to be parboiled before it could be eaten. Thicker cuts of meat, like ham, did not need parboiling, and the kids snitched bits whenever they could.

"One year," said Jim, "the family had moved down to the Getta Creek ranch. We came up to Joseph and butchered and, since it was cold, left the carcasses covered up with a piece of canvas for a few days. John and I—we were then about 8 and 12—came back later to take the carcasses inside the house. By then they were frozen. We stacked them in the pantry. There was a package of Paris Green, a poison used for insects in the potato patch, on the shelf and we knocked it down. It spilled on two carcasses. I remember what an awful time we had cleaning that off. We scraped and scraped until we couldn't see any left on the meat. After that we washed them off with water from the well. Even then we were afraid someone might be poisoned."

Hog drives were necessary to get the hogs to market. They were usually taken on the same route as the cattle, but driving them was much different. The hogs spooked at the many wooden bridges crossing Rice Creek. The dogs controlled some of the stubborn ones, and Colonel often grabbed a pig by its hind leg until the men got a rope around it and kept it moving.

At the Salmon the hogs were taken across the river on the ferry 20 or 30 at a time. On the other side of the river, the men held them overnight at the mouth of Graves Creek or on Bug Slope. At first light they headed up Graves Creek, again fighting one or two hogs at every wooden crossing bridge. Eventually, after a long day, they arrived at the stockyards. Sometimes they bought young pigs in Cottonwood and had them delivered by truck as far as the Salmon River or Box Flats, trailing them back to Joseph from there.

Raising hogs, like everything else at the ranch, took more time than projected, particularly if things went awry during farrowing or a trip to market. Problems with one project at the ranch delayed work on another. An immense amount of labor was necessary to keep up with the daily chores and accomplish the seasonal tasks.

"At times I resented the workload, but I learned to accept it as a necessity to help perpetuate our livelihood," reflected Jim. "When I was in my teens I worked hard, as I was determined to develop a larger spread. We didn't always get it all done. We just did the best we could."

Chapter 14

BACK AT THE RANCH HOUSE

*"We didn't see our neighbors often in the summer be-
cause we were too busy. My mother sometimes complained, when my father couldn't attend some social
function, that all we ever did was work."*—Narcie
Aram See 1986

WITH THE EXCEPTION of a few purchased staples, the Arams were
self-sufficient. Their cattle, hogs, and chickens provided milk, meat,
and eggs. Fresh fruits and vegetables grew in gardens and orchards at
both Getta Creek and the Joseph ranch. Game and wild berries sup-
plemented what they raised. Out of necessity Phebe devoted most of
her time, particularly in the summer months, to gathering, preparing,
and preserving all this food.

The girls worked with their mother, whose day started at 6:00 A.M.
in the winter and 4:00 or 5:00 in the summer. Each morning, sometimes after helping their brothers milk the cows and carrying the milk
to the house themselves, Rosamond and Narcie separated the cream
with a hand-turned cream separator in the pantry. Even if John or Jim
Jr. helped, this was a monotonous job. When the separation was complete, the cream was poured into five-gallon milk cans for delivery to
the creamery or into jars for their own use. The remaining skim milk
was taken out and fed to the hogs.

At 7:00 A.M. the huge ranchers' breakfast, prepared by Phebe and the
girls, was served and quickly devoured by the hungry men. Phebe,
Rosamond, and Narcie then cleaned up, washing and rinsing the dishes
in basins of hot water placed on the work table in the kitchen. "We also
took the cream separator apart and washed it," recalled Narcie. "That
was a particularly loathsome job for there were many little disks. Each
disk was washed separately, rinsed carefully, and dried. Then the machine was put back together."

Food preparation for other meals usually filled the morning. Narcie gathered eggs from the chicken house or churned butter in a wooden churn, the kind with a handle that turns beaters inside a round barrel. Rosamond helped her mother start the day's baking, four to six loaves of bread every few days and pies, cakes, and cookies on other days. They also baked custards, rice pudding, and bread pudding for desserts. Phebe made cottage cheese twice a week by setting a pan of milk at the back of the stove to curdle. When curds formed she strained them in a clean flour-sack cloth by hanging it outside on the clothesline and squeezing it occasionally to force out the whey. Once all of the liquid was squeezed out, she took the curds back to the kitchen and added cream, salt, and pepper.

Fresh food such as cottage cheese and whipped cream was usually consumed quickly by the hungry cowboys, so the lack of refrigeration at the ranch house didn't create a problem. However, in summer items prone to spoilage were placed in a box sunk in the ground outside the kitchen or carried to a springbox set in a spring about 300 feet from the house. The pantry remained cool enough to prevent spoilage during the winter.

"We didn't really worry about keeping things cold," said Narcie. "Usually we kept our own cream on shelves in the pantry and we never cooled the cream we sent to Cottonwood. The creamery could use it even if it had soured. None of us were big milk drinkers as the milk was raw and tasted like what the cow had eaten, wild onion or whatever. Most of our milk was used in cooking or baking, so we really didn't have to worry about it spoiling. What we didn't use we fed to the pigs."

Dinner was at noon whenever the men were home. It was a large meal of meat, potatoes, vegetables, salads, desserts, lemonade, and coffee. During harvest, when the crew was in the fields, the women wrapped the meat—steak, pork, or ham—in newspapers to keep it warm, filled half-gallon fruit jars with cole slaw, potato salad, or fresh lettuce salads seasoned with vinegar and bacon grease. The food, plates, utensils, desserts, and jars of coffee and lemonade were then placed in pack boxes. James returned to the ranch house, loaded the meals on a packhorse, and delivered them to the men. When James couldn't return for the meal, Narcie packed it to a shady spot near the field, spread out an oil cloth tablecloth, and served the food.

If the men were riding after cattle or fixing fences far out on the range, they carried a lunch with them in a saddle pack. Lunch usually consisted of sandwiches made from homemade bread and spread with peanut butter and honey, ham, or beans. Pie or cake finished these lighter meals, while water from pure springs and streams scattered across the range quenched the men's thirst.

The evening meal, or supper, was served about 7:00 P.M. It was a full meal with meat, potatoes or rice with gravy, occasionally potato salad, a fresh or canned vegetable, sometimes navy beans cooked with ham hocks, and a dessert. A cut glass pedestal bowl with a lid always sat in the middle of the table. Every day it was filled with canned fruit, peaches, or applesauce, or in summer with fresh fruit. Whatever was in this dish could be added to anyone's plate at breakfast, dinner, or supper.

During the height of harvest, when Phebe fed ten or more men plus the family, everyone sat wherever they found room—at the table, in a chair, or on the porch. After supper the women carried the dishes to the kitchen, separated the cream from the evening milk, and washed the dishes and the cream separator once again. They put the dishes away in a corner cupboard, washed the floor, and organized the kitchen for the next morning. By then it was between 9:00 and 10:00 P.M. and time for bed.

Sometimes Phebe needed to leave the ranch during the busiest times of the year for medical treatment in Spokane, or to pick fruit at Getta Creek. She then relied on her daughters to feed the men. "I remember one time standing on the front steps as Mother was leaving," recalled Narcie. "Rosamond was about 12 and I was 8. We were both pretty tearful and I imagine Rosamond felt even more like crying than I, because she was the one left in charge. We did the best we could and the men never complained, but we couldn't cook like Mother. On another occasion, when I was 14 and Rosamond was away at school, Mother left me in charge. I made a pie and the crust was so awful and hard. It tasted terrible, but none of the men said a word to me even when Jim teased me about it."

When the children were left alone with no hired men to feed, they improvised their own menus. Narcie and Jim Jr. fixed pancakes and syrup, which they especially liked, for every meal. On one occasion there was plenty of canned food, but the kids wanted something fresh so Jim Jr. killed a turkey, plucked it, and cut it up. Rosamond took the fresh meat and tried to fry it for dinner, but it never cooked properly.

Cooking and baking for daily meals was only one aspect of keeping food on the table. Phebe, Rosamond, and Narcie helped pick peaches, apricots, cherries, pears, plums, and apples at Getta Creek and pack them up to the Joseph ranch where still more cherries, pears, plums, and apples grew. There were also tame gooseberry and raspberry patches on Joseph. All the fruit needed to be eaten, cooked, or preserved within a few days after picking, requiring some juggling of time and chores. These harvests provided the children with delightful memories of stuffing themselves full of wild strawberries and climbing into the Royal Anne cherry trees to gorge on cherries.

The fruits were canned in half-gallon, wide-mouth economy fruit jars, a day-long process, fit carefully between all the other chores. The women gathered in the kitchen as soon as they finished the breakfast dishes. They washed, cut, pitted, and cooked the fruit or prepared a syrup to cover it. After they filled the jars they cleaned the rims of residue, placed a lid over a rubber seal, and pushed a metal clamp over the lid. The fruit was processed in a kettle by boiling for 15 or 20 minutes. The jars cooled on the kitchen table overnight and in the morning Phebe made certain each was sealed properly.

The women also made jams and jellies and pear and apple butter. They preserved whole apples by placing them in a ground pit lined with straw and covered with 18 inches of dirt. This protected the apples from frost and kept them somewhat fresh. They were dug up throughout the winter and used in applesauce and pies, but could remain in the pit until the following June.

Phebe was in charge of the gardens and each spring ordered seed from catalogs and onion sets and tomato plants from Cottonwood. In late March the family went to Getta Creek to plant a garden. Cantaloupe, watermelon, and squash did well there, as did tomatoes, which were planted later. They planted a larger garden at the Joseph ranch in late April with cabbage, tomatoes, onions, lettuce, green beans, peas, potatoes, carrots, parsnips, beets, rutabagas, pumpkins, and corn.

Green beans, corn, beets, and tomatoes took a full day to can. Phebe used the cabbage to make sauerkraut and canned or stored it in a five-gallon stone crock. She put potatoes, carrots, parsnips, and other root vegetables into a pit like the apples and used them until the first fresh vegetables began to appear at the Getta Creek garden the following spring. "Those apples and vegetables kept in the ground had sort of a musty, earthy smell to them," remembered Narcie. "They didn't smell too appetizing, but when cooked they tasted fine."

Canning wasn't limited to produce—beef, mince meat, and pork were put up in the fall after cattle and hogs were slaughtered. On occasion, Phebe canned wild grouse abundant in the pine trees shading the barn lot and the canyons of Rice Creek. "Grouse were thick there in the '20s and early '30s. We could just walk out and shoot them with a .22," recalled Jim Jr. "I was pretty young then, but one of the old fellows on the harvest crew took me down in the canyons on Sundays to hunt grouse. Often we'd bring back enough to feed the crew a couple of times. You had to be a pretty good shot to hit a grouse, but if Mom needed some she went out to the barn lot and shot them herself."

James was not a hunter, but Jim Jr. was. Any wild game he brought home was added to the dinner menu. Phebe also made use of the wild berries growing in the region. There were wild blackberries at Getta Creek and wild gooseberries and strawberries on Joseph. Occasionally, the children gathered enough wild elderberries for a pie.

All of this food preparation kept Rosamond and Narcie busy and allowed little time for play. In the summer when Aunt Minnie was visiting, the day passed quickly with lively conversations and stories spun by the women.

"The most fun times were when Aunt Minnie visited," remembered Narcie. "One time when she was there I was pretty small, but I was making a cake. I was so busy listening to them, I suddenly realized I couldn't remember how much sugar I had added. With a great amount of teasing and laughter, Mother and Aunt Minnie took over the cake and fixed it so it tasted fine."

The few staple items not raised on the land were purchased in bulk at Cottonwood, Grangeville, or White Bird: flour, rice, beans, coffee beans, oatmeal, cream of wheat, farina, sugar, baking powder, soda, salt, pepper, macaroni, spices, peanut butter, tapioca, and honey. The honey was always purchased in large five-gallon cans and kept behind the stove where it stayed warm and wouldn't crystallize. Other staples were stored on the shelved back walls of one of the upstairs bedrooms or in cupboards in the pantry, as were the many jars of home-canned items.

For most of their years at the ranch house, the family drew water from a well under the pantry. A hand pump brought the water directly into the house—a great convenience. In the middle 1930s the water began to taste bad, so James decided it was contaminated. After that they hauled their water from two springs located down a slope about 300 feet from the house. This was a daily chore usually undertaken by Jim Jr., who carried the water back on a saddle horse. At the spring Jim filled a five-gallon milk can, attached a strap or rope through the handle and hooked that over the saddle horn. It took several of these cans each day to supply the household.

Fortunately for Phebe, by the time the well went bad only Jim Jr. and Narcie lived at home and James was running a smaller spread. In the early days, with no well, four small children, and large crews of men, her workload would have been much heavier, particularly on weekly laundry days when clothes, towels, linens, and bedding were washed once a week in a big galvanized washtub set on a bench in the pantry. Phebe used a washboard and a bar of good soap, which she made once a month from lye and lard or fat drippings and scraps. White items were rinsed in water with blueing in a built-in sink in the pantry, then boiled in a copper boiler on the stove.

The women hung all the laundry outside on a clothesline. In the winter, when the clothes froze, they brought them inside to finish drying wherever they could hang or lay them around the kitchen. The day after washday was ironing day. An ironing board was set in the kitchen near the stove where the flatiron could be heated on the stovetop. Almost every item washed, from Levi's to sheets, needed to be ironed.

The hot water reservoir on the stove held about five gallons, so warm water was always available. If more hot water was needed, it was heated in the copper boiler on the stove. In the summer a basin of water and a bar of Ivory soap stood on a bench in the pantry for "sponge" baths. As they came in from work, the men cleaned up at the basin and tossed the water out the window. In the winter the basin was moved to a bench in the kitchen.

The family took full baths once a week, usually on Saturday night. They set the washtub on the kitchen floor and filled it with hot water. While one person was having a bath the next person's water was heating on the stove.

James knew Phebe had enough to do and never asked her to help with the outdoor ranch work. "I remember one of our neighbors had a wife who did all the milking," recalled Jim. "When she got sick her husband carried her out to the barn and sat her on the stool next to the cow so she could do her job. Our father would never have asked Mother to milk cows. The girls helped, but never Mother."

Since Rosamond was older and more help to her mother, Narcie was often the extra ranch hand. "Going after the milk cows was my job, especially during the summer," remembered Narcie. "As summer wore on the cows wandered farther and farther from home. We used to say they could go to New York if they wanted. Sometimes it would be after dark before I found them all. One time, when going through some especially dense brush, my horse couldn't seem to go any farther, and I couldn't seem to go back the way I had come. So I tied him to a tree and walked home. My father had come looking for me, but it was too dark to get the horse, so we left him there all night."

Because so much of Phebe's time was devoted to feeding the family and keeping them clean, housecleaning was haphazard. The kitchen and dining area were cleaned daily. The kitchen walls were covered with a durable blue-and-white-striped oilcloth, which was easily washed. The downstairs floors were linoleum for easy cleaning, while the upstairs had wooden floors. The rooms were devoid of ornamentation and bric-a-brac, so dusting, when it could be done, was simplified. Toilet seats in the outhouse were washed down frequently and fresh catalogs set out in place of toilet paper.

Most of the house received minimal attention, except during fall and spring housecleaning, which was conducted after the harvest and before the busy summer season. During those few slower months Phebe had time to turn her attention to other matters. She wallpapered the rooms of the house every three years with paper ordered from books sent to her by Sears, Roebuck, making her own paste and accenting the rooms with floral borders.

During these months Phebe had more time to read and write letters in the evenings or play card and board games with the family. She also tried her hand at some sewing—curtains, pillow cases, and mending—but by her own admission was not very good. Narcie and Rosamond learned to sew simple patterns for aprons and dresses and some embroidery, but there was little time for any "fancy work."

"Those early years on Joseph developed in me a strong work ethic," said Narcie. "I've often felt if I wasn't working at something I was useless. But many times I was miserable, especially during long horseback rides in the winter when my hands and feet were always cold. I often felt dirty and unattractive, particularly when I was about 15. I did hear Mother complain about all the work and I remember how tired she always was. It was just so frustrating sometimes because, try as we would, we just simply couldn't get all the work done."

Chapter 15

SCHOOL, HOLIDAYS, AND HOOPLA

> *The social life of the community revolved around events that occurred at the schoolhouses. For the most part these were Saturday night dances. Sometimes there were basket socials where the dances were discontinued around midnight, long enough to auction off the baskets prepared by the ladies. After dinner the dance continued until 3:00 or 4:00 A.M.*—John Aram 1984

THERE WERE NO churches, town halls, saloons, general stores, dance halls, or hotels on Joseph. Consequently, the center of the community's social life remained the schoolhouses scattered across the plateau. In the early years, the residents optimistically built five schools about six miles apart on land donated by the residents. Three of them were in the northern part of Joseph Plains—McCarval to the south of Boles, Yellow Pine to the north, and Spring Camp to the west. Two more schools, Sunset and Star, were built on South Joseph. Star was located about six miles southwest of the Aram ranch, while Sunset was built on Canfield land a little over a mile to the north.

Each schoolhouse boasted its own stage, which was located at the back or jutted off the side of the main room. The stages were utilized by itinerant ministers, public speakers, musicians at community dances, and students performing in amateur productions. For convenience, each school was built along a main route on a fenced acre of land. There was an outhouse in both corners at the back of the schoolyard, one for boys and one for girls.

The Sunset School, where the Aram children began their education, was located along the main mail route from Doumecq to Boles. The school was built largely through the efforts of William Reed, James and Phebe's neighbor and friend. It was wood frame with a stage at the back of the room and windows on one side only. Oak desks formed rows facing away from the stage. On the front of each desk was a hinged seat, to be used at the desk immediately ahead. Behind the teacher's desk, on which sat a globe, hung a very large picture of George Washington. Two blackboards were on either side of the Washington picture with two more on the windowless side of the room.

In the center of the room, but slightly toward the back, was a warming stove. On cold days the teacher started a fire before the students arrived. A water bucket with a communal dipper sat on a bench at the back of the room. Older students filled the bucket from a nearby spring. An organ stood near the steps leading to the elevated stage, which was framed by curtains drawn to each side. Another layer of curtains ran along the sides and back of the stage, providing a hidden retreat during plays for cast members, and storage area for props.

The school year ran from September to May and transportation was often difficult because of severe winters. Students walked to school or rode their horses. John, Rosamond, Jim Jr., and Narcie particularly enjoyed going on foot in the spring after the snow melted. It was in those early warming days that the first wildflowers splashed vibrant colors across the hillsides and returning meadowlarks and robins sang their greetings.

At other times they each rode their horses, leaving them in a barn a quarter mile from the school on the Canfield land rented by their father. When the weather was bad, the four took a team and either the surrey or a canvas-covered bobsled. They drove into a little shed near the barn, unhitched the team, left the buggy or sled there, and took the animals into the barn for food and shelter.

When the boys drove a bobsled or surrey to school they went as fast as they could, often racing other students, sometimes using their father's lively span of mules for a team. One snowy, wet, cold day the boys drove the mules with the bobsled. They dropped Narcie and Rosamond off at the schoolhouse and headed down the small hill to the barn and shed. The team started to run and John, who was driving, urged them on, but suddenly he lost control.

"Jump, Jim," he yelled just as the mules careened into the shed, turning wide and slamming into the doorframe as they entered. The boys landed safely in the snow, but the roof of the shed caved in on the bobsled, breaking it. That afternoon the four young Arams walked home through the snow leading the mules. Their father never said much about the broken sled, but it was some time before they had another.

The day at Sunset started when the teacher rang a hand bell, calling the students inside to recite the Pledge of Allegiance as they faced a flag at the front of the room. Then the teacher led the students in song, usually a few patriotic tunes such as "America" and "America the Beautiful." "We sang every day," recalled Narcie. "One time a teacher noticed I was not singing and said, 'Narcie, you aren't singing.' Well, I just didn't feel like singing that morning, but since she was watching I opened my mouth and pretended."

All grades from first through eighth were taught in one room, usually by a young and inexperienced teacher who boarded with one of the local families. Often it was difficult to find someone willing to come to such a remote area. One year, just prior to 1920, Phebe was asked to take the job until a permanent teacher was hired. She left Narcie and Jim Jr. in the care of Mrs. Dodge and went to school each day with John and Rosamond.

At school she faced 29 students. Some were 17 and still in eighth grade, partly because they weren't interested in school and partly because they missed often to help their families ranch or farm. One day a boy arrived at school after an encounter with a skunk. Although she felt sorry for him, Phebe made him turn around and retrace the three miles home. Discipline proved to be a problem even for a veteran like Phebe. Several of the kids came from feuding families and they fought during each lunch period and recess. This animosity proved greater than Phebe's ability to stop it. Later she told her own children, "I took one day at a time and just prayed I would make it through the day."

School ran from 8:00 A.M. to 4:00 P.M. with one hour off for lunch and a morning and afternoon recess. After the morning song time, the teacher worked with different age groups on arithmetic, geography, reading, spelling, writing, penmanship, and some art, usually watercolor painting. Spelling lessons were done on the chalkboards or with spelling bees. Arithmetic was practiced during class hours with students challenged to beat others' times while doing their tables. Homework consisted usually of some reading and the memorization of poetry or a story that was recited back to the class.

When Narcie was in the third grade she won the county spelling contest, a written test given to the students. "I knew how to read before I went to my first year of school," recalled Narcie. "I was good at spelling, reading, and geography, but I developed a mental block to math because I was embarrassed when another girl in my class could add up the math ladder quicker."

Students carried their lunch to school in metal lunch boxes or lidded "lard pails." After eating and during recess, they played steal sticks, Mother Goose, blindman's bluff, softball and ante over the schoolhouse. Another "game" was walking the top rail of the five-foot fence surrounding the schoolyard. In the winter they had snowball fights, built forts, and coasted down a hill on sleds.

"For me, recess was the best part of school," said Narcie, who was quiet in the classroom. "When I first started school my young teacher couldn't understand what I was saying when I told her my name as it is very unusual and I spoke in a tiny voice. Finally, she asked what my mother's name was. I was called Phebe for the rest of the day. By the next day that had somehow been straightened out."

When the young Arams returned home from their school day, chores took over. Homework waited until after dinner was finished and the kitchen cleaned. James and Phebe took the children out of school whenever they needed their help. Each fall all four stayed home to harvest potatoes, a duty Narcie found herself resenting. Most springs they missed school to plant the gardens, while John and Jim Jr. were taken out more frequently to help with the animals. The elder Arams maintained a pragmatic attitude about this, feeling that "what they don't learn now, they'll learn later."

School activities were an important part of the social life. Phebe and Mrs. Lou Brust started a competition among the five Joseph schools to encourage student plays. They made a bright yellow and purple banner that went to the school having the best program for the year. All the students were involved in a play or in singing or reciting poetry. Phebe usually helped with the plays and programs at Sunset School—it provided a social and creative outlet for her. With her help and direction, Sunset School frequently won the banner.

Community members planned fairs, dances, and basket socials, also held at the schools. Entire families attended the fairs during the day, with dances and basket socials continuing into the evening.

All the ladies brought their best needlework, largest vegetables, canned goods, cakes, breads, and pies to the Thanksgiving Fair, which was always held at the Star School. One year Phebe, who thought she was not considered a great cook, was delighted to win first prize for all her baked goods. In her personal memoirs Narcie Aram described the Thanksgiving Fair:

The best times were the fairs and basket socials. We would all arrive at about eleven o'clock and the ladies would set up the displays for the fair. The men and boys ran their horses in barrel races out in the school yard. By noon everyone would be starving. Tables had been set with all the food: turkey, chicken, potato and macaroni salad, coleslaw and of course cakes, pies and cookies. After dinner the judging of the fair went on and there were races and games in the school yard and games indoors for the children.

Usually about four o'clock people who lived nearby went home, while those of us who lived farther away would go visiting at a nearby house for several hours until it was time to go back to the dance, which started about eight o'clock. We usually went to the Brusts' home. They only lived a few miles away. I loved Mrs. Brust; she was a pretty, small, dark-haired lady. Of all the women I knew, I would have preferred to look like and act like Mrs. Brust.

As soon as we got back to the school, the musicians started tuning up. It was usually Mr. Dodge on the violin and Mrs. Graham at the piano. Mr. Dodge used to say that Mrs. Graham could make a piano talk. They would put floor wax all over the floor, and we kids would slide on it getting it slicked up good before the dancing started. We also did our sliding in between dances. The ladies all sat along the sides on one end of the room and the men usually all congregated down by the door. The men dutifully danced with their wives for the first dance; after that they would dance with whomever they wished. Sometimes they would have "tag" or cut-in dances or ladies' choice. They also had square dancing. Everyone danced. The kids that were old enough to walk danced together, or their parents would dance with them.

About midnight the basket social would start, and my father was always the auctioneer. He had a very loud and commanding voice. The baskets were made of cardboard covered with crepe paper and some of the ladies' baskets were very attractive. One year a lady gave me a windmill for my basket, orange with green trim which I admired tremendously. It was common practice for a girl to tell her best beau which basket was hers so he would bid on it. I told a boy about my age that the windmill was mine. He bid on it, and so we ate supper together. One time Mr. Dodge, who had not been told by Mrs. Dodge which was her basket, bought my pumpkin one. I started crying because I didn't want to eat supper with Mr. Dodge. So my mother ate supper with us.

The men would keep slipping out for a smoke and fresh air as well as a sip of moonshine or white lightning. As the evening wore on, some of them became more boisterous and about 3:00 a.m. a fight usually started, right in the middle of the floor. If it went on too long, some of the more sober men would throw them outside to finish up their fight. My sister had nightmares about those fights; she'd worry about whether they'd have one every time we went to a dance. The dance started breaking up after the fights, and we'd get in the wagons and start home. Ordinarily it would be five or six o'clock when we got home. My mother would have to start breakfast, and the men would have to start milking and doing other chores, but my sister and I were allowed to go to bed.

After the Thanksgiving Fair, the schoolteachers and students concentrated on the Christmas program, which was held at one of the five schools, usually on the Friday evening before school vacation started. The students decorated a tree with handmade ornaments and hung paper bells and twisted green and red crepe paper streamers from the ceiling; gas lanterns provided the lighting. All the students attended with their families. Poems, little plays, acting out the Nativity, and singing Christmas carols started the evening. Students each brought a little gift to exchange with another student and there were candy treats for the kids. A potluck dinner and dance followed.

Schools closed for about a week at Christmastime. The Aram children didn't have to wish for a white Christmas—the elevation usually ensured it. Bobsled rides across the white landscape and fast sled runs down a snowy hill were a Christmas reality. The entire family rode into the canyon below the house to find their Christmas tree. After much discussion, because no one could agree on the same tree, they usually cut a fir. It was hauled home and set up in the parlor. Phebe brought out a box of decorations and tinsel, and the children added paper chains, popcorn strings, and homemade ornaments.

"We anxiously awaited the mail with all the cards and letters. The most anticipated presents were in the big box from Aunt Minnie," wrote Narcie. "They were all gaily wrapped in Christmas paper and we couldn't quit looking at them or speculating about their contents once we had placed the gifts under the tree. Her gifts were magical. There were two or three presents each—books, puzzles, games, and toys. Only one year was I disappointed. That was when Rosamond received Nancy Jane, a beautiful porcelain doll that said 'Mama.' She had long hair and eyes that opened and shut. I was given a simple baby doll, obviously because I was younger and my aunt thought it was appropriate. Still, I was downright jealous and thought my aunt liked Rosamond better."

On Christmas Eve the children each took one of their father's large wool socks and left it by the stove in the dining room for Santa to fill. In the morning the stockings were stuffed with small toys, candy, and oranges. They opened the long-anticipated gifts from Aunt Minnie, as well as gifts from their parents, which had been ordered from the Sears, Roebuck catalog.

The men tended to the chores while Phebe, Rosamond, and Narcie fixed a large dinner of ham, turkey, potatoes and gravy, vegetables, oyster stew, and mince pie. Phebe brought out a white linen tablecloth and napkins and set the table with her best china and tableware. She used many of her nice wedding gifts only at Christmas and the children would point to a particularly lovely serving dish or utensil and ask, "Who gave us this?"

Another Christmas treat were the boxes of Red and Golden Delicious apples sent by Phebe's brother Henry Smith who owned an apple orchard in Washington. The children religiously wrote notes to their aunts and uncles thanking them for their gifts and giving them a glimpse of ranch life.

On January 4, 1925, Rosamond wrote her Uncle Henry and Aunt Margretta, "We enjoyed the apples very much and many many thanks for them. We have eaten one box and I guess we would eat the other if Mamma would let us. Narcie and Junior are writing but don't know whether you can make some of it out or not . . . this [the paper] is what I got [for Christmas]. Mamma got quite a lot of paper for Xmas. We children got her a big box of paper with correspondence cards with gold edges, purple, pink and white envelopes with paper with gold edges. . . . Then Aunt Minnie sent her a box of white paper. Aunt Minnie sent me a dress and Narcie one also. She sent John a basketball and Junior a ball and mitt. John is in the eighth grade I am in the seventh grade Junior is the fourth and Narcie third. I expect you will be surprised to hear from nearly all your nieces and nephews. Junior says he can't write his letter he doesn't know what to say. I have read five books this term of school. Mamma gets after us and makes us read. I wish you would come over and see us this winter but I know you won't but do come in the summer."

In his letter Jim Jr., thanked Henry for the apples then went on to say, "We are milking five cows. Rosamond and Narcie and I milk the cows most of the time. John helps Daddy. We have two orplan claves [orphan calves] and a colt to feed milk. I have two other cows to feed with the milk cows. We liked our vacation very much, but now it is over and we have to go back to school in the morning."

In her thank-you note, Narcie informed her uncle that they were saving the second box of apples for school and continued, "I will be seven tomorow. I am in the third grade now. John has a sore knee. . . . It is ofell [awful] cold now sometimes I have to helep milk. I feed the chikens to and get in the wood and wipe the dishes. We play lots of games lots of times. I have read three books this year. I get ten cents for eche [each] book I read. For Xmas I got this paper and a necklace from mamma."

The games Narcie referred to in her letter were not just those played in the schoolyard with her classmates but also the ones with her brothers and sister—jacks, marbles, tiddlywinks, and checkers. Old Maid and Oats were popular when they were young; as they grew older they played solitaire, pinochle, and dominos.

About once a month residents organized a community dance at one of the schoolhouses. These were not part of a fair or school event, but were for pure entertainment. Entire families attended; the hoedown was accompanied by one or more talented neighbors on a fiddle or harmonica and a woman or young girl chording on the organ. Rosamond sometimes chorded, and all four Aram children learned to dance to the lively tunes at an early age. Even though it was Prohibition, moonshine flowed freely. Still, James and Phebe allowed their children to attend the events alone from a relatively early age.

Once, when the family was staying at Getta Creek, John and Jim Jr., ages 12 and 9, were given permission to go to a dance at Star School on

Joseph. They rode some three miles up the Fir Gulch Trail to get out of the canyon and then another mile to the school. When they arrived several men offered them a drink. Both boys declined, but stayed at the dance until the wee hours of the morning. The next day, when James asked about the dance, they told him about being offered a drink. James became very angry and threatened to have something done with the men. The boys asked him not to do anything, and by the time James ran into the culprits a month or two later, he was no longer mad.

"In my early years I didn't know who was doing the bootlegging, but the whiskey was always abundantly available," recalled John. "After any dance there were many fruit jars or small, empty pint bottles around the schoolhouse area, especially where the horses had been tied. The young men drank whiskey like water, so someone almost always got unduly intoxicated and got into a fight. They might even forget that they had been in a fight, would pass out, and become ill. Some just went to sleep and slept out the night. The young men of the community spent most of their time talking about one of two things—the fights at the dance and their horses. They discussed who won the last fight and what the next one would be about. They talked about their horses because they were their most intimate friends."

The Aram brothers didn't get involved in the heavy drinking or brawling, even though as teenagers they rode their horses to Saturday dances all over the region. They traveled the 15 miles to Yellow Pine, 8 to McCarval, 5 to Star, and 6 or 7 to the schools on Doumecq. When Narcie became 13, she was allowed to go with Jim Jr. to the dances.

The young teen lived from one dance to another, planning what she would wear and how she would do her hair. Whiskey flowed freely, but women and girls did not drink openly; however Narcie remembers sneaking a sip of white lightning in the dark of the schoolyard. "Someone offered me a sip," recalled Narcie. "Out of curiosity I took it. It was awful potent, so I spit it out."

As the 1920s waned, the population of Joseph Plains dwindled. Class size at the Sunset School went from nearly 30 at the start of the decade to 6 when Jim Jr. and Narcie were finishing seventh and eighth grades. Eventually the Sunset school was sold to Lester Taylor for $50 and Jim Jr., then in his late teens, helped tear it down. The property reverted to the Canfields. The Star School burned down when a student, sneaking back after the teacher was gone, stuffed a gunnysack down the stovepipe. To replace Sunset and Star a new building, known simply as the Joseph School, was built a few miles from the Aram homestead. Narcie attended dances at the new school during the summers of her high school years. Today, it is the only school still standing on Joseph Plains. The original five have all disappeared.

In the 1930s, young men—those who returned after high school to run their fathers' ranches—traveled farther and farther to find entertainment. "One time Bill Lyda and I went to Yellow Pine to a dance, then to White Bird the next night without any sleep," remembered Jim. "The bridge was out on the Salmon so we left our horses and crossed the river in a rowboat, walked the mile to White Bird, and then walked back after the dance. I got home the next morning."

Arriving home after a dance at daylight, particularly in the summer was not uncommon. The people of Joseph and the surrounding communities worked hard, but when they played they played hard, too. "We saw each other so seldom that no one really worried about how long a dance lasted," said Narcie. "They were usually held on a Saturday night and people could grab a couple hours of sleep after their chores on Sunday. It was the one time the neighbors gathered to visit, gossip, dance, and eat together. They talked about their kids, their problems, their work, their crops, and the neighbors who weren't there. The drinking and fighting eventually sent the families home, but even that wasn't until the wee hours of the morning. My sister and I used to laugh about it years later when we had a sleepless night. Then we'd say we felt like we'd just been to a Joseph dance."

Chapter 16

MOONSHINE, RODEOS, AND RUSTLERS

෮

There was always booze in varying amounts. The quality wasn't important, only the quantity. The Joseph country was isolated, being about 50 miles from Grangeville, the county seat, where the sheriff hung out. He would not make a move unless a complaint was filed. Due to this lack of law, moonshiners felt free to ply their trade.—Jim Aram 1987

THE REMOTE JOSEPH community held an appeal to a few men who chose to make their living outside the law. Those with illegal stills were identified, but their activities rarely curtailed. Law-abiding citizens, all too familiar with hard times themselves, didn't fault a man for making his living off moonshine. They held a "live-and-let-live" attitude, a position assumed by the non-teetotalers largely because they enjoyed a nip themselves from time to time.

Some of the moonshiners kept stills going on and off throughout the year to supply steady cash. Others, determined to make some easy extra cash, just "fired up" their stills for the dances. Production of whiskey by outsiders increased during the summer months when stills were brought into Joseph and set up in the woods, far away from the eye of the law. One summer several men operated a still on Rice Creek where the road crossed to Doumecq. Their camp could be seen clearly by those who passed by, but the still ran unhampered throughout the summer.

One of the most prominent moonshiners was a man who lived with his family on Doumecq. When he got word about an upcoming dance he immediately put his still into operation, then bottled the whiskey in pint bottles to sell at the dance. As soon as he felt his oldest son was ready for the job, he sent him as his salesman.

"His son was a few years older than I, but he was a good friend of mine," remembered Jim. "The trail from Doumecq to Joseph went right by our house and the son came by on horseback when acting as his father's salesman. Often, when I was about 13 or 14, I went with him. He had two gunnysacks containing the pint bottles hung over each side of the saddle horn. The bottles were not wrapped, but loose with eight or so in each sack. They sold for a standard price of $1 each. My friend kept one pint as a sample and each customer got a free drink out of that pint when he bought a bottle. Since I had an 'in,' I got a few nips free.

"However, that was 'fighting whiskey.' It was raw, unfiltered, terrible tasting, and generally laced with a poison we called fusel oil, which should have been removed by charcoal filtering. To avoid getting a straight shot of it and getting sick, the men shook up the bottle. Still, the fusel oil seemed to frequently make men mean. There were problems between people during the course of their workdays, and when they got full of that moonshine they really got ugly.

"One young man had a reputation for getting pretty mean when he got drunk. In the early hours of the morning after one dance, I watched him play cat and mouse with another man, who was husky but not as big or strong. The drunk man pushed the other one around for a while, then acted like he was going to let him go. As soon as the victim started to move away, he was grabbed, lifted up, and held overhead at arm's length, then twirled around. This went on for quite some time until the drunkard got tired of the game and let him go."

One summer a Joseph resident made whiskey for a dance at the Yellow Pine School. He was in such a hurry he didn't filter or age the whiskey and bottled it "green." Jim Jr., who was in his midteens that summer, attended the dance. Generally, he wasn't much of a drinker, but that night he took a couple swigs of the moonshine and became so violently ill he thought he would die. More than two years passed before he could even smell whiskey without getting sick all over again.

This same bootlegger had a relative who sometimes played his violin at the dances. This violinist loved whiskey and his foot-tapping and swaying to the music became more pronounced as the evening wore on. At one dance he drank so much he swayed and tapped happily while his violin bow moved rapidly back and forth, never once touching the strings.

The most notorious bootlegger in the area was a bachelor who lived on the breaks of the Salmon River. He pretty much made his living from his stills and had the reputation for making a very good whiskey. He not only kept the locals supplied with a constant source of moonshine but also plied his trade in Cottonwood. Unfortunately, he was his own best customer, and by the time he sold his supply in town he was so drunk he hardly knew who he was. One of his loyal customers always put him back on his horse and headed him on the trail for Joseph.

The Aram boys were aware of moonshine from an early age. John, while working with one of his dad's harvest crews, was offered stealthy nips from one of the hired hand's bottles. He never had enough to show, so his parents never knew. Later, his father offered John sips out of his own hoarded fifth of "Johnny Walker" label whiskey purchased from a bootleg operation in Grangeville or Cottonwood. He even offered John some dandelion wine made by one of his sisters.

Jim Jr., on the other hand, had his first taste of moonshine at the age of 8 after watching some of the farm hands taking a nip out of a bottle hidden in the rafters of the barn. "They had been passing that bottle around, and as each took a sip he shook his head back and forth like it was really good stuff," recalled Jim. "I decided I better try some, so after they left I went and got the bottle down. Boy, after one swig of that, I ran as fast as I could to the water trough."

The moonshiners gladly sold their bottles to regular customers one at a time, but they preferred to trade wherever a large group of thirsty men gathered. Besides the dances and various socials, bootleggers profited from the Flyblow rodeos during the 1920s. Flyblow was a timbered area west of Boles between Yellow Pine and Spring Camp. The region earned its name when some of the first cowboys working the range at the turn of the century discovered the shady, moist area was so conducive to fly eggs that a fly could "blow"—or lay—its eggs in almost anything and they hatched. Cowboys were fond of saying the flies could blow a log chain or lariat in Flyblow country.

The rodeos were started at Flyblow in the early 1920s by W. I. "Bill" Rook and his sons Mark, Vance, and Jack. With several enthusiastic neighbors, they built a large arena that doubled as a racetrack. Bleachers to accommodate some 200 people, as well as chutes to handle the animals were built. They erected outhouses in the woods and located a good spring. Rook held the rodeo for three days around July 4 and developed a show by inviting professionals from other states, as well as local riders. To pay for the prizes that lured professionals to the rodeo, and to make a little money himself, Rook charged admission.

Despite the remoteness of Flyblow, the rodeos became very popular. Residents of Joseph and Doumecq attended, but so did families from Cottonwood, White Bird, and even Grangeville. Most came by horseback or in wagons, while a very few prosperous townfolk actually showed up in cars that had managed the new Joseph-Cottonwood road and the wagon route across the plateau.

The Arams attended the rodeo for several years, traveling the 17 miles to Flyblow with a team and wagon loaded down with a tent, camp stove, boxes of food, and hay and grain for the horses. As people streamed into the area a little "town" of tents, small cabins, and a few businesses came to life. It was a thrill for the children to be in the midst of all this excitement, and their eyes and ears filled with sights and sounds they never forgot.

Rodeo events included bronc riding, calf roping, steer riding, rope twirling, and races. Jackson Sundown, a famous Nez Perce bronc rider and rope twirler, delighted the crowds with his talent. Jim Jr. was thrilled to watch Bill Rook ride a beautiful bay back and forth across the center of the arena while the racehorses streamed around him on the track. Bill's horse was a pacer and its high-stepping show awed the little boy.

After the rodeo the few little businesses operating temporarily at Flyblow came alive. A central attraction was the the Bowery, a dancehall that provided nightly entertainment. On one end of the Bowery Mrs. Brust ran a little restaurant and on the other end the Gunter family sold concessions and Kewpie dolls. Mrs. Lyda, with the help of her entire family, ran a little cook shack where she served family-style meals. Hamburgers and candy available at these businesses were rare treats for the Aram children.

One night Jim Jr., drawn by the music and laughter, crept away from his campsite alone to see what was happening at the Bowery. Remembered Jim, "I was trying to see what was going on when two men came outside. One pulled a bottle out of his pocket, took a sip, and passed it to his friend. They stood there passing it back and forth, acting rather secretive about it. I was a pretty little kid, about 7 or 8, but I'll never forget the eerie feeling I had watching from the shadows."

The Rooks' Flyblow rodeos were colorful and well attended and they remained popular for many years, but as Joseph and Doumecq residents continued to sell their homesteads and move away, the Flyblow era ended. In later years some of the Joseph residents put on small rodeos for fun. For one July 4 celebration George Dobbins built a corral and with the help of some neighbors put on a little show. The Arams took some of their cattle and local cowboys tried their luck at roping the calves or riding the young bulls. These neighborhood rodeos were just for fun—none compared to the Flyblow rodeos in size or as a market for local moonshine.

Making and selling whiskey was not the only illegal activity on Joseph, for this rugged cattle country harbored its share of thieves and rogues. Two or three families were well known for their "long lariats," which didn't always distinguish between their cattle and another man's. Some of these dubious characters were also known for their gambling and cheating abilities in the poker halls of Cottonwood and Grangeville. Their activities were frowned upon and occasionally stopped, but generally the law-abiding citizens gave these men wide berth, particularly if one of them was loaded with whiskey and looking for a fight.

It wasn't unusual on the range to have a cow or horse disappear without a trace. A rancher never knew for certain if a missing animal had accidentally been mixed with an honest neighbor's herd or gone to market with a dishonest man. Some settlers were reputed to butcher only other men's cows for their family larder. On the other hand, most went out of their way to notify a neighbor if they found one of his strays with their herd—a rancher's reputation went a long way in determining guilt or innocence in the eyes of the owner of cattle in question.

Many honest errors were made due to wandering cattle, poor brands, and long hair that obscured good brands. On one occasion James purchased several yearlings in Cottonwood and took them to the Joseph ranch, where they were put out in nearby pastures for two to three weeks until the men had time to brand. As they were branding one bunch, Lester Taylor came by looking for some of his strays. He stopped to help the Arams and was holding one animal down, when he suddenly yelled, "Hold it. I think this animal is mine." On close inspection the men discovered Taylor's brand under a mass of long hair. The rest of the yearlings were checked, but it was the only stray who had wandered into the Aram herd.

"It was just sometimes hard to see those brands," said Jim. "Because of that, an honest man might inadvertently brand another man's animal. I can remember one big steer I saw out on the range had the Aram brand on one side and the Brust brand on the other. Obviously one of us didn't see the other brand. I don't know who ended up with that steer, but one of us must have."

Jim Jr. once met a couple of cowboys taking a herd of cattle across the Salmon River bridge. It was the late 1930s, and he was on his way from Cottonwood to Joseph in a GMC truck. "As the cattle went by me, I recognized two of our yearlings," recalled Jim. "Of course I told them and they said that they hadn't been able to identify the cattle properly because of their long hair. I followed them to their ranch and took our yearlings back to Joseph in the truck. In those days brand inspection wasn't enforced, or if it was and you hauled cattle in the dark, the brand inspector checked with a flashlight and took your word on the validity of the brands. We tried not to sell cattle belonging to other ranchers, but it sometimes happened."

On the range, unbranded cattle were referred to as "slickears"—fair game for anyone who could rope and brand them. Some cowboys made a real art form out of slickearring another man's cattle, but nothing could ever be proved since the animal had not carried the owner's brand.

One year during the Depression, when cattle weren't worth much, a strange herd appeared on Joseph; some were branded, some weren't. It was rumored that a bunch of cowboys had brought them up from southern Idaho, picking up any cattle they encountered along the way. When they arrived, there was no pastureland so they abandoned the animals. Many of them were on Aram land, so James notified the sheriff and then ran an ad in the *Idaho County Free Press* stating that if the cattle were not claimed by a certain date he would take possession of them as payment for grazing privileges. No one responded and the cattle became an Aram asset.

On another occasion a herd of 100 yearlings belonging to Bill Platt simply disappeared. He had taken them to graze in the Dry Creek country along the Snake, but when he went back to check on them a month later they were all gone. His search all over the Snake country, Joseph, and into Oregon proved fruitless. He finally concluded that rustlers had forced the cattle across the Snake and into Oregon where they were probably sold. They were never seen again.

Others were much bolder in their actions. One character was known to "prefer stealing to eating." Some thought he stole just to see if he could get away with it. One evening he was invited to stay for supper at a farm outside of Grangeville. He left after dark, taking one of his host's horses with him. Each time he was caught he apologized, which got him off the hook several times, until someone finally pressed charges and he served time in the penitentiary. After that he had his sons and hired hands do his stealing for him.

In the fall of 1924, James, John, and Jim Jr. were on Grouse Ridge, a steep hill above Rice Creek, fighting a lightning fire. A young man, Hugh Bentley, galloped up, having ridden hard from Doumecq with a message for James. Bentley pulled the older man aside and spoke briefly to him. Without an explanation to his sons, James mounted his horse and rode away toward Doumecq. The boys and a couple of hired hands finished putting out the fire. Later, they learned Bentley had brought news that some Aram cattle had been stolen and were in the White Bird area.

The 25 head had been taken from the Rosey place, a homestead James owned on the southeast side of Rice Creek. The rustlers rounded up the cattle one evening shortly after James had ridden out to check on them. As soon as it was dark, the men drove the cattle along a ridge toward Camp Howard and then down the county road across Doumecq. However, the road ran close to Newt Otto's ranch, and when he heard cattle passing in the dark he knew something was wrong.

At daybreak Otto set off to investigate. At the Salmon River he discovered a yearling shot dead because of a broken leg. The animal bore the Aram brand. Otto rode on to White Bird where he learned the Aram cattle had been driven right down the main street of town at night. Witnesses identified the rustlers, and Otto sent for James.

By the time James arrived at White Bird, a posse had formed. The posse—some seven armed civilians—and James followed the fresh trail from White Bird to White Bird Creek. From there it led up a ridge into the mountains for some 20 miles, ending at a meadow where the Aram cattle were grazing. Across the meadow stood a dilapidated cabin with saddled horses tied in front. The posse approached the cabin, but before they could "tighten the noose" on the culprits their presence was discovered. The rustlers ran outside, covering their faces, jumped on their horses, and rode away before the posse was able to stop them.

James retrieved his cattle and herded them back to the Rosey place. On the word of witnesses in White Bird, two men were arrested. One was a young man James had recently asked to work as a cowhand for him. Both men were quickly let out on bail. While the case was waiting to go to trial, the father of one bragged openly that he had planned the theft and if his boy hadn't been drunk and driven the cattle through White Bird, he might have gotten away with it.

The man was a tough character with a hard reputation. Twice he came to the Aram ranch to convince James to drop the charges. Both times he arrived when James was away and sat for hours waiting for his return, leaning back in a chair with his feet on the dining-room table. Phebe and the children avoided the man as best they could. Each time James firmly told his visitor, "No, I won't drop the charges. We caught them red-handed and they'll go to jail."

After that there were rumored threats against James Aram's life, and for the first time in his family's memory James carried a loaded .45-caliber handgun with him. "He carried that old .45 for quite a while," remembered John. "I'm sure he wouldn't have known how to use it. Anyway, if someone had tried to shoot him, they probably wouldn't have faced him head on. They would have ambushed him."

When the case went to trial, the prosecutor discovered that only one man would testify against the duo. He had seen the rustlers herding the cattle through White Bird. But the defense attorney brought up the fact that the witness was a known liar and then produced several citizens who testified to that knowledge. Even though several people had originally claimed to have seen the defendants with the cattle, the prosecution could produce no more witnesses. The two men were acquitted.

Rumors ran rampant. Some said the witnesses were threatened by families of the defendants. Others claimed the jury had been paid off. No one knew for certain what had happened. However, most agreed that, in this case, justice had not been served. James continued to wear his gun, but eventually talk of the stolen cattle and rumors of threats disappeared and the .45 was put away.

Generally there was little need to carry a gun for there was no violent crime on Joseph—no murders, felonious assaults, or armed robberies. Besides breaking the law on Prohibition, most other crimes would have constituted theft and in some cases, such as fistfights, simple assault. Some of the "lawbreaking" was merely conjecture or rumor and much of what went on was more fuel for the gossip mill than for the court system.

Men generally let "bygones be bygones" and often socialized amicably with a neighbor they suspected of taking some of their stock. As for the men who rustled the Aram cattle? "Well," said Jim. "Dad and I ran into one of the culprits in town some time after the trial. He and Dad spoke and both were very cordial. I knew the guy pretty well from dances and such and, when he wasn't drunk, he was really a pretty nice guy."

Chapter 17

DEPRESSION

❧

After the cattle rustling incident, the bank was afraid we'd lose more cattle to rustlers. They called Dad's bank notes early. In the spring they sent in their own hired wranglers to round up the collateral—some 1,000 head of Aram cattle.—Jim Aram 1992

The attempted theft of the Aram cattle and the resulting trial marked the beginning of a decline in James Aram's business ventures. Poor markets, yielding a scant return on his investment, made it difficult to repay the bank loans used to finance his cattle operation. In early 1926 his Lewiston bank, concerned about the downward spiral of the farm economy and the potential for more cattle rustling, notified James that they were calling his notes.

James had a good relationship with his bank and approached the loan officers with the diligent proposal to wait until fall. He could then fatten his herd over the summer, bring a better price for them and pay off the notes. Much to his surprise, the bankers refused, pointing out they had the option to demand payment prior to the actual due date. Late that spring they sent in several hired men to round up the cattle. For several days the wranglers rode the range while the family stayed at Getta Creek, watching as the cows and their new calves were taken.

"The bank sent in their own wranglers. Those cowboys were ruthless and didn't give a damn," recalled Jim who, though only 10 at the time, retains bitter memories of that spring. "They drove cows away from their little calves. Some starved before we were able to go out and bring them in. They delivered about 1,000 head of cows, calves, and yearlings to Cottonwood for shipment to market. The cattle were some of the best Herefords we ever had, beautiful white-faced cattle, but they brought only $40 a head. That wasn't enough to pay off the debt, so the notes weren't canceled. By fall cattle were going for $60 each. If they had let Dad wait, he could have paid off the notes and been ahead."

John shared Jim's bitter memories of those dark days just months before his 14th birthday. "I had a cow and calf Dad had given me. He had given me very few things, but in this instance I was the owner, at least on record with my family. I had them corralled near the house at Getta Creek. The cowboys—a hardy, rough and tough lot—were going to take them away. I stood guard at the gate and insisted they were my animals and didn't belong to anyone else. I defied them and after some verbal confrontation, they left me with my cow and calf and went on their way."

As the herd was driven roughly toward Cottonwood, James and John followed on a heartbreaking ride to the rail station. Among the cattle headed for market were several bearing the 111 brand, those financed by Aunt Clara. James had not been able to pay her back, so she was still part owner. At the railway station he politely asked the representatives of the cattle buyers to give him a separate tally of those cattle with the 111 brand.

"They refused to grant it and told him to go to hell," said John who was standing nearby. "I didn't hear all the language, but they abused him terribly, accusing him of being dishonest and a thief. Dad didn't say anything. He and I rode that evening on the train from Cottonwood to Grangeville to see Aunt Clara and spend the night. He was terribly hurt. He didn't ever explain the dispute to me and I didn't hear enough of the discussion to know all that was going on. I'm sure that if I'd heard it all, as a brash young man, I would have gotten into the dispute. It's probably better that I didn't, because if I had, we probably both would have come out much worse for the experience."

While James and John were gone, the rest of the family brought in calves left behind, penned, and bottle-fed them. When James returned he and his sons rode out, crisscrossing the range to gather up any strays bearing their brand. With these leftovers, John's hard-won cow and calf, and the few abandoned calves, they created a little herd, but the future looked bleak. Offering his reputation as his only collateral, James approached a bank in Cottonwood for credit. It was granted, as was credit at the local hardware store.

Summer brought the usual flurry of activity—fence repair, haying, and harvest. However, the absence of large numbers of cattle grazing peacefully in nearby pastures or scattered across the green expanse of the summer range at Center Ridge cast an eerie pall over those usually bright days. This somber mood was intensified by John and Rosamond's imminent departure for high school in Grangeville. The spring before, John had finished ninth grade at Sunset School, a grade taught with special permission and under the auspices of Grangeville High School; Rosamond had completed eighth grade. Their only chance at further education lay in Grangeville, where they could live with Aunt Clara and attend high school.

Throughout the summer John insisted he didn't need to go to high school. All he wanted to be was a Joseph cowboy. Phebe cajoled, listing all the advantages—an education, a glowing future, life in a larger town or maybe a city where there were museums, symphonies, and theaters. "Our plays are just as good here as they are in New York," John retorted. By fall he agreed to go, but only for one year. For 12-year-old Rosamond, homesickness set in the minute her father's Dodge pulled away from the ranch house.

The following year the bankers in Lewiston told James they wouldn't back him in cattle, but they would finance a sheep operation. Facing the potential loss of his entire "Little Empire," the then 64-year-old reluctantly agreed. With a new loan he traveled to Southern Idaho in the fall of 1927 and purchased 1,400 sheep. John stayed home from his second year at Grangeville High to help. His father called and directed him to hire another man, go to White Bird, buy camp equipment, and meet the trainload of sheep at McCall.

Winter's first snow was on the ground and it was cold and blustery when John and his hired hand set up camp outside of McCall. The two went into town looking for James, who they found settled comfortably in a hotel room. Over the next few days, the men drove the sheep out of McCall and down Highway 95 for about 60 miles to White Bird. From there they drove the herd across the Salmon River bridge, up the county road crossing Doumecq, and on to the Biddle place on Joseph. The trip took four days and three nights.

"Dad wanted me to be camp tender for the herder, but I didn't know anything about doing that," said John. "It meant I was to keep the camp supplied with food, find water, take camp down, and then set it up again as the herd moved from place to place. It was a lonely job and I didn't like it. I know I had a psychological block against the sheep business. We were cattle ranchers and cowboys, not sheep men. I told Dad I couldn't do the job. He would have to hire someone else or do it himself. He didn't argue with me, and I pitched in and did a lot of other work. I just couldn't do that."

To help with the sheep herd, James bought Queen, a female sheep-dog. He paid $100 for her, but she proved to be the best investment he ever made. She was almost human in her actions. If the band was disturbed at night, Queen went out on her own and brought them back to their bed ground. If they started to move at daylight and the sheep herder was not yet up, Queen woke him.

Over the years they raised several pups out of her and many of them went to work at six months with very little training; however, none of her pups was ever as smart as Queen. Jim Jr. observed Dave Daniels, who herded for James on Getta Creek one winter, send Queen for a mile or more after stray sheep. He directed her by walking left or right because she couldn't see his arm wave from that distance. The valuable dog was almost lost when she ingested poison set out by government trappers for coyotes. Fortunately, Daniels quickly identified her symptoms, took her to his camp, and poured all the lard he could find down her. Queen was pretty sick, but after a month was back on the job.

When the sheep arrived on Joseph they were grazed out from the home ranch. The herder, Mr. Fix, stayed at the house while the sheep were so close. "I don't know if he was a good sheep herder or not," said Jim. "But he was somewhat of a character." On cold nights when the fire died down in the dining-room stove, Fix would get up to put on more wood saying, "I best reblemish the fire." He had several spotted horses that James allowed him to pasture on Aram land. One day he discovered his horses were missing. Fix suspected a certain Joseph resident had a hand in the disappearance and approached the man. After a severe "dressing down," Fix told the culprit, "You have 48 hours to get those horses back where they belong." Before the allotted time was up the horses reappeared. Nothing more was ever said about the incident.

For the lambing season, the Arams built sheep corrals, lambing pens, and sheds to protect and shelter the ewes and their newborns at Getta Creek. Shortly before the first lambs arrived, the men penned the ewes and trimmed off tags of wool from around their udders, hind legs, rumps, and eyes. This was called tagging and was done to discourage blowflies from laying eggs in these areas when they became moist. The tags from around the udder were removed so the new lamb would not mistake a string of wool for a nipple.

That first spring many of the ewes were young and gave birth for the first time. Several men were needed to keep them under constant surveillance. During the day the sheep grazed on the range, but at night the men herded them into the corrals where a night attendant kept a careful watch over them, helping any ewes in trouble. 25 to 30 ewes gave birth each night. Once a lamb was born and suckled, the attendant penned it with its mother and others. The next day the newborns and their mothers were watched closely by another man. If there were any problems, it was his job to solve them.

There were enough lambing pens to hold 50 to 60 ewes and their offspring. On the second day those that were doing well were let out to pasture to make room for more newborns. After two or three days the herders started forming bands of 50 to 100 from the ewes and their young based on birth order. Once the lambs no longer had trouble finding their mothers the herds were increased to 300 or 500.

About three or four weeks after birth, the men again corralled the lambs and separated them from their mothers. They cut off their tails with a sharp knife to prevent the lamb from becoming filthy and attracting blowflies. They also inoculated all the lambs and castrated the males. The testicles were so tiny it was hard for the men to grasp them with their fingers, so they learned to use their teeth. Jim Jr. and John used this technique, but their father, who had false teeth, needed to use his fingers. When all the procedures were done, they branded the lambs and their mothers with the letters JA using a cold metal brand dipped in a mixture of linseed oil and lampblack. The mixture dried on the wool and remained visible all summer and in fall, when the brands had faded, the process was repeated.

After the lambs had healed from the castration and tail removal, they were combined into one large herd. John or Jim Jr. counted the sheep as the herd passed through a gate. For every 100 head they dropped a rock in their pocket then counted the rocks to figure a total. Once the entire herd was together, the herder watched carefully for any sign of coyotes. Still, the predators caused some loss because they were cunning and slipped around a large band, attacking at the point farthest from the herder.

In May the men drove the sheep to Joseph for shearing by a crew of men who camped while they worked for various ranchers, but one year James drove his sheep out to Mike Sloviaczek's sheep ranch northwest of Boles. Sloviaczek had a large operation with corrals for handling sheep efficiently. The men on his shearing crew stood on platforms with roofs for protection from the elements. Sheep were forced one at a time up to the platform on a ramp built from an adjacent pen where 15 or 20 could be held. Using gas-powered shears, each shearer finished 60 to 100 sheep a day. That year, after the shearing, several of the Arams' ewes and lambs sickened and died when a late snowstorm caught the sheep out on the range without their woolly coats.

When summer arrived the herd was moved to summer range. James didn't have enough high grazing land, so he arranged with the Forest Service to summer them on Green Mountain beyond Elk City and Red River Hot Springs. Mr. Fix had moved on, so Billy Rankin agreed to take the job as summer herder, and James hired another man to tend camp. James helped drive the sheep the hundred miles to Green Mountain, but returned to Joseph after the two-week trip.

At the end of the second summer, Jim Jr. accompanied his father to Green Mountain to bring the band back to Joseph. On the trail they used a castrated buck, known as a bellwether, to lead the other sheep. The bellwether wore a bell and was led on a rope. "I was given the 'great honor' of leading this big, gentle bellwether," recalled Jim. "What a boring job for a young boy. The road from Elk City to the Clearwater was through tall timber, so tall in fact that on a cloudy day the trail was dark. In the deep forest the band might be strung out for a mile or more.

"One day I was leading out without knowledge of how the main band was trailing, for the road was crooked and I could only see those few directly behind me. We went near a meadow and about half the sheep broke off and went in there to graze. Billy came up and stopped me, but by then I'd gone a mile too far."

The trip out of the national forest was grueling. Young Jim was up with the herders by 3:00 every morning, ate breakfast, helped pack the camp, and was on the road by daylight. There wasn't much for the sheep to eat on the timbered route and little time to graze them. When they crossed the old bridge at Harpster, the men let the sheep graze on the open green hills where they ate goat weed, which caused their heads and ears to swell to three times their usual size, killing some of them.

The rest of the herd was moved on to Grangeville where they were held in stubble fields for a few days while the lambs were separated and sold. Some of the remaining sheep got sick on wheat spilled during harvest and the herd suffered more loss. A few days later the remaining sheep were trailed from Grangeville, across the Salmon, and on to Joseph.

After he acquired his sheep, James kept hearing about the advantages of keeping a ranch band, a small herd of sheep allowed to graze freely around the home ranch with no herder. They were used to keep weeds down, provide fresh meat, and bring in ready cash from the sale of the wool and lambs. The Aram ranch band was started with the bum lambs, usually one of a set of twins who was rejected by its mother and could not get enough to eat. Often the sheep herders just hit the bum lambs over the head, because they didn't have facilities to care for them. The Arams, however, took theirs into a pen built inside the Getta Creek house where they were kept warm.

Ten-year-old Narcie was in charge of the orphans and sometimes had as many as 15 to care for. They needed feeding every four to five hours starting about 4:00 A.M. and continuing around the clock. Narcie warmed enough cow's milk for five or six and filled several bottles, feeding the hungry lambs with one bottle in each hand. When those lambs were full, she warmed enough milk for six more. Narcie fell in love with the little lambs, who in turn mistook her for their mother and followed her all over the Getta Creek ranch. Phebe particularly enjoyed the sight of her youngest daughter running up and down a little hill near the house with all the lambs following. When the lambs were old enough, the men trailed them back to Joseph.

James added to his little ranch band when he heard of a small herd for sale at a farm north of Boles. He made a deal at $4 or $5 a head and sent Jim Jr. to collect the sheep. "I arrived at the farm about dark," remembered Jim. "Two boys were the only ones home. I was invited for dinner and while the boys were doing the dishes, I noticed the towel one was drying with was practically black. Just then he said, 'Mother had better come home soon, because this is our last clean dish towel.' They got up the next day about 3:00 A.M. and killed a chicken then fried it for breakfast. It must have been an old hen, for it was so tough I couldn't stick my fork in it.

"The three of us drove the sheep to the ranch that day. The herd was all right, except that to care for them was just another chore. They started lambing in late March and early April when our heifers were calving and had to be watched day and night. Sometimes, between cows and ewes, I wouldn't get much sleep at night and then spent the day feeding and caring for more cows and ewes. We had been sold on the idea they would keep the weeds down around the house, but it seemed to me they preferred grass. That ranch band didn't mix with other sheep. They could go through another herd and come out the other side intact."

During the two years they were busy with sheep, the Arams continued to add to their cattle herd. James, most likely on credit from his Cottonwood bank, purchased some shorthorns. When the Lewiston bank learned the Arams still had cattle on the range, they told James to deliver them to White Bird for sale and they would forgive the notes still held from the 1926 cattle sale. Jim Jr. and Narcie rounded up about 50 head and drove them to White Bird, where they turned them over to a buyer procured by the bank, and the notes were forgiven.

James also tried to raise turkeys at Getta Creek. He kept the hens in an enclosed half acre until after their eggs hatched in spring. When the little turkeys were two months old, they transported the flock to Joseph. The young were carried in boxes lashed on each side of a packhorse with another riding in the center on top. The older turkeys rode in burlap bags with their heads and legs sticking out of holes cut in the burlap. This unusual cargo was held in place by another slit in the top of each bag, which slid over the horn of a riding saddle. Several turkeys were transported this way, while the rest rode two or three on each side of the packsaddle.

At the Joseph ranch the men built pens, but when the young were more than half grown they were let out in the barn lot and fields to feed on vegetation and insects. Sometimes, when feeding a quarter mile from the house, something startled the turkeys and the entire flock took flight, sailing into the protection of the farm buildings.

About two months before Thanksgiving, James penned the birds and fattened them on grain. A few days before Thanksgiving they were butchered in the woodshed behind the house, hung by their feet, and plucked. The next morning the family packed the birds, folding the wings neatly and leaving the heads on. The packed boxes were sent by mail stage to Cottonwood where the train took them to Spokane. The entire operation, from butchering to market, was all accomplished without refrigeration.

By the summer of 1929 the sheep operation, funded so willingly by the Lewiston bank, was breaking James. He had paid too much for the sheep, and by the time he was ready to sell wool in spring and lambs in fall, the bottom had fallen out of both markets. Just prior to the October 29, 1929, stock market crash heralding the Great Depression, James sold his sheep. He kept only the small ranch band. What little money was raised from the sale left nothing to pay his mortgages.

In 1930, at age 67, James Aram lost his land. His good friend and attorney, A. S. Hardy of Grangeville, had tried to help earlier by advancing him money on the Getta Creek ranch. When James continued to get farther and farther behind on his payments, Hardy reluctantly foreclosed. The Federal Land Bank foreclosed on all the rest of the land, including the 500 acres comprising the home place. They allowed the Arams to continue working and living on the Joseph ranch, but the loss of Getta Creek put their best winter range and the bountiful orchards and vegetable gardens beyond their reach. The family made do with the variety of fruits and vegetables grown on Joseph and with steeper winter range for their small herd.

That same year John spent his last summer working on Joseph. When he left to attend his senior year at Grangeville Phebe didn't need to convince him to go. "After watching what my father was going through in '29 and '30 I changed my mind about being a Joseph cowboy," said John. "I just couldn't figure out any way to make the ranch operation work. Besides, I had seen some of the rest of the world and had an idea of how other people lived. I left the work on Joseph that fall of 1930 and never looked back."

Young Jim remained on Joseph working with his father for most of the Depression years, with the exception of the months he attended high school in Grangeville. "After all that bad luck Dad couldn't get started again very easily," said Jim. "In desperation, to generate some income, we raised potatoes for the market. We had about three acres a couple different years. It was a tiresome job to plow, plant, cultivate, hoe weeds, and finally dig, sack, and transport the potatoes to a central point. Then we had to keep them from freezing. There were so many it was not feasible to put them in a ground pit so we piled the potatoes in the old log building just north of our house and covered them with a lot of straw and canvas.

"I remember helping load out a ton another rancher bought for $25 to feed his hogs. Each sack had to be filled by hand and weighed by putting a rope around it and lifting it up to hang on the scales. It would be interesting to know what we made an hour raising potatoes.

"Dad also somehow heard about the silver fox business. He traded 20 head of horses and a note payable yearly for a pair of silver foxes. Fox farming was popular at that time, but the only ones making money at it were the promoters selling breeding stock. We paid around $800 for that pair—this in a day when hay-hand wages were $1 per day and board. The horses constituted some credit, but the rest was paid in hard cash. After all the work, expense, and care, we sold a few pelts. But it was no bonanza as it had been pictured. In fact, it was just a waste of time and money."

As the Depression deepened, the land on Joseph became practically worthless. The Federal Land Bank told James they wanted to help him get his land back and offered him "bargain basement prices" with no down payment. Borrowing from his new bank in Cottonwood and from his friend Hardy, James repurchased the home ranch, several hundred acres of steep winter range in the Fir Gulch area above Getta Creek, and other parcels of grazing land. He bought some of it for a mere $1 an acre. James continued to lease about 1,000 acres from Eva Canfield and rented other acreage owned by Attorney Hardy. By then the beloved Getta Creek ranch, scene of their warmest childhood memories, had been sold and was lost to the Arams forever.

"Dad worked so hard for so many years on his cattle business and, for a while, success was almost in his reach," reflected Jim. "Then the bank called his notes, he went broke in the sheep business, and the Depression set in. He tried desperately to find something that might be a better gamble than cattle. Of course there wasn't anything better for that country. Dad always knew that. He probably should have borrowed again and gone right back into the cattle business in a big way. Many years later one of the bankers who called Dad's notes in 1926 told me, 'I wish we had never forced James Aram to sell his cattle. We made one big mistake.'"

Chapter 18

NO 911

∽

The telephone—that was our main source of quick communication. We could contact our neighbors in an emergency or a doctor in White Bird or Cottonwood. Of course, no one could get to us very quickly.—Narcie Aram See 1992

DURING EMERGENCIES THE residents of Joseph relied on their wits and each other. The telephone lines provided the only quick link to neighbors and the outside. These lines, which ran through rugged country, were often hard to maintain, particularly during bad weather. Then, the only means of quick communication was a fast horse. Sometimes the call for help came too late.

Such was the case for the young Boles family who lived on a ranch near the Snake River at the mouth of Wolf Creek. Hazel Boles was Phebe's good friend. She and her husband, Saxby, had their river ranch and a homestead, High Breaks, on Joseph. Saxby also caught sturgeon in the Snake. He sold the eggs for caviar and the sturgeon for meat, loading his fresh catch onto the mail boat as it made its return trip to Lewiston. On August 1, 1924, Saxby and Hazel took their three children—Matha (pronounced May-tha) age 7, Mark, 6, and Betty, 3, on an outing in their boat.

Saxby rowed his family across the swiftly moving Snake to a sandbar on the other side. The children splashed in a pool in the sandbar, while their parents ventured into the river. The current, which had undercut the bar, quickly drew Hazel in over her head. She panicked and called to Saxby for help. He attempted to reach her, but was also pulled under.

The children watched, horrified. Their mother struggled toward the sandbar, while their father surfaced two or three times, then disappeared. As Hazel came up for the third time, her feet touched rocks and she pulled herself up and out of the water. She asked the children where their father was. Silent and wide-eyed the three pointed to where they had last seen him.

Hazel screamed her husband's name over and over as she prodded the depths near the sandbar with an oar. After a time she gave up, put the children in the boat and, although she had never rowed before, delivered them safely back across the swiftly flowing river to Wolf Creek and their home. The grief-stricken young mother tried to reach several neighbors, but was so incoherent it took several calls before someone understood her.

While she waited for help to arrive from distances of 10 to 15 miles away, Hazel sobbed her distress as the three children stood frozen at the foot of her bed. As soon as a group of neighbors reached the ranch, a distraught Hazel led them to where Saxby had disappeared. Searchers dragged the river all night. By dawn they had located Saxby's body on the river bottom in 15 feet of water, his arms clasped tightly around a rock.

The Snake claimed another friend in the mid-1930s when Dale McDougall, son of the Joseph postmistress, drowned in its treacherous waters. Dale had married in late spring and spent his first months of marriage haying and harvesting. When the neighbors came to the McDougall farm to thresh that year, Dale drove a bundle wagon with his new bride, Alma, at his side. After harvest the young couple went down to the Snake for a few days. They were fishing from a large rock just above the mouth of Getta Creek when Dale fell in. He was in deep water and couldn't swim. Alma got on her horse and rode to the Qualey home for help. The Qualeys rode back to the river with her, but all they could do was retrieve Dale's body.

Jim remembers the sad days that followed, "The body was laid out in the little room in the back of the post office. It was there for two or three days. The Qualeys were good carpenters and they built a coffin that was very simple and made of planed, unpainted lumber. I was called on to help dig the grave and be a pallbearer. There was an old graveyard with a few graves on the Lou Brust ranch about a mile east of the McDougall home. We picked a spot and started to dig. There was about three feet of soil and then fractured basalt, which was really tough. The going was so hard that we finally gave up. I don't know if we ever got it six feet deep, but it was close.

"The funeral was a primitive affair. We put the body in the wooden box and had a team and wagon for transportation to the grave. We sat on the side of the wagon box for the trip to the graveyard. I can't remember who read the Bible and said a few words for the departed, but I think it was Mother as she usually conducted funerals. Later, Alma married Tom Qualey and they bought a ranch near Grangeville."

Other emergencies had happier endings such as the time Jettie Lyda's appendix burst; two doctors were summoned. The appendix had ruptured, so the doctors put in a drain. Jettie's 12-year-old brother Cecil took the doctors back to the Salmon River by hack. En route he heard one doctor tell the other they would never have to come back to finish that job. However, Jettie was a fighter. A month later they were back performing a successful surgery by the light of a kerosene lamp as Jettie lay on the dining-room table.

The Arams, too, had their share of mishaps requiring attention beyond what Phebe could give. When the children were small James broke his leg when his horse fell on him. A doctor came from White Bird to set it. After a short recuperation, James went back to work, hobbling around for several weeks. Phebe also suffered a painful break while wallpapering the upstairs hall with young Jim's help. While standing on a bench she leaned over too far. The bench buckled and Phebe fell. Jim helped her downstairs and splinted the leg with sticks and clean cloth strips. He called the doctor in Cottonwood and a car was sent to take Phebe out of Joseph. She suffered the pain stoically while waiting the hour and more it took for the car to arrive. Then she rode in pain for another hour over the bumpy road to Cottonwood where her leg was finally set.

Considering the type of work they did, the elements, and terrain, serious accidents and illnesses were fortunately few and far between. However, during the winter of 1928-29 the Arams suffered more than their usual share of near tragedy. John and Rosamond were living with the Abercrombie family in Grangeville for they couldn't live at Aunt Clara's again because they had fought so much during the previous year. It was a cold, windy winter with unusually heavy snow and in December all the kids came down with colds.

John was miserable by the time Christmas vacation arrived. He and Rosamond boarded the stage, an open-air truck, for White Bird. Their father was to meet them there with horses for the trip back to Joseph.

The two teenagers arrived in White Bird before James and sat on a bench outside the hotel until he came. John's cold was much worse by the time he reached the ranch. He was wet and chilled through. The next morning he went out to the barn to help his father with the chores, but by then he was terribly sick. James sent him back to the house where Phebe put him to bed.

Christmas was quiet while the family watched over John. Phebe and James took turns applying onion poultices to his back and chest to ease his congested lungs. New Year's Day came and went. By then it was obvious John was not getting better. Rosamond returned to Grangeville with neighbors and James called Dr. Orr in Cottonwood. Because it was snowing, the doctor drove out to the Salmon River where James met him with a horse. By then it was the middle of the night. After examining John the doctor said, "I need to get this boy to the hospital. He has double pneumonia."

While Dr. Orr drew fluid off John's lungs with a long needle, James and Phebe discussed what to do. It was snowing hard and both realized the necessity of getting their son off Joseph before the roads became impassable. Dr. Orr suggested he return to Cottonwood and send a car back for John. Early the next morning a young man, Sid Triplett, arrived in a Dodge touring car. John was bundled into the backseat with his mother for the slow, two-hour trip. By the time they arrived at the house used for a hospital, John was hot and sweaty. The medical staff removed his warm layers of clothing and wrapped him in cold sheets. By the next morning John was deathly ill. Even the doctor held out little hope for his recovery.

Phebe, however, never gave up. The hospital was primitive, medical knowledge limited, and there was no miracle drug such as penicillin to cure her critically ill son. Against all these odds, Phebe prayed. Night and day she stayed at John's bedside, talking to God, then to her son, urging him to pray and get well.

John was so sick he could barely respond, let alone pray, so Phebe continued to pray for her own miracle. James arrived in Cottonwood and wandered in and out of the hospital to check on his son's progress. John hovered near death for two weeks but then "turned a corner." Gratefully, James and Phebe watched their son slowly come back to them. "Mother's prayers got him through it," said Jim years later. "It couldn't have been anything else."

As James and Phebe hovered at the bedside of their oldest child, their youngest faced her own crisis back on Joseph. An old man, a family friend, was staying at the ranch with Jim Jr. and Narcie. Winter storms swept across the plateau with regularity. In mid-January the worst storm of the winter hit, dumping several feet of snow across central Idaho and inundating Joseph, Doumecq, and Camas Prairie. Roads were impassable. The January 31 issue of the *Free Press* described the storm under the headline "Camas Prairie Has Deepest Snow Cover For Many Years." It read:

> Severe winds, that at times reached almost blizzard gale, have marked the time since last Thursday. These winds, which were interspersed with downfalls of snow, have tied up the stage service in and out of Grangeville for over a week. The Boise Stage has tried several times to get even as far as White Bird but has been turned back each time by insurmountable drifts between Grangeville and White Bird Summit.
>
> On Sunday and Monday the mail was taken to Salmon River points by a caterpillar pulling a sled full of mail. The road crew, under the direction of Harry Benson, has been at work most of the day and night for over a week trying to force its way through with a snowplow and has succeeded several times opening a road to Cottonwood, only to have the cuts in low places filled before the return trip. The Lewiston Stage left for that point Sunday and following the snowplow to Cottonwood finally reached its destination. It did not return the next day, although the freight truck made it to Grangeville. The trains on Camas Prairie have been on time, but this has been possible only by using the big rotary snowplow every day. Old timers say its the most complete tie-up "since the Grandad's whiskers froze to his vest in 1895."

One evening after supper, in the midst of this storm, 11-year-old Narcie suffered terrible pains in her right side, intensified versions of milder pains she had felt off and on over the summer. The old man staying with them was of little help, so Jim Jr. called their closest neighbors, the Grahams. Mrs. Graham came over to the house to see what was wrong and, when she discovered how much pain the girl was in, immediately contacted James and Phebe in Cottonwood.

After consulting with Dr. Orr, they determined Narcie should be brought to the hospital. Al Graham fixed up a covered bobsled and hitched a double team of four horses to it. Soon he had Narcie loaded in the sled and the two started off for Cottonwood. It was snowing heavily and large drifts blocked their route. Eventually they reached Clyde Morrow's house at the top of the hill just before the road started down the steep switchback grade leading to the Salmon. Realizing he could travel no farther in the dark, Al stopped at the Morrows' and helped Narcie into the house.

It snowed all night and was still snowing the next morning as Al readied the bobsled for the trip down to the Salmon. Narcie was feeling better and asked for something to eat. Concerned that giving the sick child solid food might make her worse, her hostess gave her fruit juice. She was then bundled up warmly and tucked in the bobsled. They started out, but kept bogging down in the snow.

A call for help went out from the Morrow house. Soon Clyde Morrow arrived with Bob Dobbins, Wirt Jackson, Ernest Box, and 11 horses. The men couldn't see where the road had been, so they drove the horses across the snow where they thought it might be. This packed the snow and created a path for the team and sleigh—it took three hours to reach the Salmon River.

At the top of the hill, on the other side of the river, a man from Cottonwood waited with a bobsled and fresh horses. Al transferred Narcie to the other sled and with the best wishes of her Joseph neighbors she was sent on her way with her new escort. Narcie asked the driver if she would be able to eat when she got to Cottonwood. "They'll just give you soup," he responded. "And you'll get an enema."

It was after 6:00 P.M. when they arrived at the hospital, the same house where John lay critically ill. Phebe gathered her daughter into her arms before Narcie was whisked off for an examination by the doctor. The driver's prophecy came true. She got her soup, but she also later got the enema.

After a night's rest Narcie was taken to surgery at 8:30 the next morning, a procedure that took place in what was once the dining room of the house. As the nurse lowered the mask with its ether drops over Narcie's face she heard Dr. Orr rattling his instruments and quickly said, "Don't start yet. I'm not asleep." Phebe, tired and strained from her long vigil at John's bedside, went in the next room and cried.

The surgery went well; Narcie's appendix was inflamed but not ruptured. Meanwhile she was lauded in newspapers across the nation and around the world as the little girl whose life was saved by a courageous band of cowboys who, with their horses, broke a trail through impenetrable drifts to bring her to civilization. James and Phebe stayed in Cottonwood until both children were out of danger. Meanwhile, 13-year-old Jim Jr. was the only Aram left at the ranch.

"There I was with that old man," remembered Jim. "He didn't like me, or anybody, I think, and cooked for himself only what he ate, did up the dishes, and left nothing for me. We had about 60 head of cattle and some horses to be fed, but he wouldn't help at all, so I fed the livestock. Then I got on my saddle horse and went out to the sheep camp which was on the Kerlee Place about a mile across the canyon, where Billy Rankin was tending the sheep and I helped feed them.

"There was a storm and wind nearly every day, so it was some job digging that loose hay out of the snow. We used a team and sleigh and the wind often blew the tracks full between loads. We fed two big loads a day. I helped load and then drove the team while Billy unloaded. Billy always had a pot of beans and cooked up something else to go with it, so I got my one good meal each day."

It was during those weeks when Jim Jr. worked alongside Billy that he grew to know his father's friend better than he had before. At a time when most of the ranch operation was falling directly on Jim's young shoulders, the boy knew he could rely on Billy to take care of the 1,000 head of sheep. Jim missed his family, but he didn't feel so alone when he warmed himself by Billy's fire, filled up on his beans, and visited with the older man. He heard Billy's stories of his early days herding sheep in the Imnaha and Grande Ronde River regions. He also became well acquainted with one of Billy's favorite sayings proclaimed at the end of most meals, "Well, that doesn't taste so sweet anymore. I guess I've had enough to eat."

Because of the demands of the ranch, Jim Jr. quit going to school and missed half of his eighth-grade year. Finally his father returned, but Phebe stayed with the two patients in Cottonwood. When John was well enough to travel, he was sent to Clarkston to recuperate with the Reeds, former Joseph neighbors. His illness caused him to miss his junior year. Narcie, who missed several weeks of school, returned in time to complete seventh grade.

Only Rosamond, probably at Phebe's insistence, remained in school throughout that extremely difficult winter—a time the family believes they survived largely because of Phebe's prayers and affirmations. When spring finally arrived, the Arams counted their blessings and were infinitely glad they had each other. However, it was a winter the family never forgot—a winter during which the physical hardships seemed a cruel reflection of the harsh economic times engulfing their world.

Chapter 19

JIM

As we ponder our childhood experiences, our lives were busy and by the standards of our present culture we endured hardships. In retrospect these experiences were good for us, especially Rosamond, Narcie and I, who each were released by our parents to reach out in search of more comfortable situations. Jim stayed on . . . it is Jim who endured the most and did the most on Joseph.—John L. Aram 1993

IN THE MONTHS after James Aram lost his ranch to foreclosure, the Depression deepened. The market for farm products dropped dramatically. Cattle that had once sold for 10 to 11 cents per pound were practically worthless. The value of land plummeted. Ranch hands on Joseph were happy if they found jobs paying room and board. Few ranchers or farmers had spare change jingling in their pockets.

With Phebe's encouragement, young John and Rosamond turned hopeful faces to an outside they knew offered greater opportunities. James, however, clung to the hope that his oldest son would return to the ranch. Several times he pleaded with him to come back, but John stuck to the final agonizing decision made during the summer of 1930. Life on Joseph was placed firmly in the past.

After high school graduation in the spring of 1931, John took a summer job with the Forest Service. Rosamond had graduated a year ahead of him and that fall he joined her at the University of Idaho in Moscow. Both young Arams paid their own way. Rosamond worked as a secretary in her cousin Oren Fitzgerald's office on campus, while John worked as a bellhop for the Moscow Hotel during the school year and reclaimed his Forest Service job each summer.

The following fall, Jim Jr. reluctantly left Joseph to attend high school. Charlie Campbell, the owner of the Imperial Hotel in

Grangeville, hired Jim as a bellhop just as he had John before him. At the hotel Jim's responsibilities included greeting people, carrying their luggage to their rooms, and maintaining the hotel lobby floor, windows, stairs to the first floor, and the hall to the dining room. Jim studied in a small room adjacent to the lobby while waiting for customers. For his work, he received room and board plus tips, usually 10 cents or, if he did something extra, 25 cents.

Life at the hotel was an education in itself for a boy straight from Joseph Plains. Interesting people came and went, and something was always happening. One day the kitchen door flew open and Charlie Campbell ran past Jim, pursued by his Chinese cook waving a meat cleaver menacingly at Charlie's retreating back. Young Jim made a mental note never to upset the cook.

A few months later the cook was called back to China by his family. The night before he left he called down from his room and requested that Jim come up and help close his trunk. Hesitant to go alone, Jim asked a steady boarder at the hotel to accompany him. In the cook's room they discovered a trunk so overloaded it took both of them standing on it to lock it. When they were finished, the cook handed each of his helpers a dollar.

Once, when Jim showed two men to their room, they asked him if he could get some whiskey for them. Jim was aware of several bootleggers in Grangeville, but declined any information. Later, the two men called down for some ice and mixer. When Jim took it up they quizzed him again. Weakening, he suggested they try a business where he knew a classmates's father kept a supply of whiskey. The next morning at school Jim learned the father had been arrested. He realized then that the two young men were federal agents. Covering his chagrin and embarrassment at being used by the agents, Jim acted surprised at the news.

Jim was so busy with school and work, he had no time for extracurricular activities. However, the track coach asked him to compete in the mile run in the upcoming meet. Without any training Jim came in second in a race against 11 other young men; however, he wasn't able to pursue the sport because he had no time. Midway through his junior year, Jim grew weary of school and left. After a brief visit to his Uncle Henry's in Washington, he returned to help James at the ranch.

Phebe, however, was determined Jim would finish high school. The following fall she took him back to meet with the superintendent. The three decided Jim should complete his remaining years—half his junior year and all of his senior—in one year. Phebe made arrangements for him to join Narcie at Aunt Clara's. He wouldn't have to work while staying there and could concentrate on his studies.

Phebe spent much of the winter at Clara's coaching Jim. By late spring he had completed his high school requirements and was able to graduate with Narcie, who had caught up with him. "I graduated in the spring of 1935," remembered Jim. "I bought a new suit from Sears for $14. When graduation came, I had the measles and wasn't able to attend."

During young Jim's absence, an aging James and one hired hand kept the ranch going, but just barely. Jim was anxious to return and help, but first he stopped at his father's bank in Cottonwood and requested a loan of $500 to buy more cattle. Jim realized banks were loaning little money in those deep Depression years, but that didn't stop him from walking confidently into the bank and asking.

The loan officer talked to the 19-year-old and told him to come back at two o'clock that afternoon. When Jim returned the bank director was with the loan officer. After visiting with Jim, the director said, "Lend him the money." They issued a check enabling young Jim to select several head of good cattle to add to the Aram herd.

The next years were busy ones as Jim Jr. worked almost single handedly to win back his father's ranch. He bought and sold cattle and hogs, purchased available land and leased more, rode miles across the range tending the growing herd, delivered calves, helped lamb and shear the remaining ranch band of sheep, harvested hay and grains, built and repaired fences, constructed log water troughs with Hilt Thrapp, drove herds from one part of the ranch to the other with the sole help of the ever faithful Major, and generally did the work of three men. During the spring of his 20th year, to make some pocket cash, Jim worked for a sheep rancher herding ewes and newborns on Getta Creek land once belonging to his father. He worked for a full month, but never saw the promised dollar a day.

Jim then turned his attention to improving the home ranch. Tired of hauling water up the 300 feet from the spring, he devised a line from the creek to a pressure tank at the house, with a gas-engine pump located midway between the house and spring. The pump needed a building to shelter it, so Jim set about designing one. He had never built anything but fences, hog pens, pole gates, and pole-log corrals; however, he believed he could construct a simple pump house. First he tore down an old homestead shack for lumber. Then, since there was no cement for a foundation, he gathered flat rocks and used them. When he completed the building, Jim stepped back and looked at it with satisfaction. Not only was it solid but it also looked just fine. Encouraged, he tore down structures on another homestead and built a garage and aboveground root cellar.

Once the three small structures were finished, Jim decided to replace their old ramshackle barn. With the building plans in his head, a 50-by-50-foot barn with a 20-by-50-foot haymow and an attached shed on each side, he set to work. He decided to frame the barn with 10-foot-long fir poles for uprights and with logs 12 to 14 inches in diameter and 15 to 20 feet long as the bottom plate. First he framed and completed one shed, which he used over the winter, and then he framed and completed the barn, haymow, and other shed the following year. To finish the barn he ordered manufactured lumber, a rough fir selling for $15 dollars per thousand board feet. Jim did virtually all of the construction himself, working at odd hours. Only when the heavy trusses needed to be hoisted into place over the haymow did he ask for help.

As he took more control of the day-to-day operations of the ranch, young Jim looked for ways to reduce the number of men needed for a job. He felt branding required too many cowboys, and, although he had never seen a structure built to make branding easier, designed a branding chute. Along one side of his corral he constructed a small holding pen for eight to ten cattle. A gate opened from the corral, so the cattle could be released directly into the pen.

At the far end of the holding pen he built a 25-foot-chute just wide enough for a cow to go through, but too narrow for a calf to turn around in. At the end of the chute he built a squeeze box long enough to hold one cow. The cow was forced down the chute and into the squeeze box where a movable side was pulled tight with a system of pulleys and ropes until the cow was immobilized with its head sticking out the front. Jim then clamped an iron bar over the cow's nose to further control it. The cow was quickly branded, inoculated, or dehorned, all with much less manpower than needed to throw and brand an animal.

Gradually Jim Jr.'s efforts and innovative ideas improved the Aram holdings. Farm markets improved. Cattle sold for around nine cents a pound, about three times the price in the early 30s. There was more money available to buy products on the "outside." Young Jim purchased a brand new Ray Holes saddle in Cottonwood for $60, a pair of chaps for $15 and a used GMC pickup truck to take small loads of livestock to and from town and haul heavy equipment. He bought Phebe a gasoline-powered wringer washing machine to ease her workload.

In 1938, at the Idaho County Fair in Cottonwood, Jim watched proudly when his father served as grand marshal for the annual parade. This honor, much like that bestowed on Tom Aram at the Grangeville 4th of July parade in 1893, recognized James Aram as one of the leading citizens of the county.

Although much of Jim Jr.'s life was consumed by work, he did take time to attend the dances and socialize with his friends. He also made quiet note of the young, available women in the area. One day, after a cattle drive to the stockyards in Cottonwood, he was visiting with Ben Lightfield who received, weighed and sold the cattle and hogs brought to the stockyards. Jim had known Ben most of his life and vaguely remembered staying overnight at the Lightfields' former Rocky Canyon Creek home while on a hog drive from Joseph to Cottonwood when he was about 8. Since then Lightfield had opened the Cottonwood Sales Yard and moved his family to a house nearby.

A car drove up to the house as the two men talked and Lightfield's two sons, Bill and Mark, and daughter, Ruth, got out. Jim watched Ben's petite daughter with interest as she hurried toward the house, her long blond hair swirling around her shoulders. Shaking his head as if he had just seen a vision, Jim said his goodbyes to Ben and mounted his waiting horse. Looking back at the closed door of the Lightfield house as he turned toward Joseph he thought, *There's no way a girl like that would be interested in a Salmon River hillbilly like me.* The following summer Jim caught a glimpse of Ruth Lightfield again at a rodeo, but it was another year before he met her face to face.

In the meantime, Ruth had heard of young Jim Aram from other Salmon River ranchers. According to most of them he was the "best-looking, hardest working, strongest man on Joseph Plains." It was the early summer of 1939 when the "Joseph Legend" stepped into Ben Lightfield's office to collect a check for a load of hogs.

When Ruth looked up from her desk to greet the tall, lean cowboy, her words nearly caught in her throat. She knew exactly whose blue-green eyes she was looking into. If she had never before believed in "love at first sight," 21-year-old Ruth did then. After a few cordial words and a mutual "sizing up," young Jim reluctantly took his check and went on his way. As he walked out the door, Ruth thought, *Oh, if I could have a man like that, I'd be happy.*

A few days later Ruth received a letter from Jim inviting her to the 4th of July celebration at Grangeville. However, Jim could only attend at night and Ruth couldn't accompany him since she took tickets at her father's new moving-picture theater. On his next trip to town, Jim made certain he went to the movies and then returned on the second night to buy a ticket for the same movie. Ruth gave him a free ticket and then joined him after the show in the empty theater. The couple had their first real visit and Jim asked Ruth three questions: How old are you? What are your politics? What is your religion? They matched on the first two for Jim was 23, just two years older than Ruth, and both were Republicans. But religion was a complete mismatch. Ruth was a devout Catholic; Jim came from a long line of Protestants.

The next morning Jim left with a load of cattle bound for market in Portland. While there he visited with his sister Rosamond, who had graduated from the university and was employed as a secretary for Bonneville Power Administration. His stay was shorter than originally planned. He told Rosamond something had come up and he needed to get back to Cottonwood. The "something," of course, was Ruth.

He stopped in Cottonwood long enough to invite Ruth to an up-coming dance in White Bird. On the night of the dance Jim arrived in his pickup, and when he came to the door he was chuckling. Ruth asked what he was laughing about. Jim said, "Well, I brought two of my ranch hands down with me and realized on the way I forgot to bring a comb. I gave one of them some money and asked him to go buy a comb for me while I ran another errand. He came back with an ice cream cone."

Still chuckling, he offered Ruth his arm and escorted her to his wait-ing pickup. After the dance they drove back to Cottonwood. The Lightfield home near the stockyards had burned down, so the family lived in an apartment over the theater. Sitting on the steps leading up-stairs, just off the hushed and dimly lit foyer, they talked and talked. It was then Jim told Ruth he planned to marry her as soon as his financial position stabilized. "But," he warned, "that might be three years."

The couple continued to see each other throughout that summer and into the fall. One day Ruth was stopped on the street by a man who worked for the Arams. "Treat that young Aram right," he told her. "You don't find men like that around anymore." Already head over heels in love with Jim, Ruth didn't find his advice hard to follow. For Jim the future had never looked brighter. He recognized that ranching was more a way of life than a huge money maker, but he believed that within three years he would have a fiscally sound operation. Jim loved the life he had on Joseph, and in Ruth he had found someone he wanted to share that life with.

It was just such happy thoughts that were tumbling through his mind in early November when he and Ernest Wells returned from a hog-buying trip to Kooskia, a town on the Clearwater River. Night arrived before they headed up the Harpster grade toward Grangeville on a narrow gravel road. When they met a farmer driving a wide-bed truck Jim realized, even in the dark, that the road was not wide enough for the two vehicles. He forced his pickup as far to the right as possible, almost against the inside bank. Still, the truck sideswiped Jim, spinning the pickup with its load of hogs around and forcing it off the road where it came to a stop in an upright position.

When Jim and Ernest crawled out, they discovered Jim was bleeding profusely. His arm, which had been resting along the open window of the truck, was all but severed in the impact. Ernest tied a handkerchief around the upper arm just above the torn limb and helped Jim into a passerby's car. He was rushed to Dr. Chipman's office in Grangeville where the primitive tourniquet was taken off. Miraculously the bleeding had stopped, but the doctor felt Jim should be taken to Dr. Orr in Cottonwood for proper treatment.

Ten years before, Dr. Orr had seen John and Narcie through their critical illnesses. Now, he faced the heartbreaking task of amputating their strong, healthy brother's left arm just below the shoulder. Since Jim was in pain and suffering from shock, the doctor attempted to reach James and Phebe for permission to amputate. Unable to find them, he contacted John, who had graduated from the university, married, and was working for Potlatch in Lewiston. "If the arm needs to come off," John choked out, trusting Dr. Orr completely, "then take it off."

Once John granted permission, Jim was taken into surgery at the new Cottonwood hospital. James and Phebe were finally located on Joseph and immediately rushed to their son's side. John arrived with his wife, Mary Jane, as soon as possible, but Rosamond, who was still in Portland, and Narcie, who was attending St. Luke's School of Nursing in Spokane, could only send their love and concern. "That was the saddest time our family ever faced," remembered Narcie. "I guess up until that time we had all been pretty lucky to be as healthy as we were."

Ruth at first knew nothing of the accident, as she had left to visit cousins in Boise just after Jim stopped to see her in Cottonwood on his way to Kooskia. The accident happened on Thursday, November 2, but on Saturday Ruth still knew nothing of it. "I was supposed to leave on Saturday with my cousins to visit Sun Valley. I had never been there and was looking forward to the trip," recalled Ruth. "But on Friday night I dreamt Jim was in the Cottonwood hospital. Upon waking I had the strong feeling I should return home. I arrived that afternoon, learned of Jim's accident, and went to the hospital immediately. Jim had been somewhat despondent because I hadn't come to visit him. He was afraid I might not want anything to do with him because he lost his arm. That never even occurred to me."

Ruth's reassurances eased Jim's mind. After a week in the hospital, he was sent to recuperate at the Cottonwood home of the Agnews. Within a few days the stump became infected and Jim returned to his hospital bed where poultices were applied to draw the infection out.

As he lay there, Jim remembered how his first thoughts after the accident were for survival. Now that he knew he was going to live, he wondered how. His life's work required a strong body, two strong arms, and two hands. With his left arm gone, life was changed forever. Some people might even consider him a cripple. Right then he decided no one would ever have the opportunity to feel sorry for Jim Aram, Jr. He would get on with his life and do whatever needed to be done. Nothing would stand in his way.

Chapter 20

GOODBYE JOSEPH

Many of the scenes from Joseph Plains will remain forever in my memory—the Snake and Salmon rivers, Seven Devils, Camp Howard, and the view from the top of Fir Gulch looking toward Getta Creek. Over the years I have met others who lived at one time or another on Joseph. The time spent there seems to be the most memorable of their lives.—Jim Aram 1992

JIM'S STRONG, YOUNG body fought a winning battle against the terrible infection in his arm. At the end of a week he was again released to recuperate at the Agnews. One day Mrs. Agnew served tea while Ruth was visiting. Jim hated tea, but politely accepted a delicate cup and saucer. As he held them the full cup tilted dangerously. Mrs. Agnew looked at Ruth as if she should do something, but Jim placed the saucer on a nearby table and waved her away. Then, grinning at Ruth, he lifted the cup to his mouth, crooked his little finger and took a dainty sip.

In the following weeks this natural sense of humor took Jim over many rough spots. He returned to Joseph and helped his father around the ranch, discovering some things could be done with one hand while others were awkward or impossible. Phebe watched her son struggle with tasks such as opening a door while carrying an armful of firewood. Gently, she urged him to attend the University of Idaho and prepare for another career.

When Jim finally agreed, thinking he might like to major in agriculture and become a county agent, Phebe helped him prepare by giving him crash courses in mathematics and English. In mid-January 1940, he once again left Phebe and James alone at the ranch to pursue his education.

Jim took his studies seriously, but when spring break arrived he was glad to return to Joseph and help his father. Cows that were calving were fenced on bench land along Getta Creek, land the Arams had purchased the year before. Jim, who was still an expert horseman, rode down to check on the animals. Two of the new mothers were in distress. One had too much milk and needed milking, so Jim roped and milked her. The other had a calf, but her afterbirth had not cleared. Remounting his horse, Jim roped the cow and inserted pills designed to expel the afterbirth. Since he was the only person around, he was relieved it was no longer necessary to throw and restrain the cow.

When Jim returned to his speech class after break, he made a presentation on how he had spent his spring vacation. He told of helping on the ranch and roping cattle. His classmates were astounded. "It amazed me the way the class listened spellbound," remembered Jim. "When I was finished, they all sat there with their mouths open. They couldn't believe I could do all that with one arm."

That same spring a man who sold prostheses contacted Jim and asked if he would like to be fitted with an artificial limb. Jim agreed and met with him to have a cast taken of his stump. In a few weeks the man returned with a lightweight arm carved of willow wood. It cost Jim $150 and had both a hand and hook that could be screwed into the end of the arm, giving Jim the option to use one or the other. The arm attached by a series of straps that went over the shoulders and across the chest. Jim could open or close the hand or hook by moving his shoulders in a certain way, causing one of the straps to pull or release the movable parts.

When classes ended for the summer, Jim returned to the ranch. By approaching old tasks in different ways he discovered his new arm allowed him to do some of the work he hadn't been able to before. He couldn't pound fence posts or use a crosscut saw to cut a tree, but he could pitch and shock hay, use a variety of tools, and carry things while opening a door.

Earlier he used a $250 credit on his wrecked pickup as a down payment on a new Ford tractor and plow. Up until then he had used horses in the field, but that summer the tractor was his salvation. He didn't need to harness and unharness the team or stop to rest the horses. He drove the tractor with ease and ran it all day and all night when necessary.

Throughout that first spring and summer after his accident, Jim was either in Moscow or on Joseph Plains. However, he managed to see Ruth at infrequent intervals when passing through Cottonwood. Between visits they corresponded. When Jim returned to the university in the fall, Ruth enrolled also. For the first time, they were close enough to see each other often. They talked of marriage, but the difference in religion—which had seemed a minute obstacle during the first bloom of courtship—rose like a specter between them.

Ruth would marry, but only in the Catholic church. Jim, uncertain of what that might require of him, wanted a civil ceremony. Hurt and confused by the other's unwillingness to budge, they drifted apart. Both dated others. "We didn't see each other much that year at the university," remembered Ruth. "But any time Jim walked into a room I knew he was there, even before I saw him. I dated many nice men, but I really couldn't see anybody but Jim. We were constantly drawn together like a couple of magnets, but each time we couldn't resolve our differences we went our separate ways."

At the end of that school year, Jim left the university, even though he was a good student and had excellent grades. "At 24 I was a grown man who had already been operating my father's ranch for several years. I had dealt with banks, bought and sold livestock. I couldn't see any future in economics, sociology, and philosophy. It just didn't make any sense to me, so I decided to go back to the ranch."

Jim was able to do much of the work, but not as efficiently as he had before his accident. To complicate matters, his father was 75 and his chores were taking much longer. Together, with the help of one hired man, the Arams finished the summer work. However, that fall, poor health forced James and Phebe to leave the ranch for the first time in over 30 years to spend the winter in a Lewiston apartment near John, Mary Jane, and their daughter, Jane. John picked his parents up in Grangeville on December 7, his daughter's first birthday. While there he learned the Japanese had bombed Pearl Harbor.

Once again, the world shifted under the young Arams as their country plunged into war. John, who would have served in uniform if called, was never drafted because Potlatch requested a deferment for his war-essential plant supervisor position. Instead, he worked on bond fund drives, neighborhood security patrols, Lions Club war-related activities, and served as regional representative for the War Production Board's Training Within Industry Program.

Jim Jr., who also would have served if it had been possible, didn't face the threat of draft because of his arm. Still, the war brought another battle to Joseph Plains as cowboys departed to join the military. When his last hired hand left for the army that winter following Pearl Harbor, Jim struggled alone to take care of his cattle, farm animals, and crops. James returned in the spring, but the work was more than father and son could realistically manage. Phebe was recuperating from a heart attack and could not keep up with the work at the ranch house. That summer James, Phebe, and Jim Jr. made the heart-wrenching decision to sell out.

In September they finalized a sale with Slim and Mary Johnson, who many years before had purchased the Arams' Getta Creek ranch from A. S. Hardy. Neither Jim nor James felt they had lost the battle to reclaim their ranch, for they had well over 2,000 acres of land owned free and clear. In addition, they held leases on another 1,000 acres of Canfield land and over 600 acres of School Section land. Johnson took over the leases and paid $10 an acre for the Aram land, ten times what James and Jim had paid for some of it during the Depression.

Not only did they have the land, but they had rebuilt their cattle herd—over 300 head which they sold for 13.75 cents per pound, the highest price ever. The Arams were free of debt for the first time in their lives and they had money to invest. Their departure from Joseph was difficult, but it was in no way a failure.

When they left in December of 1942 to move to Lewiston, Jim drove the Ford tractor to Cottonwood where he stored it in a garage over the winter. The following spring and summer he used it to plow gardens and mow fields in the Lewiston area. They purchased a house in a development called the Lewiston Orchards in the summer of 1943. Phebe, whose years of hard work had taken a toll on her heart, needed more rest. For the first time in her life, she could read and write at her leisure. As an added bonus she had neighbors to visit. James, on the other hand, was quite lost without his livestock and land. To keep occupied, he dabbled in real estate investments.

Jim Jr. was also a little lost and continued to look for his niche in Lewiston. The next spring and summer he worked for the University of Idaho's entomology department, touring the state and giving farmers demonstrations on a new method of controlling grubs in cattle. He also took samples of insects found on row crops and returned them to the university for identification. When that job ended, he went to work at Potlatch Forests, Inc., for a month and then, without giving notice, went hunting for two weeks.

"Potlatch should have fired me for just leaving like that," Jim recalled, "but help was hard to get during the war. I wasn't in a critical job, so they overlooked my absence. I only worked for them for two more weeks and then quit to go into the real estate business with Clyde Jungert. To get my real estate license all I needed to do was post a thousand-dollar bond and have six property owners sign a petition. The state of Idaho then issued me my brokerage license."

Just as Jim entered the real estate business, his "on again, off again" relationship with Ruth reached an all-time low. She had graduated cum laude that spring from the University of Idaho and had taken a job as secretary in the purchasing department at Jantzen Mills in Portland, Oregon. The couple remained at an impasse, and by that fall Ruth was convinced there was no future in the relationship. In October she enlisted in the SPARS, the Coast Guard's Women's Auxiliary. "I was heartbroken," said Ruth. "I was simply going off in a huff. To me it was the equivalent of joining the Foreign Legion."

Without saying goodbye, Ruth left for boot camp in Florida, then an office job with the Coast Guard in New York City. Jim kept busy with his new business. In 1945 he and Jungert bought the Ford tractor agency and moved the real estate business into the same building. "Both businesses were lucrative," recalled Jim. "People were making good money and there wasn't much to buy. Nearly everyone had saved up a few thousand and of course wanted a home. The war brought the price of farm commodities up, so the farmers had money and were starved for machinery."

Jim's years of hard work on the Joseph ranch continued to pay off in Lewiston. He was still lean and strong. When farm equipment needed to be moved on the showroom floor, Jim grabbed one end of it with his good arm and did the work of two other men working on the opposite end. He also had a natural understanding of land and money. By 1946 he felt he could afford a new car. He came back to the office with a new Hudson.

Late that spring, Ruth was discharged from the Coast Guard. Her time of self-exile had convinced her life would be miserable without Jim. In New York she dated men from all over the country. Not one of them measured up to the cowboy from Joseph. News of Jim reached her through friends and relatives, and she knew he was still unattached. By the time she arrived in Lewiston, Ruth was almost willing to forgo a Catholic wedding just to have him back in her life—but first she had to see whether Jim was still interested. After buying a new outfit, Ruth arrived unannounced at Jim's office. When she entered he blinked three times, as if he couldn't believe his eyes.

"Well," Ruth said, "I'm going to be here for a while. Do you want to take care of my social life?"

"Yes," replied Jim, still bowled over by her sudden appearance.

"Okay, then, you're on for Saturday night."

"How about Wednesday, too?" grinned Jim.

"Even better," answered Ruth.

Thus their stalled relationship resumed. Ruth stayed in Clarkston for a few weeks caring for her grandparents and then took a secretarial job with Empire Airlines in Lewiston. The couple dated all summer, seeing each other three or four times a week. With other young couples they went to movies, dances, and beach parties along the riverbanks.

A mechanic at Jim's shop was dating a Catholic girl; when he decided to marry, he took six weeks of instruction in Catholicism. Jim watched the entire procedure with interest and decided he, too, could take the instruction and learn about Ruth's religion. That fall when Jim, once again, asked Ruth to marry him it was with the understanding the ceremony would take place in her church.

After that, there was no more waiting. On November 24, 1946, after seven years of courtship, Ruth and Jim were married. Only Rosamond, who lived in California, could not attend the wedding. The long-awaited occasion was one of the last times the family was together. Phebe died in October of the following year. She was only 68, but her heart finally gave out. Ruth was with her mother-in-law when she had her fatal attack. Phebe seemed to know the end was near, telling Ruth quietly, "I don't think I'll survive this one."

The family was crushed at the loss of Phebe. A lonely James, then 84, went to live with Rosamond, her husband, Edward Neale, and their two youngsters, 2-year-old Betty and infant David. Within months, John and his family moved to Boise where John took a job with Boise Payette Lumber Company. Narcie was living in Portland where she worked at the veterans hospital, but later transferred to

Santa Monica, California, to be near Rosamond and her father. Only Jim, Ruth, and their infant son, Vance, born the year after Phebe's death, remained in Lewiston.

And so it was, the children of James and Phebe Aram scattered like so many seeds in the wind. They left behind the remote country settled by their family more than 80 years before, but they took with them a strength of character that was to serve them well in their individual lives. It was a strength inherited from their pioneer parents and grandparents—a strength tested daily in their youth by a wild and beautiful land.

EPILOGUE

The years of my boyhood seem now like a dream rather than reality.—John Aram 1993

AFTER SOME TIME in Santa Monica with Rosamond's family, James Aram returned to Lewiston to live with Jim Jr. and Ruth. When asked about his return he simply responded, "There was too much traffic and not enough trees." He also reminded his family that he had already seen California, referring to his honeymoon some 40 years before.

Following his father's return, young Jim became restless. Both men missed their life on Joseph, and Jim wanted to try ranching again. In the summer of 1951, he bought a 40-acre ranch and some cattle near Weiser, Idaho. Jim left his Lewiston real estate business and moved the family to the ranch. He bought an additional 1,400 acres of dry pastureland and settled into ranch life.

For James, then 88, the move was like a return home, a last chance at a life he had always known. He loved the ranch and enjoyed being near livestock once again. In late March 1952, James's health failed, due largely to old age. After two weeks in the Weiser hospital, he died on April 8, just three months short of his 89th birthday. Many Joseph residents attended the funeral in Lewiston, paying their last respects to a man they held in high esteem.

Phebe and James lived just long enough to see their oldest son become a rising star in the forest products industry. In 1936, after graduation from the University of Idaho with a B.S. in business, John married his college sweetheart, Mary Jane Pace. He was offered a job as a sales trainee with Potlatch Forests in Lewiston and quickly rose to a management position.

In 1949 he transferred to Boise Payette Lumber Company, predecessor to Boise Cascade. By 1956 he was president. He then moved to the Weyerhaeuser Company in Tacoma, Washington, and was elected a corporate vice president. He retired from Weyerhaeuser in 1973 and became a vice president of Pacific Denbamann Company in Seattle until 1981. By the end of his career, John was recognized as one of the most effective and respected business leaders in the forest products industry.

Even during his busy career years, John served as an officer on numerous forestry industry associations. He was active in local community activities, the Episcopal church, and the Republican party. He also served as a trustee of several colleges including Gonzaga University where he was chairman of the board of trustees from 1979 to 1980. Gonzaga lauded him with the honorary degree of Dr. of Laws in 1987 and the John L. Aram Professorship of Business Ethics in 1988, an endowment whose major contributors included Weyerhaeuser and Boise Cascade.

In 1989 he was honored by the University of Idaho School of Business Administration as one of ten outstanding graduates. John also served on the board of directors of several corporations, resigning from the last one, chairman of the board of directors for the North Pacific Bank, in January of 1993 after 20 years of service.

Looking back on his career John says, "I was never really given an assignment in the forest products industry that I was trained for, but I was always willing to learn and had a can-do attitude. People around me recognized that and were helpful. They appreciated my willingness to work. I also read and studied a lot, particularly the *Harvard Business Review*. One book that helped me the most was *A Business and Its Beliefs*, by Tom Watson Jr., the head of IBM. Like my father, I was always willing to take risks, look for a better way of doing things, and either follow or lead, whichever was necessary. And, of course, I had a wonderful and supportive family."

John and Mary Jane had three children—Frances Jane, born in 1940, John David, born in 1943, and James Pace, born in 1951. After 45 years of marriage, John lost Mary Jane to cancer in 1981. He later married Margaret Harris, who died in 1987. In February, 1989, John married Anne Gibson. Together they share a life of travel and involvement with their extended families— Anne's three children and grandchild, John's three children, five grandchildren, and two great-grandchildren, plus two stepchildren and grandchildren from Margaret's family.

Rosamond, once referred to by John as "the bright spirit of our family," left Joseph at an even earlier age than her older brother. She was a serious student and never really returned to the ranch for any length of time after leaving to attend high school in Grangeville. Rosamond graduated from high school a year ahead of John and started at the university in Moscow.

While at college she changed her name to Bobby, mainly to avoid the abbreviation of her given name to Rosie. The name stuck and "Bobby" Aram, who had always excelled at shorthand and typing, graduated from the university with a business degree in 1935, passed the civil service exam, and left for a government job in Washington, D.C. From Washington she went to work for the Soil Conservation Service in Colorado Springs, Colorado, and later transferred to Portland, Oregon. There she met Ed Neale. When he was sent to Texas with the navy during World War II, Rosamond joined him; in 1943 they married.

Rosamond returned briefly during the war to live with her parents in Lewiston while awaiting the birth of her daughter, Betty Frances, in 1944. At the end of the war, Ed and Rosamond were reunited. They moved to Oakland, California, where Ed completed his doctorate in education at the University of California, Berkeley. There, David was born in 1946. The family then moved to Santa Monica where Ed taught at Long Beach State College.

Ambitious and hardworking, Rosamond continued her career while raising her children, working as a secretary for a law firm in Long Beach. In 1967, at the age of 53, Rosamond "Bobby" Aram Neale, died after a short battle with cancer. "In our adult years Rosamond and I had some wonderful times together and a lot of good laughs," recalled Narcie. "Although she never said so, I always had the feeling she hated Joseph. Needless to say, I was astounded to learn her last request was to have her ashes buried there."

Ruth, Jim, Ed, and Betty took that final trip to the old, abandoned homestead with Rosamond's ashes on a warm, sunny day in July. Against the backdrop of the ranch Jim could easily visualize Rosamond as she had been in the early days. He saw her rounding up cattle, carrying milk to the house, separating the cream, hanging clothes on the line, and helping their mother in the house—all with abundant energy and a cheerful demeanor.

After his father's passing at Weiser, Jim Jr. remained at the ranch for another year. "I should never have left my real estate business," Jim says now. "I just wanted to ranch so badly I didn't realize you had to have a really huge operation to make any money. We sold out and returned to Lewiston in 1953. My old partner Clyde had left Lewiston briefly but returned also, so we went back into the real estate business. By then the state had changed their regulations and I had to take a real estate exam to renew my license. I passed on the first try."

Clyde left the partnership in 1958 to settle on a grass ranch in the Boise Valley near Star, Idaho. Jim continued to sell real estate, often buying and trading for his own investment. In the fall of 1963, his former partner approached him, asking if he would be interested in going in on a partnership to purchase 500 calves. Jim had never really gotten the idea of cattle ranching out of his head, or heart, and was intrigued with the idea. The purchase led Jim to, once again, leave Lewiston for an 80 acre ranch near Star.

Again he discovered the small ranch was not a paying proposition and, without losing money, sold the cattle and ranch at the end of the year. He returned to Lewiston, bought a house, and opened a real estate office in his new home. For the rest of his career he sold real estate, successfully buying and selling property for himself and others. Like his father and older brother, Jim was a risk taker. Fortunately, most of his investments paid off in one way or another and provided a comfortable living. Jim spent nearly 50 years as a broker and still dabbles in real estate.

Jim and Ruth have two sons, Vance Edward, born in 1948, and Thomas James, born in 1957. Both sons live nearby in Lewiston with their wives, and each has given Ruth and Jim two grandchildren, three girls and a boy. Their lives revolve around family and friends, the church, and community activities, particularly sports. When he married Ruth, Jim agreed that the children would be raised Catholic. He participated willingly in church activities with Ruth and the boys, and in 1979, after 33 years of marriage, asked to join the church. Now, Jim and Ruth's comfortable two-story home is located directly across the street from the St. Stanislaus Catholic Church where they both attend regularly.

Narcie, who finished high school with Jim, went on to the University of Idaho for one year. She joined Rosamond for a few months in

Colorado Springs, then enrolled at St. Luke's Nursing School in Spokane. After a three-year nursing program, she graduated in 1940 and took a job in a doctor's office in Kellogg, Idaho, where she doubled as a surgery nurse. Patients were not just residents of the community, but miners from the nearby silver, zinc, and ore mines.

In 1944 Narcie joined the war effort as an Air Corps flight nurse. She volunteered for overseas duty, but Phebe suffered another heart attack and Narcie returned to Lewiston briefly. After that she requested stateside duty; she flew around the country with military patients from one hospital to another. On one trip to the East Coast in 1945 she visited Ruth in New York City. The next year she was discharged with the rank of 1st lieutenant.

Narcie returned to Lewiston to be near her family and worked for a short time at the children's home. When her mother died she was nursing at the veterans hospital in Portland, Oregon. Later, she transferred to Santa Monica, where she remained after her father returned to Lewiston, but in 1956 joined the Alaska Department of Health. She was hired on a ship that sailed to the Aleutian Islands and small villages in southeastern Alaska near Juneau, providing health care—immunizations and x-rays—to the natives. After about a year, the government discontinued the program.

Those months were a life-altering experience for Narcie, not because of what she did but because of whom she met—Ben See, captain of the ship. The nurse from Joseph, Idaho, and the Seven Seas captain from Hoonah, Alaska, found they had much in common and became fast friends. On February 27, 1958, they married and settled in Seattle where Narcie continued her career in a public health hospital. Ben was the divorced father of five children, ages 12 to 17, who lived with their mother in Alaska, but spent some time in Seattle.

In addition to their chosen careers, Narcie and Ben made several successful real estate ventures, and owned and operated a charter fishing boat for a time. They also traveled to Europe, Mexico, Hawaii, China, and Hong Kong. Ben died suddenly while in Hong Kong in 1984. Narcie remained in Seattle where she still resides in her own home.

"I do have a special feeling for the land," said Narcie. "It is important to me to own property, just like my father, though I don't own a lot of it. I used to think I'd like to be buried on Joseph, like Rosamond.

It is more home than anywhere. After visiting in recent years, I've changed my mind—it just seems too lonely and remote."

Looking back on her childhood, Narcie says, "My parents instilled in me a strong work ethic. I've always felt if I wasn't working at something I was useless. They taught me respect for nature and animals. I learned to worry from my mother. She used to say when one of us wasn't home when she thought we should be, we always seemed to come when she got real worried. On the other hand, I learned to take financial and business risks from my dad. He always said he was never concerned that things would not work out."

A REUNION

by Narcie Aram See

∽

Oɴ ᴀ sᴘᴀʀᴋʟɪɴɢ, sunny day in Grangeville, Idaho, 50-plus descendants of John and Sarah Aram met for a reunion. The affair was arranged by great-great-granddaughter Linda Junes and was held on July 25, 1992, at the home of Linda's cousin, Dick Geary.

Following a coffee hour at the Geary home, the Aram clan drove to the site John and Sarah had selected for their home in 1864—a slightly elevated area with Mount Idaho in the background and a view of Camas Prairie before them. The Spencer family, who bought the farm in the early 1900s, had long ago moved the Aram's two-story house to another location. Where the old house once stood, they built a sprawling home with a swimming pool surrounded by lawns, trees, and flowers. A few of the trees planted by John Aram remain part of the landscape. Carmelita Spencer allowed us to wander around the farm and through her lovely home.

We also toured the remodeled homes of Aunt Clara and the Geary family (now Dick Geary's home), drove past the empty house of the Johnson family at Tolo Lake, and visited the cemetery where many of our ancestors are buried. We drove by, but did not enter, the relocated and well-preserved Aram home. Throughout the day we enjoyed becoming acquainted with relations we had never met, reminiscing with others, taking pictures, and eating wonderful food. How Sarah and John would have loved this day!

* * *

The day following the reunion, John and I once again visited the Joseph ranch. With us were his daughter, Jane, his son, Jim, and granddaughter, Sahaja. Jim had been there once as a young boy, the others had not.

The roads seem narrower and steeper, the canyons deeper, and the area more isolated and lonely each time I return. On that day I may have been seeing it as I thought the others might view it. Sahaja, then 13, would probably agree with her cousin, Jonathon, who visited in 1988 when he was 12. His comment? "I guess it's all right, but I sure don't see anything here."

NOTES

1. Extract of letter written by Eugene Aram to the Reverend M. Collins, Vicar of Knaresbrough.

2. The Co-Operative Publication Society, *Poems of Hood*, p. 145.

3. Jay Robert Nash, *Encyclopedia of World Crime*, p. 142.

4. The Co-Operative Publication Society, *Poems of Hood*, p. 145.

5. Noel B. Gerson, *The Last Wilderness:The Saga of America's Mountain Men,* p.97

6. The date of the Arams' arrival on Camas Prairie has been recorded in family records and published works as 1863, 1864, and 1865. For several reasons I have chosen Apr. 1864 as the most probable date. On p. 389 of the *History of Northern Idaho*, it states that when James. H. Robinson arrived on the prairie in 1865, John Aram was among the settlers already there; 1863 is unlikely because James was born in Oregon in July 1863, and they would not have made the trip in the fall or winter of that year. In addition, Sarah's obituary, printed in the *Idaho County Free Press* on Jan. 13, 1921, states that they came to Camas Prairie in Apr. 1864. That is the most specific date recorded anywhere. The fact that John Aram's obituary, printed in the *Idaho County Free Press* on Oct. 3, 1901, gives the date as 1863 could be explained by the possibility that John came to the prairie in 1863 on his way to the gold mines, saw the rich land, staked a claim, and returned for his family in 1864.

7. Wallace W. Elliott, ed., *History of Idaho Territory*, p. 99.

8. Sister M. Alfreda Elsensohn, *Pioneer Days in Idaho County*, vol. 1, p. 3.

9. Ibid., vol. 2, pp. 531, 532.

10. Ibid., vol. 2, pp. 526–27, 541.

11. Western Historical Publishing Co., *History of North Idaho*, p. 389.

12. Ibid., p. 1229.

13. Ibid., p. 389.

14. Idaho Territory Federal Population and Mortality Schedules, 1870, 2nd District of Nez Perce County, based in Lewiston Post Office of Idaho, July 20, 1870, p. 129. Camas Prairie was part of Nez Perce County until 1875 when it became part of Idaho County.

15. Western Historical Publishing Co., *History of North Idaho*, p. 1228.

16. Henry C. Johnson, "Some Reminiscences of the Nez Perce Indian War," pp. 8 and 9. Another manuscript by Henry C. Johnson, "Volunteer Survivor Recalls Battle with Indians East of Cottonwood," is in the collection of the Idaho State Historical Library, Boise.

17. Alvin M. Josephy, Jr., *The Nez Perce Indians and the Opening of the Northwest*, p. 467. The name of Ollokot has been spelled by others as Ollikut, Ollokut, Alokut, and Ollicutt, and Hin-mah-too-yah-lat-Kekht as Heinmot Tooyalaket.

18. Ibid., p. 467.

19. Ibid., p. 468.

20. Western Historical Publishing Co., *History of North Idaho*, p. 55.

21. John Hailey, *The History of Idaho*, p. 208.

22. Elsensohn, *Pioneer Days*, vol. 1, p. 116.

23. Helen Addison Howard, *Saga of Chief Joseph*. p. 176.

24. Historians disagree on the number of Indians involved in this battle with the "Brave Seventeen."

25. Johnson, "Some Reminiscences of the Nez Perce Indian War," pp. 6 and 7.

26. Helen Addison Howard, *Saga of Chief Joseph,* p. 334.

27. *Idaho County Free Press,* Sept. 17, 1886.

28. "Funeral of 'Tom' Aram," *Idaho County Free Press,* July 2, 1897.

29. Idaho County Tax Records, 1910.

30. Elsensohn, *Pioneer Days,* vol. 2, p. 523.

Bibliography

Aram, Alberta. "Let's Remember Joseph Aram." Publication and date unknown. Photocopies provided by Aram family.

—————. "She Discovered California's Gold." *California Today*, Aug. 2, 1970. Photocopies of article provided by Aram family.

Aram, Eugene. Extract of a letter written by Eugene Aram to the Reverend Mr. Collins, Vicar of Knaresbrough. Undated. Origin and source unknown. Photocopies provided by the Aram family.

Aram, Ruth. "Biographies of the Five Sons of Mathias Aram." Undated. Photocopies provided by the Aram family.

Aram, Rev. Stephan. "Descendants of Peter Aram." Winthrop Harbor, Ill.: Sept. 15, 1988. Photocopy provided by the Aram family.

Bailey, Robert G. *River of No Return: The Great Salmon River*, N.p: R. G. Bailey Printing Co., n.d.; reprint, Lewiston: Lewiston Printing Co., 1983.

Barber, Floyd R., and Dan W. Martin. *Idaho in the Pacific*. Caldwell, Idaho: Caxton Printers, 1956.

Beal, Merrill D. *I Will Fight No More Forever: Chief Joseph and the Nez Perce War*. Seattle: University of Washington Press, 1963.

Brown, Dee. *Bury My Heart at Wounded Knee: An Indian History of the American West*. New York, Chicago, & San Francisco: Holt Rinehart & Winston, 1970.

Census Records for 1870. 2nd District of Nez Perce Territory, July 20, 1870.

Chedsey, Zona, and Carolyn Frei, eds., *Idaho County Voices: From the Pioneers to the Present*. N.p.: Idaho County Centennial Committee, 1990.

The Co-Operative Publication Society. *Poems of Hood*. New York and London: The Co-Operative Publication Society, n.d.

Defenbach, Byron. *Idaho: The Place and Its People*. Chicago & New York: American Historical Society, Inc., 1933.

Elliot, Wallace W., ed. *History of Idaho Territory*. San Francisco: Wallace W. Elliott & Co. Publishers, 1884.

Elsensohn, Sister M. Alfreda. *Pioneer Days in Idaho County*, vols. 1 & 2. Caldwell, Idaho: Caxton Printers, Ltd., 1947.

Geary, Dick. Notes on the Aram and Johnson families compiled by Dick Geary of Grangeville, Idaho. Photocopies provided by Linda Junes and Verna Geary McGrane.

Gerson, Noel B. *The Last Wilderness:The Saga of America's Mountain Men*. New York: Julian Messner, 1966.

Grangeville Globe. "Obituary of Sarah A. Aram," Jan. 20, 1921.

Hailey, John. *The History of Idaho*. Boise, Idaho: Syms-York Company, Inc., 1910.

Haines, Francis. *The Nez Perces: Tribesmen of the Columbia Plateau*. Norman: University of Oklahoma Press, 1955; reprint, 1972.

Howard, Helen Addison. *Saga of Chief Joseph*. Caldwell, Idaho: Caxton Printers 1941; reprint, 1965.

Idaho County Free Press. Small news items from issues dated: June 18, July 9, July 23, Aug. 6, Sept. 10, Sept. 17, Oct. 8, Oct. 15, and Nov. 12, 1886.
————. Classified ads: July 30, 1886, Apr. 17 and May 1, 1891.

————. News items from issues dated: Feb. 11 and Oct. 28, 1887.

————. News items from issues dated: July 13 and July 27, 1888 (excerpts from an address given by L. P. Brown at the first reunion of the Idaho County Pioneer Association on June 13, 1888); July 27, Aug. 3 and Dec. 14, 1888.

————. Advertisement from issue dated June 28, 1889, and news items from July 12, Aug. 23, Aug. 30, and Oct. 4, 1889.

————. "A Sorely Afflicted Family," May 13, 1891.

————. Report on the deaths of Mina and Charles Johnson and "Fire at H. C. Johnson Home," Apr. 24, 1891.

————. "Marriage of T. J. Aram and Miss Carrie E. Moore," April 1, 1892.

————. "The Funeral of Tom Aram," July 2, 1897.

————. "In Memoriam" (Obituary for John Aram), Oct. 3, 1901.

————. "Last of Real Pioneers of Prairie Dead: Mrs. Sarah Amelia Aram succumbs to paralysis at age of 88," Jan. 13, 1921.

————. "Fights Big Drifts, Saves Girl's Life" and "Camas Prairie Has Deepest Snow Cover for Many Years," Jan. 31, 1929.

Idaho County Tax Records 1910 and 1913. Copies provided by John L. Aram, Tacoma, Washington.

Idaho Territory Federal Population & Mortality Schedules: 1870, 1880.

Johnson, Henry C. "Some Reminiscences of the Nez Perce Indian War," 1927. Photocopies provided by Verna Geary McGrane, Grangeville, Idaho.

Johnson, Mary Frances Aram. Records of births, marriages and deaths from the Bible of Mary Frances Aram Johnson. Photocopies provided by Verna Geary McGrane of Grangeville, Idaho.

Josephy, Alvin M. Jr. *The Nez Perce Indians and the Opening of the Northwest.* New Haven and London: Yale University Press, 1965.

Lewiston Morning Tribune. "James H. Aram, Indian War Survivor, Dead," Apr. 10, 1952.

_____. "Clara Fitzgerald, 84, Recalls Life of Pioneer," undated clipping from scrapbook of Jim and Ruth Aram.

_____. "Bustling, Booming Mount Idaho Now Nothing But A Ghost Town," an article by Norman Adkison, July 1, 1962.

McGrane, Verna Geary. "The Aram Family." Jan. 1992. A manuscript prepared for the author.

Miller, John Perry. *The Genealogy of the Descendants of Samuel Smith, Sr. and Elizabeth (McCleave) Smith.* Kenia, Ohio: Aldine Publishing House, 1922. Photocopies of relevant pages provided by the Aram family, pp. 39, 56, 57.

Nash, Jay Robert. *Encyclopedia of World Crime: Criminal Justice, Criminology, and Law Enforcement,* vol. 1. Wilmete, Ill.: Crimebooks, Inc., 1989. Photocopies of relevant pages provided by the Aram family. Eugene Aram pp. 141–42.

Powell, Barbara V. *Citizens of North Idaho Newspaper Abstracts 1862–1875.* Medical Lake, Wa.: Barbara V. Powell, Publisher, 1986.

Schwantes, Carlos A. *In Mountain Shadows: A History of Idaho,* Lincoln and London: The University of Nebraska Press, 1991.

Tchakmakian, Pascal. *The Great Retreat: The Nez Perces War in Words and Pictures.* San Francisco; Chronicle Books, 1976.

Wells, Merle, and Arthur A. Hart. *Idaho: Gem of the Mountains,* Northridge, Ca.: Idaho State Historical Society & Windsor Publications, Inc., n.d.

Western Historical Publishing Co., *History of North Idaho.* N.p.: Western Historical Publishing Co., 1903.

Wolfe, Matha Boles. "Seeing My Father Drown." Undated. Photocopies provided by Matha Boles Wolfe of Corvallis, Ore.

Yadon, Gordon W. "Aram More Than Library in Delavan History:

James Aram 1813–1897." An article published as a series of biographical sketches on the 46 individuals elected to the Hall of Fame in Delavan, Wisc., as part of the community's sesquicentennial observance. N.p.: N.p., n.d. Photocopies provided by the Aram family.

Index

roundups, 97, 99, 102, 104–5; rustling, 145–46, 149; slickears, 144; transporting to market by rail, 101–03

Chamberlain, Mr. and Mrs. John, 19, 20

Charity Grange #15, Patrons of Husbandry, 10

Chipman, Grangeville physician, 173

churches: Camas Prairie, 9, 28; Joseph Plains, lack of, 46

Clarke, Daniel, xix–xx

Coltman, Bill and Ester, 69, 91

cowboys: clothing for, 93–94. *See also* cattle, horses

Crooks, John, early Camas Prairie pioneer, 4, 8, 10, 17

dances: on Camas Prairie, 9, 28; on Joseph Plains, 129, 137–40

Daniels, Dave, 152

Day, Lew, 19–20

derrick. *See* hay harvest

diamond hitch, 81–82

Dobbins, Bob and Margaret, 71, 82, 113, 164

Dobbins, George and Oma, 71, 143

Dobbins, Mirabel, 71

Dodge, Russell and Minnie, 70, 131, 133–34

education: early schools on Camas Prairie, 9; literary societies, 9; Methodist academy at Grangeville, 28. *See also* schools, on Joseph Plains

Evans, B. F., 22

Excelsior Livery, 28–29, 32

fences, construction and maintenance of, 112–14

Fitzgerald, Clara H. (Mrs. John Fitzgerald), 38, 64, 189; hosts Aram children, 161, 169; partnership with James H. Aram on cattle, 98, 150–51; visited by family of James H. Aram, 55–56. *See also* Aram, Clara Helen

Fitzgerald, John P., 31, 33

Fitzgerald, Oren Aram, 33, 55, 167; career, 64; ranch hand, 49, 64, 68

Fix, Mr., 152, 154

flu, 1919 epidemic, 45–46

Flyblow, rodeos at, 141–43

food: cream, making and delivering, 108, 121; cottage cheese, making of, 122; harvesting and preserving on Joseph Plains, 124–25; planting of gardens at Getta Creek and Joseph Plains, 78, 81, 124; preparation of meals, 121–23; preservation of on early Camas Prairie, 8; refrigeration of on Joseph Plains, 122–23; staples, 125

foreclosure, 157

Foskett, Wilson, Whitebird physician, 41, 42

fox farming, 158

games: played at school, 132; played at home, 136

Geary, Dick, 189

Geary, Edna. *See* Johnson, Edna

Geary, Estaline, James and Verna, 56

Getta Creek, Aram ranch at, 80, 81

Gibbon, Col. John, 23

Girton, Ward, 9

Graham, Mr. and Mrs. Al, 69, 110, 133, 164

grains: harvesting, 109, 111; planting, 108–9; threshing, 112

Grangeville: beginning of, 10; growth of, 28, 29

Grangeville Globe, quotes from, xiii, 55

Great Depression: impact on Aram ranches, 157–58, 169

Hamilton, Bert, 116

Hardy, A. S., 157–58, 178

hay: at Getta Creek, 78, 79, 81; buckrakes, use of, 111; derricks, use of, 110–11; harvesting of, 109–11; hauling to cattle, 112; shocking, 111

Hin-mah-too-yah-lat-kekht. *See* Joseph, Chief (Young)

hogs: at Getta Creek, 81; butchering of, 117; drives, 118; meat, processing of, 117–18; raising of, 116–17

holiday celebrations, on Joseph Plains: Christmas, 134–35; Thanksgiving, 132–34

horses: gelding and treatment for injuries, 89–90; importance of, 84–85; raising of, 85; trading of, 90; training of, 85–86

housekeeping, at Joseph ranch, 126–27

Houseman, Richard, xix–xx

Howard, Gen. Oliver, 16, 18–19, 21, 38;

Perry, Col., 19, 21–23, 27
Platt, Bill, 144
post offices, on Joseph and Doumecq. *See* mail
potatoes, raising of, 157–58
Qualey, brothers (Olaf, Tom, Nelse, and Therwald), 72, 91, 160–61
Qualey, Mr. and Mrs., 72, 79, 97
Randall, Capt. D. B., 22
Rankin, Billy, 74–75, 91, 154, 165
rattlesnakes, 79–80
Reed, Biancia, 9
Reed, William ("Bill"), 70, 91, 129, 166
roads and trails: to and from Joseph Plains, 41, 51, 53–54, 57–59, 61–63, 66; Fir Gulch Trail, 77–79, 81, 105
Robinson, James H., 9–10
rockbucks. *See* fences
Rook, W. I. and sons (Jack, Mark, Vance), 141–42
Salmon River Country Store, 54, 93
schools, on Joseph: as center of social life, 130; Joseph, 138; McCarval, 129, 137; Spring Camp, 129, 141; Star, 129, 136, 137–38; Sunset, 71, 129–32, 137–38, 151; Yellow Pine, 38, 129, 137–38, 140–41
See, Ben, 187
See, Narcie (Mrs. Ben See), "A Reunion," 189–90. *See also* Aram, Narcie
sheep: herding, 151–54; lambing and care of, 152–53; purchase of, 151; ranch band, 155–56; sale of, 157; shearing, 153–54; summer range at Green Mountain, 154; trailing, 151, 154–55
Shillam, Jim, 49, 97
Shumway, Aurora, 4, 8
"Shumway Jim," 8–9
slickears. *See* cattle
Sloviaczek, Mike, 154
Smith, Harry Clarence and Hannah M., 38, 62
Smith, Henry Marshall and Margretta, 38, 61–62, 135–36, 168
Smith, Minnie Jameson, 38, 61–64, 125, 135–36
Smith, Narcissus Jameson, 38
Smith, Phebe Lucinda (later Phebe L. Aram), 38–40. *See also* Aram, Phebe L.

Spencer, Carmelita, 189
springbox. *See* food, refrigeration of
Sundown, Jackson, 142
Talkington, A. W., 29
Taylor, Lester, 137, 143
telephones, on Joseph Plains, 51, 52, 159
Terry, Henry, xx
Thrapp, Hilton, 64–68, 80, 113–14, 168
Tompkins, Elizabeth, xxi–xxii
Toohoolhoolzote, Chief, 16, 18, 24
treaty: of 1855, 3; of 1863, 3, 4, 13–15; of 1893, 34
Triplett, Sid, 162
Tuekakas. *See* Joseph, Chief (the elder or "Old Joseph")
turkeys, 156
Twogood, H. P., 52, 57
Vansise, Frank, 22, 29, 30
Wahlitits, 18, 23
War of 1877. *See* Nez Perce
Warnick, Charlie, 85, 96–97
water troughs, log, 82, 113–114
Watson, Mr. and Mrs., 18, 20
Wells, Ernest, 173
Whipple, Capt. Stephen C., 15, 22–23
White Bird, Chief, 16, 18, 24
White Bird Canyon, Battle of, 21, 27
White Bird, description of, 54
Williams, Fred, 115
wood, as fuel source, 115
Wright, Coral and Mary, 70–71
Zehner, Ross, 52

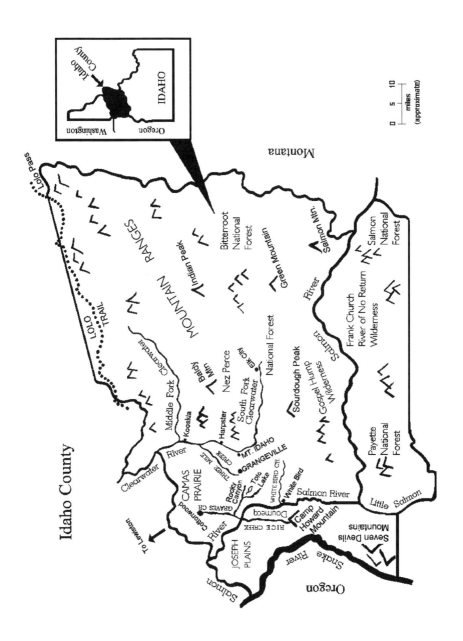

Idaho County

Joseph & Doumecq Plains
Idaho County, Idaho

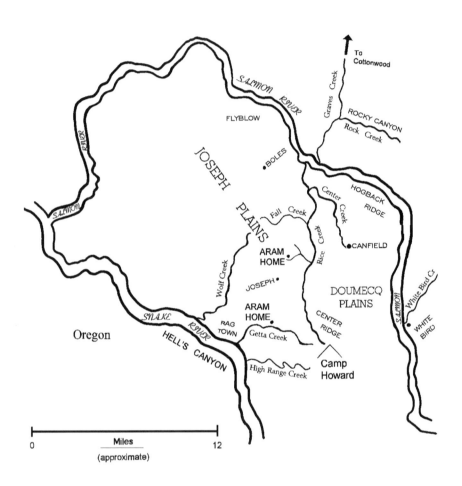